AVENGERS & THE INFINITY GAUNTLET

WRITERS **Brian Clevinger & Lee Black**

PENCILER **Brian Churilla**

INKERS **Brian Churilla** (Nos. 1 & 4) & **Terry Pallot** (Nos. 2-4) with **Sandu Florea** (No. 4)

COLORIST **Michelle Madsen**

LETTERERS **Jeff Powell & VC's Clayton Cowles**

COVER ARTISTS **Humberto Ramos & Edgar Delgado; Ron Lim, Sandu Florea & Edgar Delgado; Tom Grummett & Edgar Delgado; and Brian Churilla & Michelle Madsen**

EDITORS **Nathan Cosby & Michael Horwitz**

INFINITY GAUNTLET NO. 1

WRITER **Jim Starlin**

PENCILER **George Pérez**

INKERS **Josef Rubenstein** with **Tom Christopher**

COLORISTS **Max Scheele** with **Ian Laughlin**

LETTERER **Jack Morelli**

EDITOR **Craig Anderson**

COLLECTION EDITOR **Mark D. Beazley**
ASSISTANT EDITOR **Caitlin O'Connell**
ASSOCIATE MANAGING EDITOR **Kateri Woody**
ASSOCIATE MANAGER, DIGITAL ASSETS **Joe Hochstein**
SENIOR EDITOR, SPECIAL PROJECTS **Jennifer Grünwald**
VP PRODUCTION & SPECIAL PROJECTS **Jeff Youngquist**
BOOK DESIGNER **Adam Del Re**
SVP PRINT, SALES & MARKETING **David Gabriel**

EDITOR IN CHIEF **C.B Cebulski**
CHIEF CREATIVE OFFICER **Joe Quesada**
PRESIDENT **Dan Buckley**
EXECUTIVE PRODUCER **Alan Fine**

AVENGERS CREATED BY **STAN LEE & JACK KIRBY**

AVENGERS & THE INFINITY GAUNTLET. Contains material originally published in magazine form as AVENGERS & THE INFINITY GAUNTLET #1-4 and INFINITY GAUNTLET #1. First printing 2018. ISBN 978-1-302-91151-5. Published by MARVEL WORLDWIDE, INC., a subsidiary of MARVEL ENTERTAINMENT, LLC. OFFICE OF PUBLICATION: 135 West 50th Street, New York, NY 10020. Copyright © 2018 MARVEL No similarity between any of the names, characters, persons, and/or institutions in this magazine with those of any living or dead person or institution is intended, and any such similarity which may exist is purely coincidental. **Printed in Canada.** DAN BUCKLEY, President, Marvel Entertainment; JOE QUESADA, Chief Creative Officer; TOM BREVOORT, ...; ...AVID BOGART, SVP of Business Affairs & Operations, Publishing & Partnership; DAVID GABRIEL, SVP of Sales & Marketing, Publishing; JEFF YOUNGQUIST, ...s; DAN CARR, Executive Director of Publishing Technology; ALEX MORALES, Director of Publishing Operations; SUSAN CRESPI, Production Manager; STAN ...rmation regarding advertising in Marvel Comics or on Marvel.com, please contact Vit DeBellis, Custom Solutions & Integrated Advertising Manager, at ...l subscription inquiries, please call 888-511-5480. **Manufactured between 1/12/2018 and 2/13/2018 by SOLISCO PRINTERS, SCOTT, QC, CANADA.**

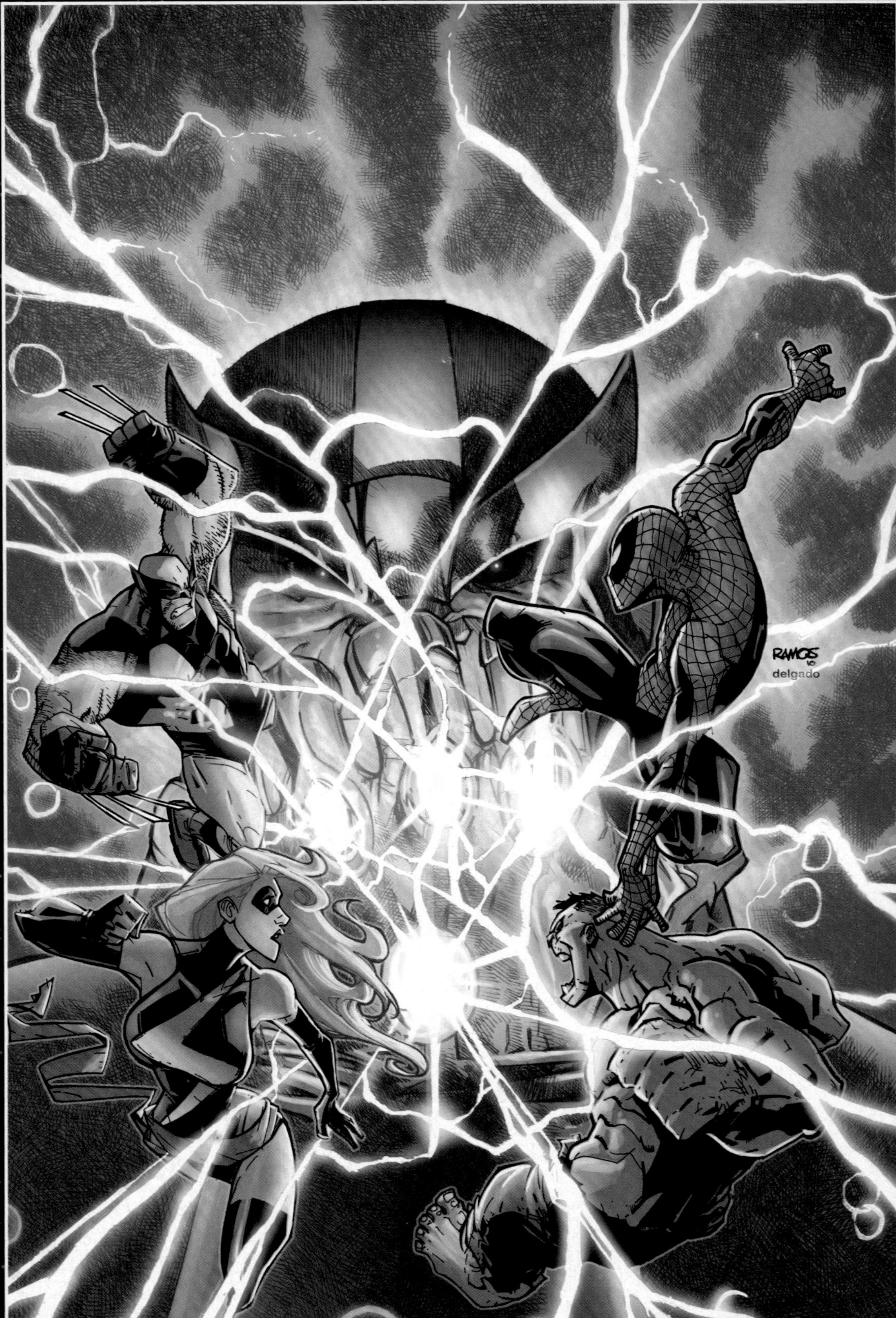
RAMOS
10
delgado

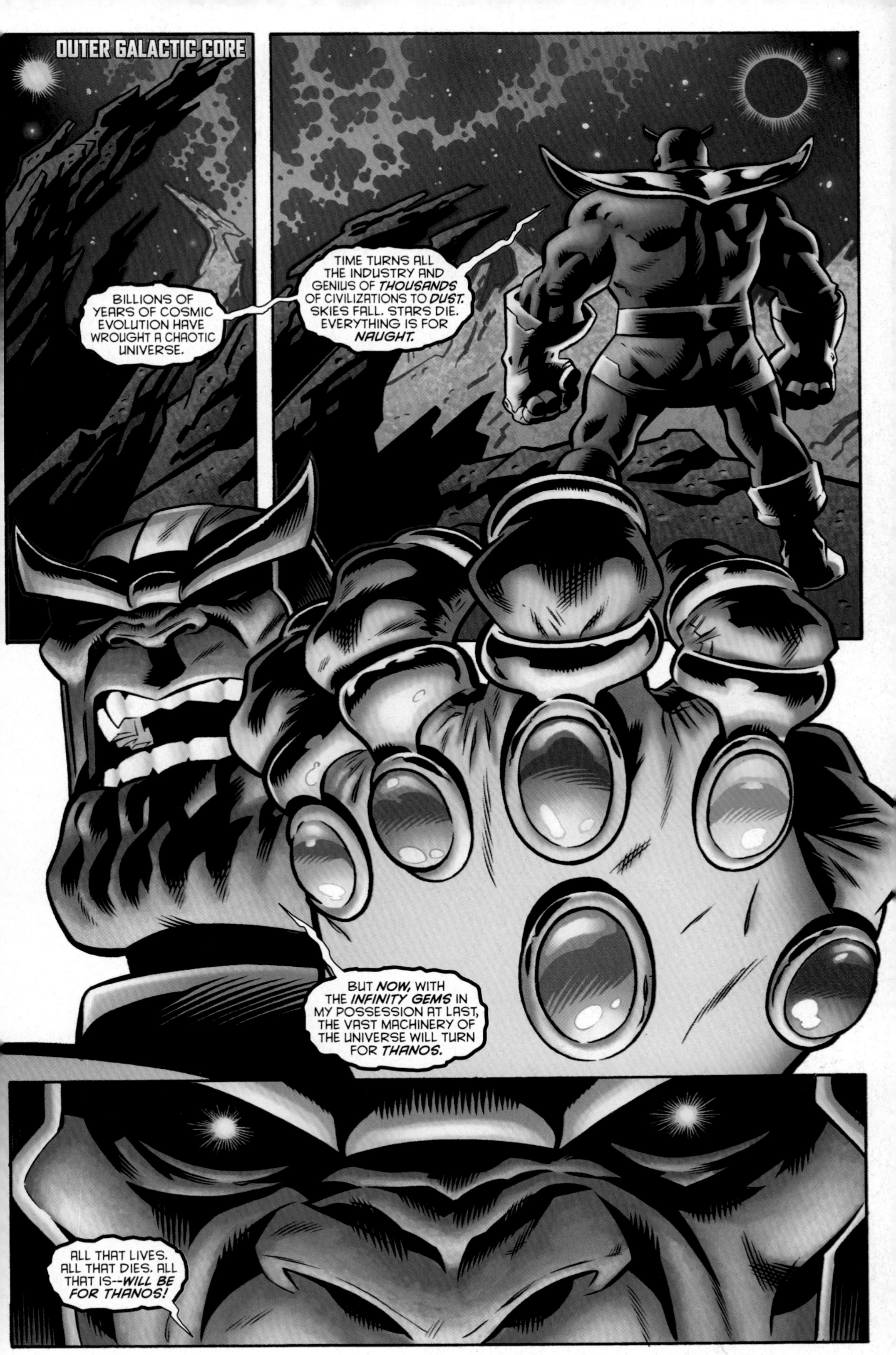
OUTER GALACTIC CORE
BILLIONS OF YEARS OF COSMIC EVOLUTION HAVE WROUGHT A CHAOTIC UNIVERSE.
TIME TURNS ALL THE INDUSTRY AND GENIUS OF THOUSANDS OF CIVILIZATIONS TO DUST. SKIES FALL. STARS DIE. EVERYTHING IS FOR NAUGHT.
BUT NOW, WITH THE INFINITY GEMS IN MY POSSESSION AT LAST, THE VAST MACHINERY OF THE UNIVERSE WILL TURN FOR THANOS.
ALL THAT LIVES. ALL THAT DIES. ALL THAT IS--WILL BE FOR THANOS!

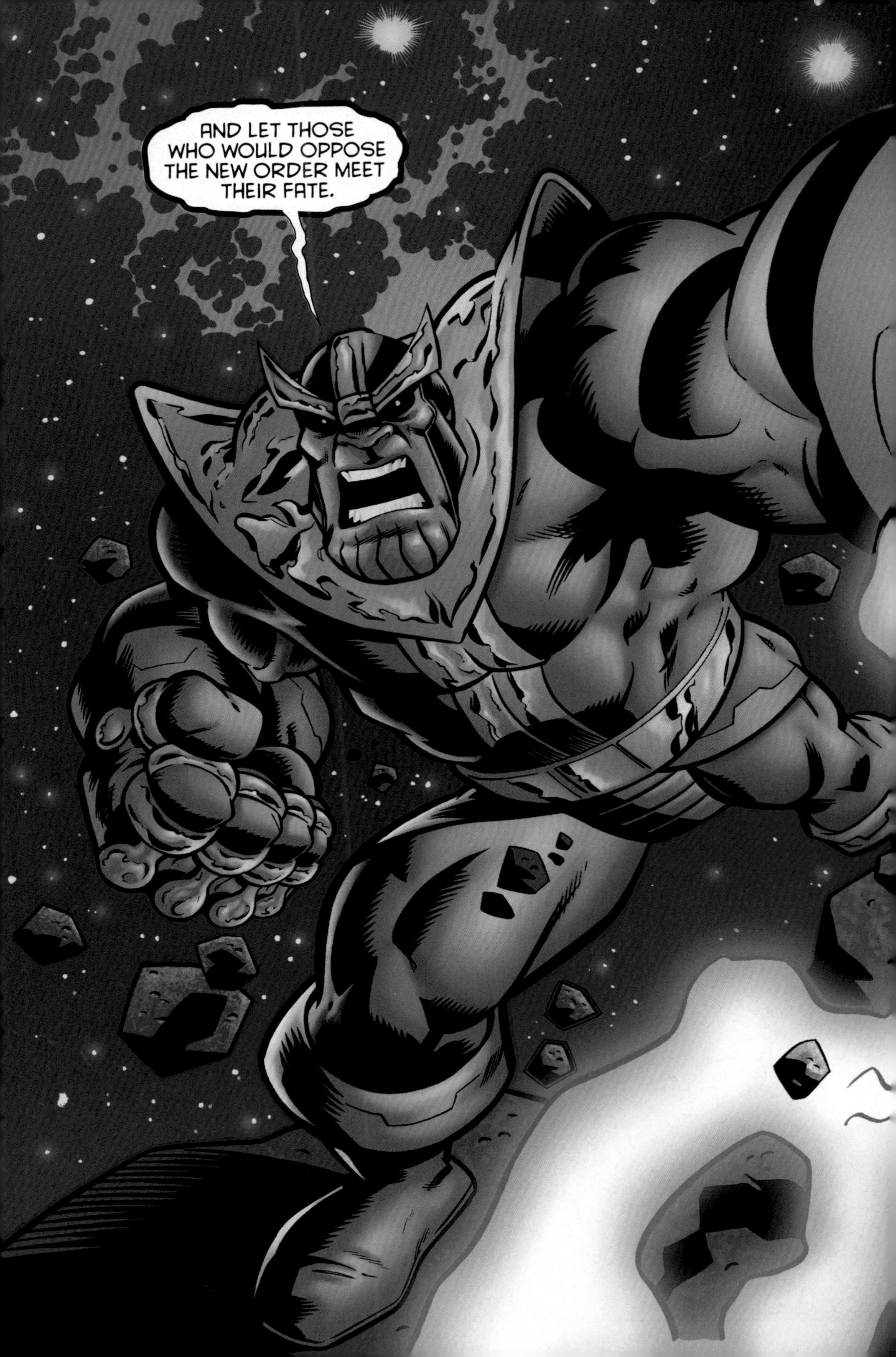
AND LET THOSE WHO WOULD OPPOSE THE NEW ORDER MEET THEIR FATE.

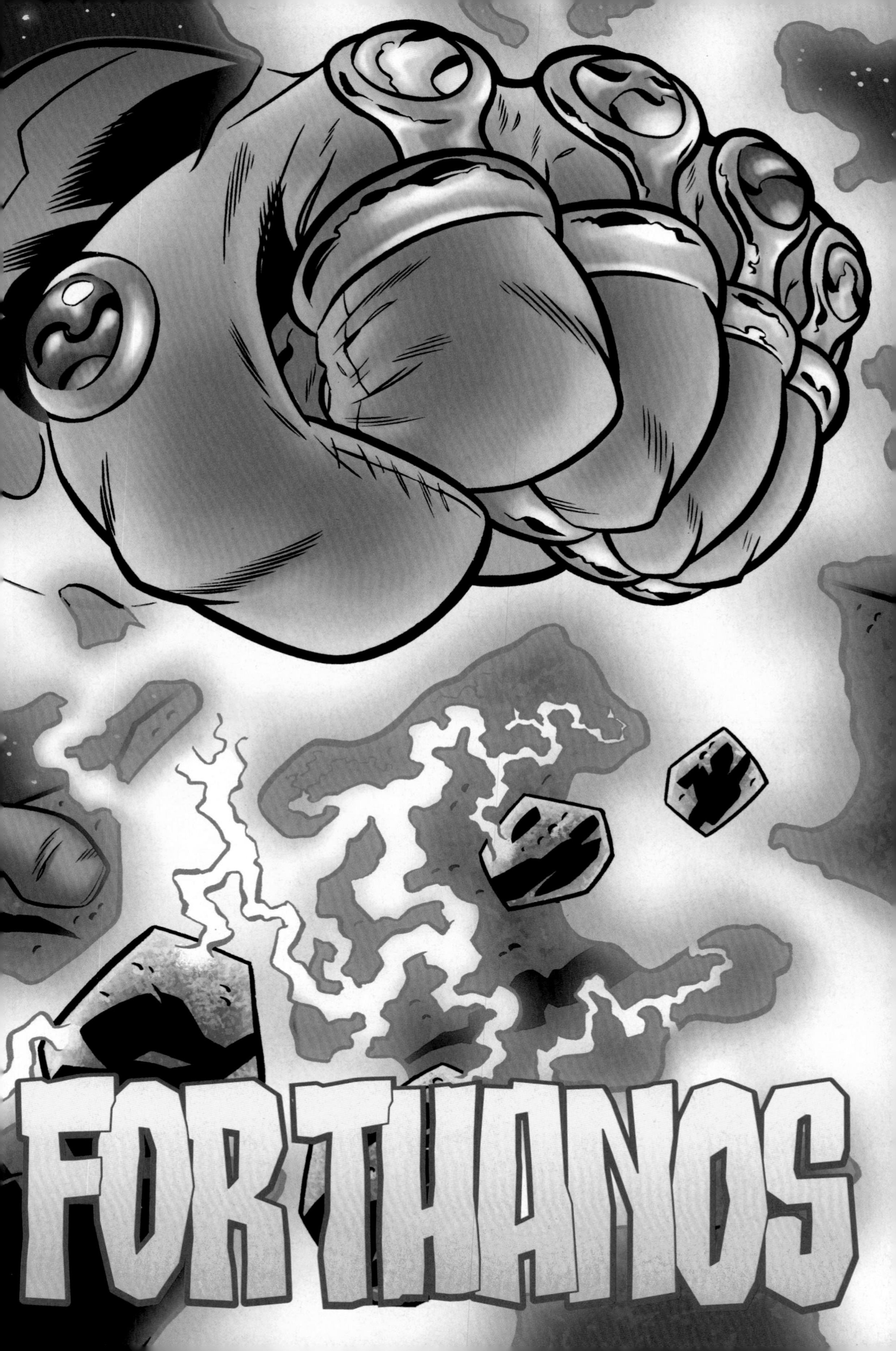
FOR THANOS

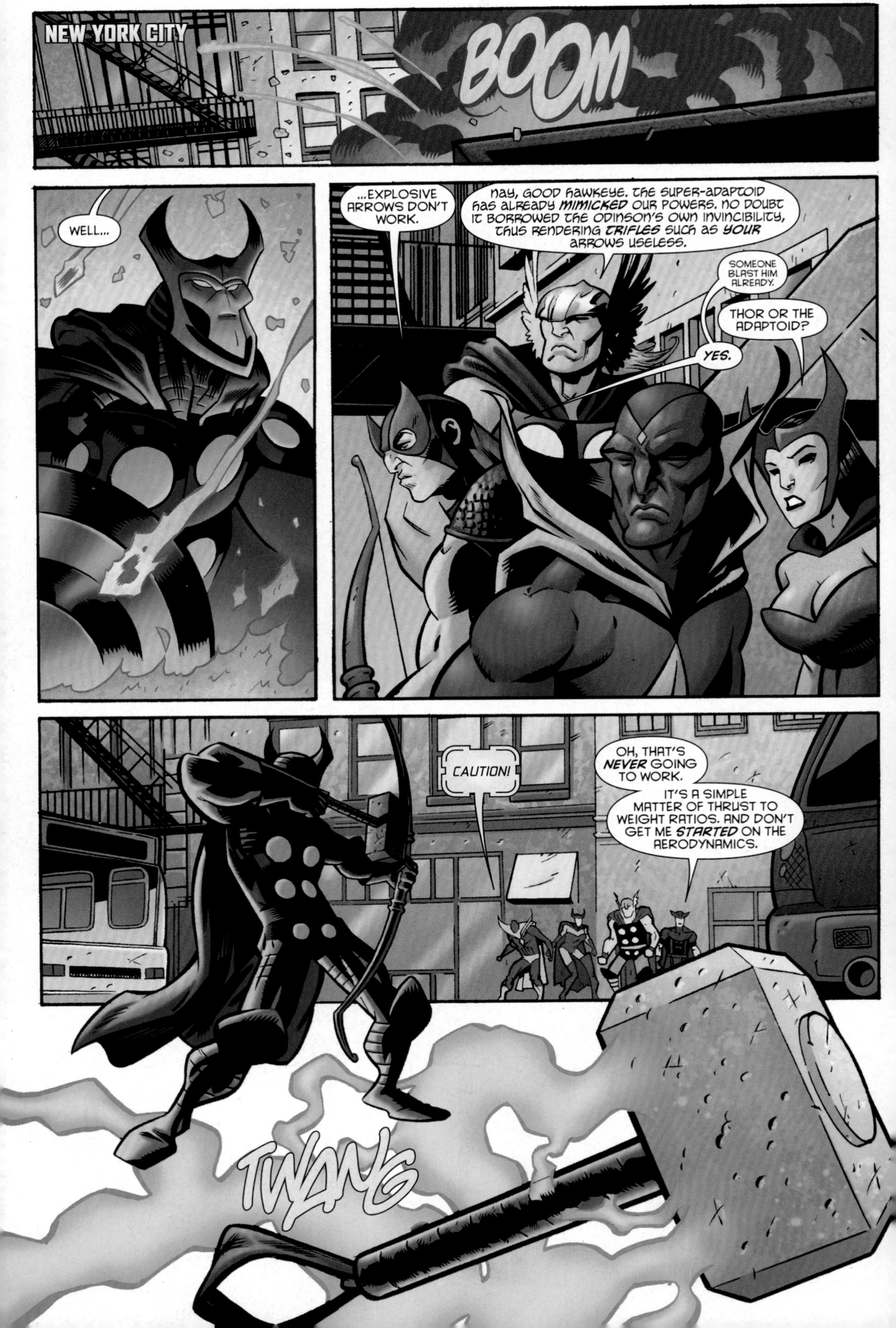
NEW YORK CITY
BOOM
WELL...
...EXPLOSIVE ARROWS DON'T WORK.
NAY, GOOD HAWKEYE. THE SUPER-ADAPTOID HAS ALREADY MIMICKED OUR POWERS. NO DOUBT IT BORROWED THE ODINSON'S OWN INVINCIBILITY, THUS RENDERING TRIFLES SUCH AS YOUR ARROWS USELESS.
SOMEONE BLAST HIM ALREADY.
THOR OR THE ADAPTOID?
YES.
CAUTION!
OH, THAT'S NEVER GOING TO WORK.
IT'S A SIMPLE MATTER OF THRUST TO WEIGHT RATIOS. AND DON'T GET ME STARTED ON THE AERODYNAMICS.
TWANG

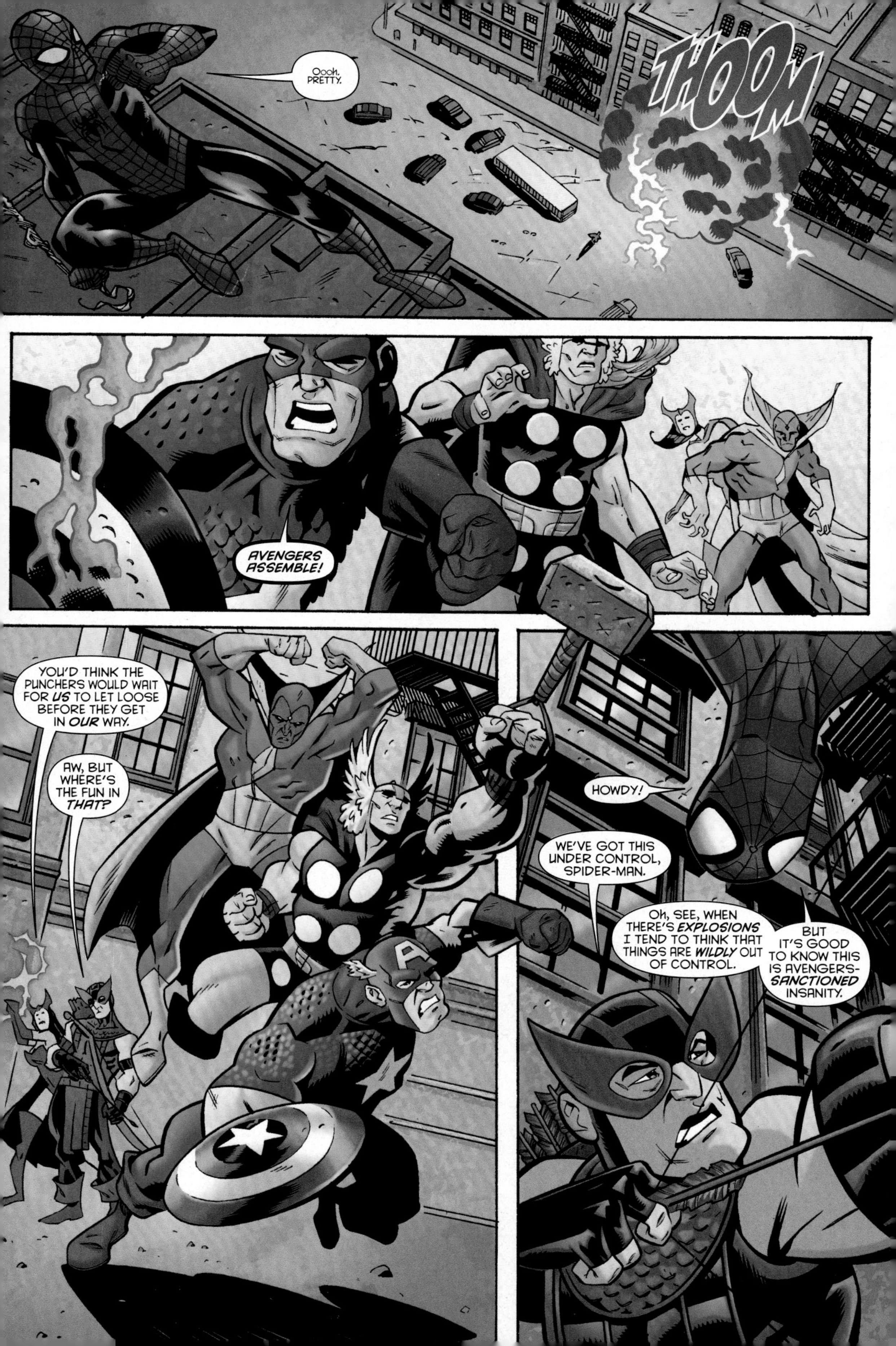
Oooh. PRETTY.
THOOM
AVENGERS ASSEMBLE!
YOU'D THINK THE PUNCHERS WOULD WAIT FOR US TO LET LOOSE BEFORE THEY GET IN OUR WAY.
AW, BUT WHERE'S THE FUN IN THAT?
HOWDY!
WE'VE GOT THIS UNDER CONTROL, SPIDER-MAN.
Oh, SEE, WHEN THERE'S EXPLOSIONS I TEND TO THINK THAT THINGS ARE WILDLY OUT OF CONTROL.
BUT IT'S GOOD TO KNOW THIS IS AVENGERS-SANCTIONED INSANITY.

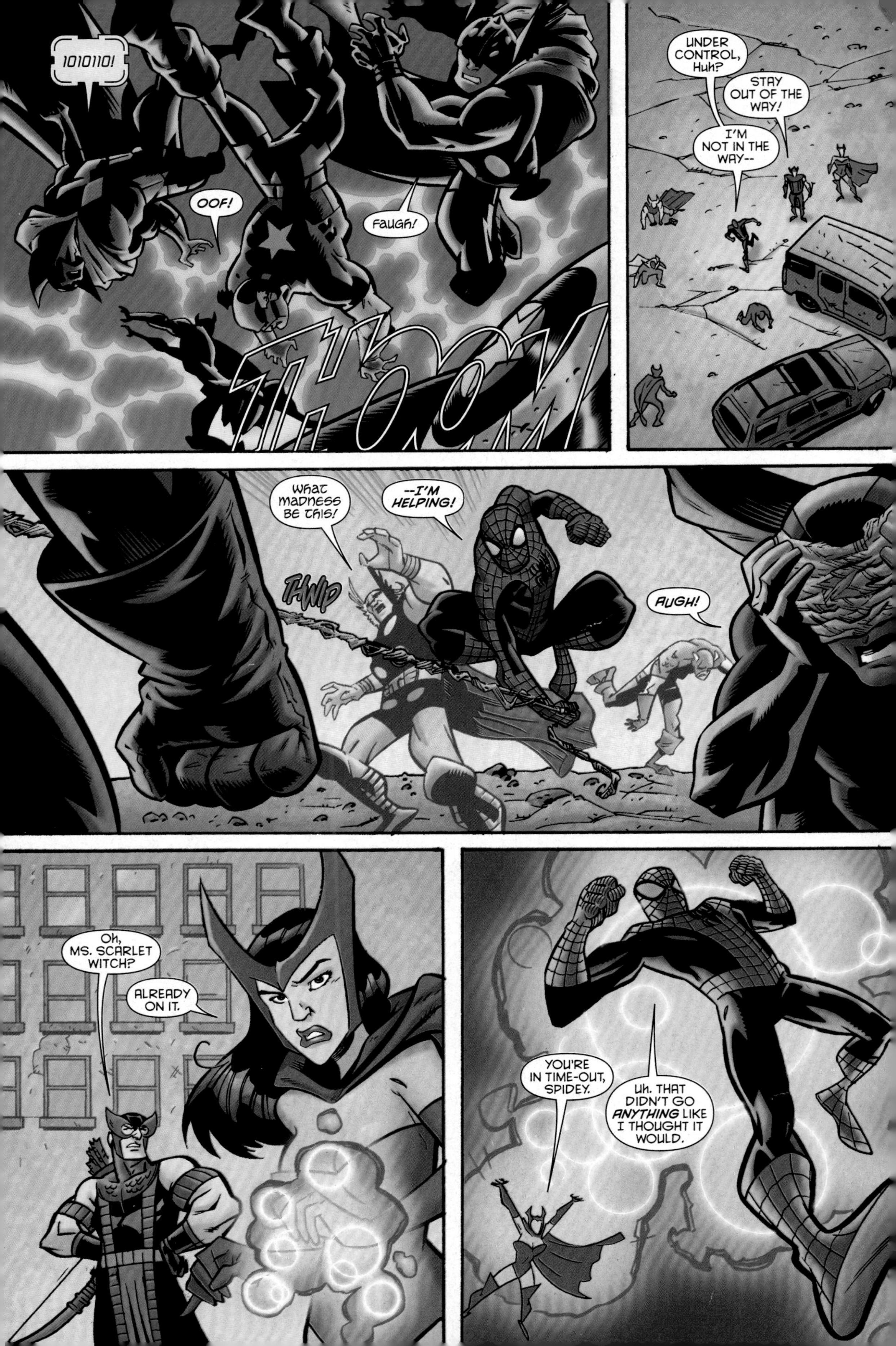
1010110!
OOF!
FAUGH!
THOOM
UNDER CONTROL, HUH?
STAY OUT OF THE WAY!
I'M NOT IN THE WAY--
WHAT MADNESS BE THIS!
--I'M HELPING!
THWIP
AUGH!
OH, MS. SCARLET WITCH?
ALREADY ON IT.
YOU'RE IN TIME-OUT, SPIDEY.
UH. THAT DIDN'T GO ANYTHING LIKE I THOUGHT IT WOULD.

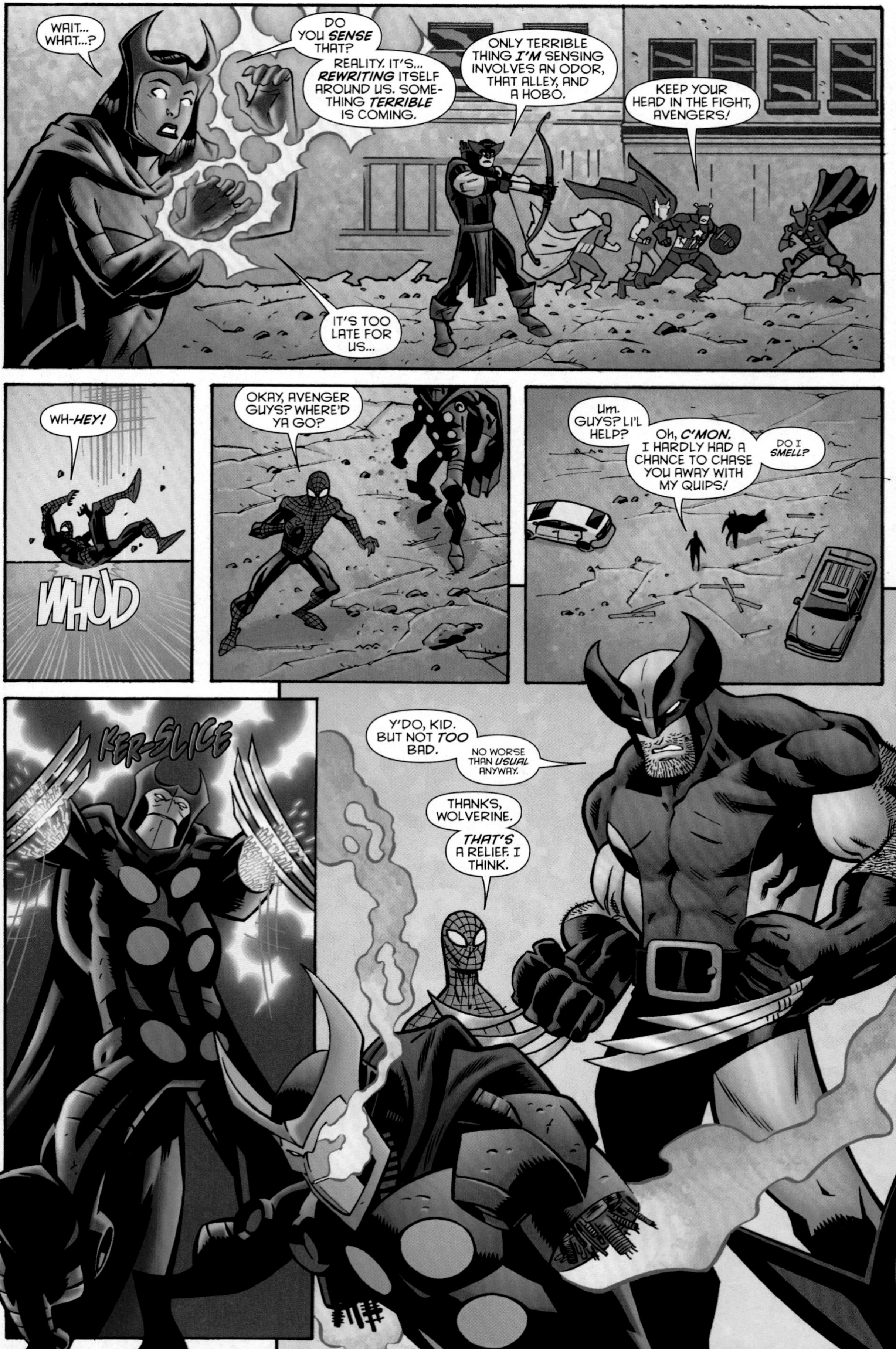
WAIT... WHAT...?
DO YOU SENSE THAT?
REALITY. IT'S... REWRITING ITSELF AROUND US. SOMETHING TERRIBLE IS COMING.
ONLY TERRIBLE THING I'M SENSING INVOLVES AN ODOR, THAT ALLEY, AND A HOBO.
KEEP YOUR HEAD IN THE FIGHT, AVENGERS!
IT'S TOO LATE FOR US...
WH-HEY!
WHUD
OKAY, AVENGER GUYS? WHERE'D YA GO?
Um. GUYS? LI'L HELP?
Oh, C'MON. I HARDLY HAD A CHANCE TO CHASE YOU AWAY WITH MY QUIPS!
DO I SMELL?
KER-SLICE
Y'DO, KID. BUT NOT TOO BAD.
NO WORSE THAN USUAL ANYWAY.
THANKS, WOLVERINE. THAT'S A RELIEF. I THINK.

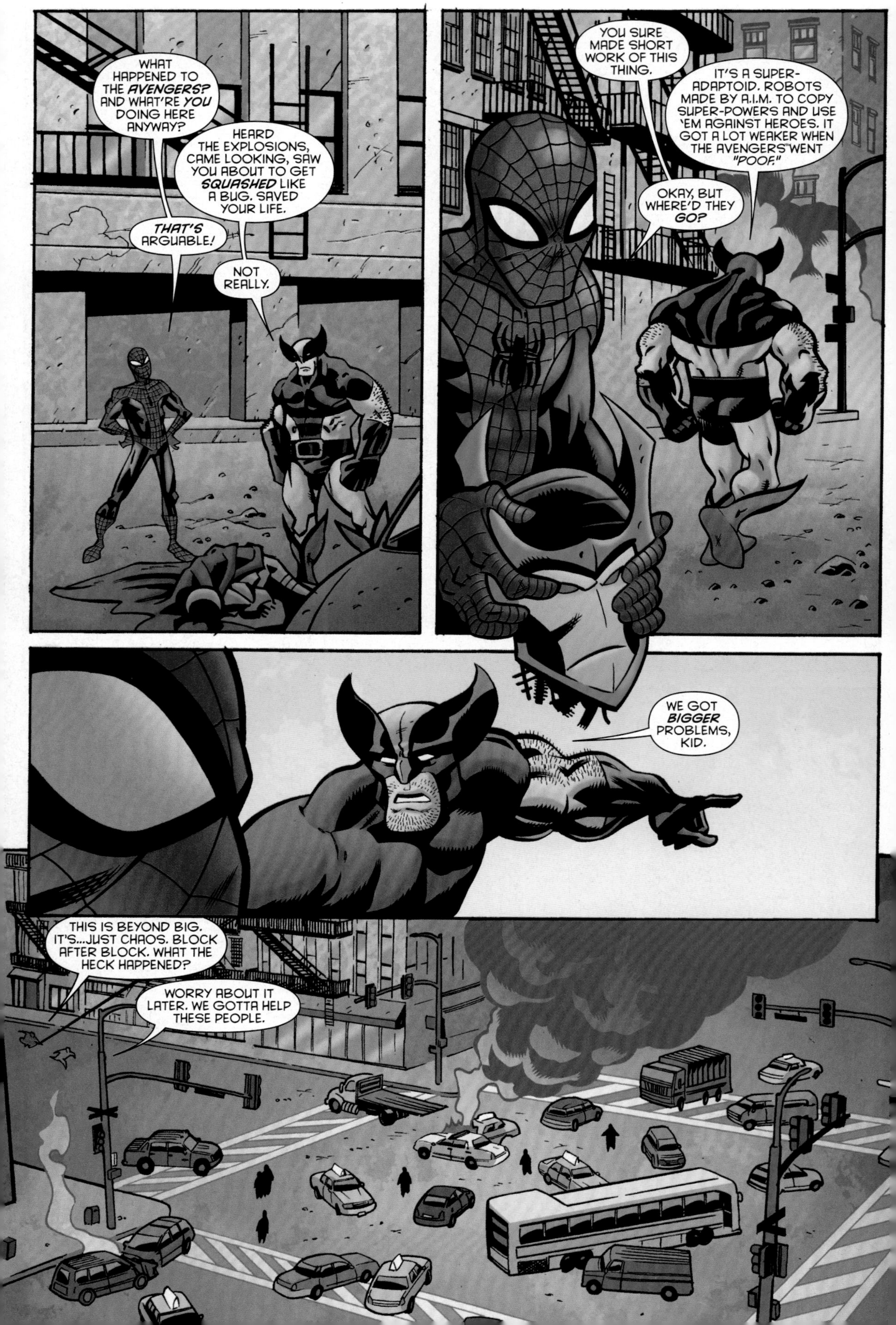
WHAT HAPPENED TO THE AVENGERS? AND WHAT'RE YOU DOING HERE ANYWAY?
HEARD THE EXPLOSIONS, CAME LOOKING, SAW YOU ABOUT TO GET SQUASHED LIKE A BUG. SAVED YOUR LIFE.
THAT'S ARGUABLE!
NOT REALLY.
YOU SURE MADE SHORT WORK OF THIS THING.
IT'S A SUPER-ADAPTOID. ROBOTS MADE BY A.I.M. TO COPY SUPER-POWERS AND USE 'EM AGAINST HEROES. IT GOT A LOT WEAKER WHEN THE AVENGERS WENT "POOF."
OKAY, BUT WHERE'D THEY GO?
WE GOT BIGGER PROBLEMS, KID.
THIS IS BEYOND BIG. IT'S...JUST CHAOS. BLOCK AFTER BLOCK. WHAT THE HECK HAPPENED?
WORRY ABOUT IT LATER. WE GOTTA HELP THESE PEOPLE.

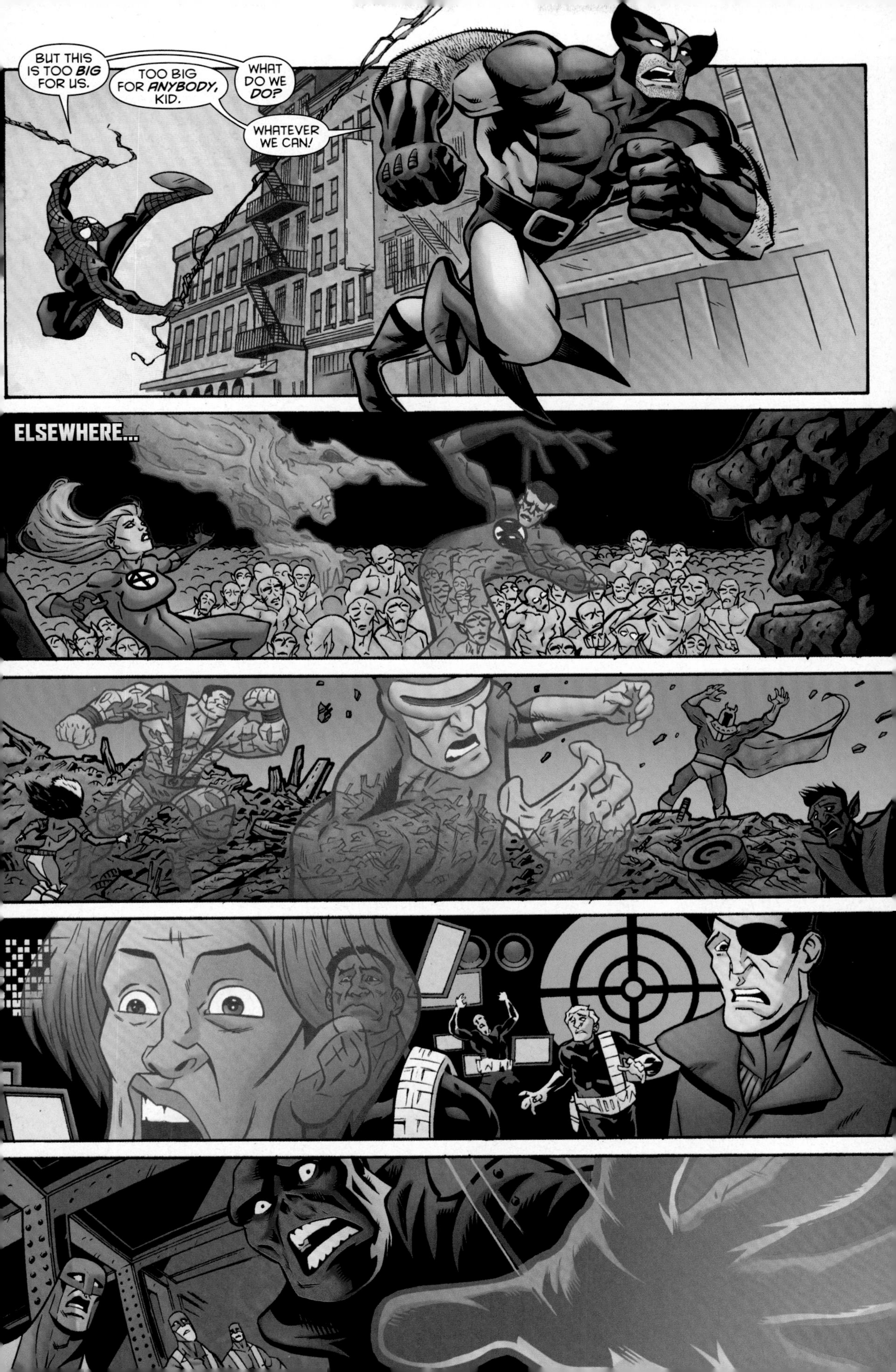

BUT THIS IS TOO *BIG* FOR US.
WHAT DO WE *DO?*
TOO BIG FOR *ANYBODY,* KID.
WHATEVER WE CAN!
ELSEWHERE...

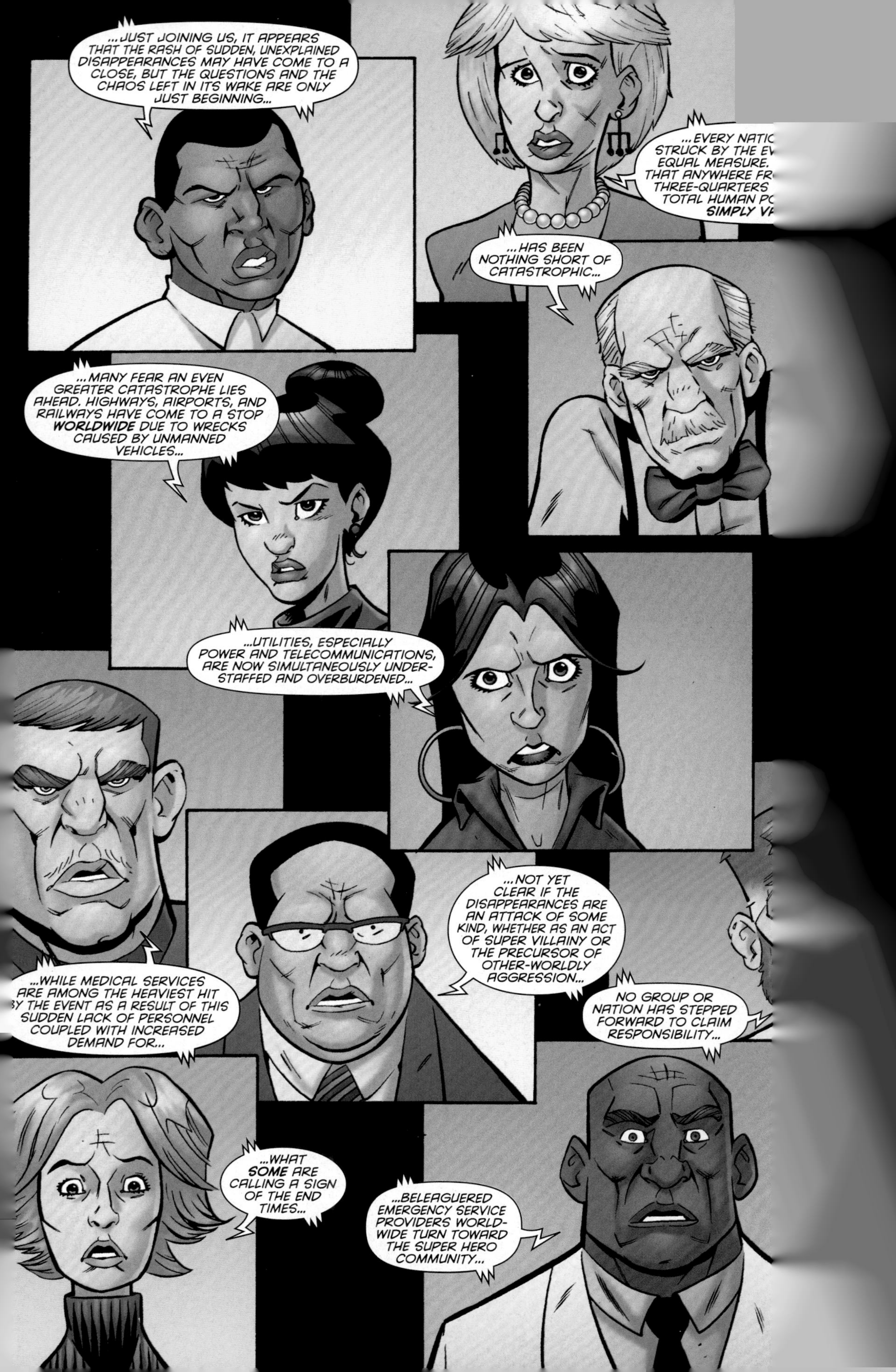

...JUST JOINING US, IT APPEARS THAT THE RASH OF SUDDEN, UNEXPLAINED DISAPPEARANCES MAY HAVE COME TO A CLOSE, BUT THE QUESTIONS AND THE CHAOS LEFT IN ITS WAKE ARE ONLY JUST BEGINNING...
...EVERY NATIC STRUCK BY THE EV EQUAL MEASURE. THAT ANYWHERE FR THREE-QUARTERS TOTAL HUMAN PO SIMPLY VA
...HAS BEEN NOTHING SHORT OF CATASTROPHIC...
...MANY FEAR AN EVEN GREATER CATASTROPHE LIES AHEAD. HIGHWAYS, AIRPORTS, AND RAILWAYS HAVE COME TO A STOP WORLDWIDE DUE TO WRECKS CAUSED BY UNMANNED VEHICLES...
...UTILITIES, ESPECIALLY POWER AND TELECOMMUNICATIONS, ARE NOW SIMULTANEOUSLY UNDER-STAFFED AND OVERBURDENED...
...WHILE MEDICAL SERVICES ARE AMONG THE HEAVIEST HIT BY THE EVENT AS A RESULT OF THIS SUDDEN LACK OF PERSONNEL COUPLED WITH INCREASED DEMAND FOR...
...NOT YET CLEAR IF THE DISAPPEARANCES ARE AN ATTACK OF SOME KIND, WHETHER AS AN ACT OF SUPER VILLAINY OR THE PRECURSOR OF OTHER-WORLDLY AGGRESSION...
NO GROUP OR NATION HAS STEPPED FORWARD TO CLAIM RESPONSIBILITY...
...WHAT SOME ARE CALLING A SIGN OF THE END TIMES...
...BELEAGUERED EMERGENCY SERVICE PROVIDERS WORLD-WIDE TURN TOWARD THE SUPER HERO COMMUNITY...

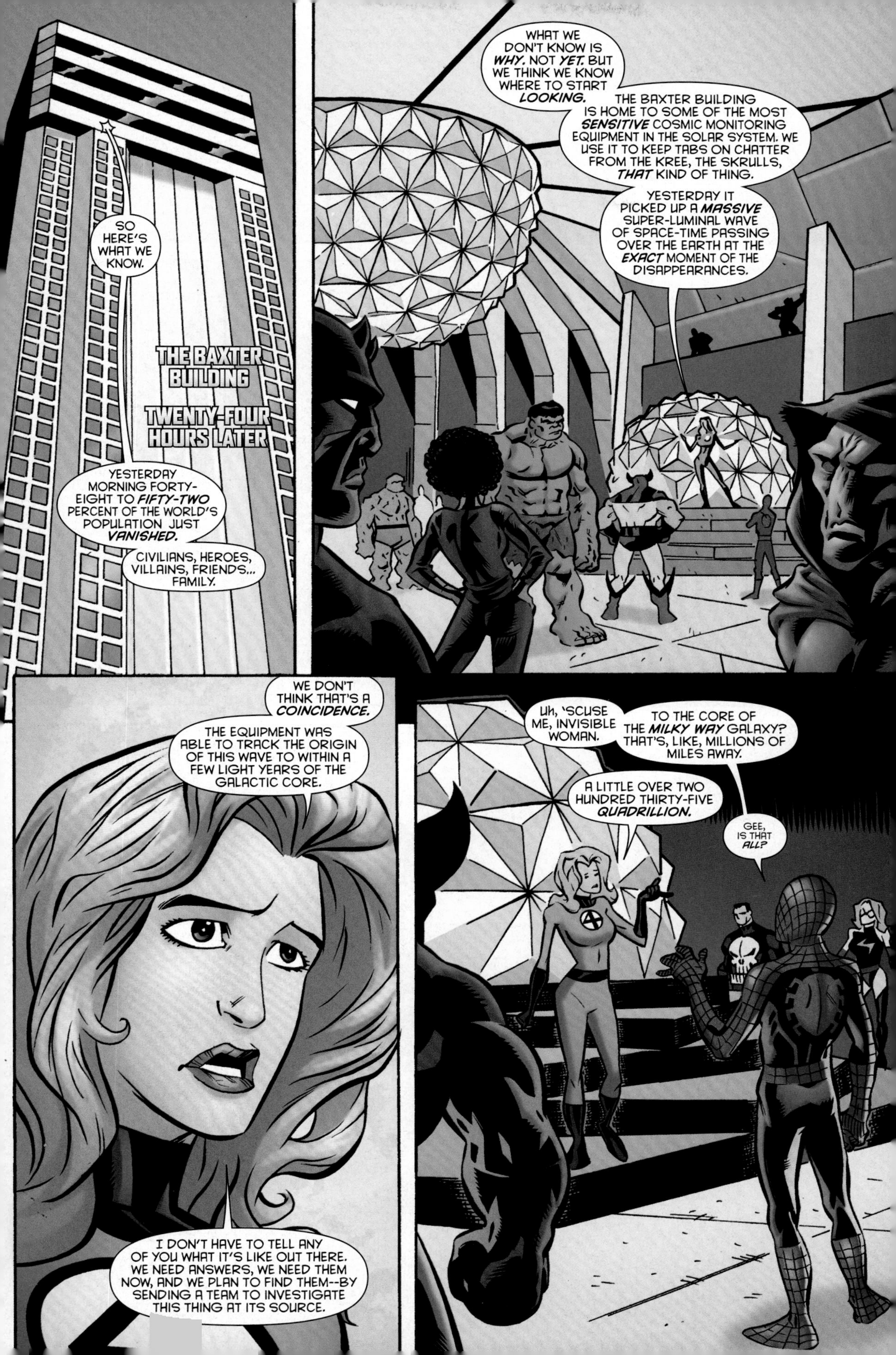
SO HERE'S WHAT WE KNOW.
THE BAXTER BUILDING
TWENTY-FOUR HOURS LATER
YESTERDAY MORNING FORTY-EIGHT TO FIFTY-TWO PERCENT OF THE WORLD'S POPULATION JUST VANISHED.
CIVILIANS, HEROES, VILLAINS, FRIENDS... FAMILY.
WHAT WE DON'T KNOW IS WHY. NOT YET. BUT WE THINK WE KNOW WHERE TO START LOOKING.
THE BAXTER BUILDING IS HOME TO SOME OF THE MOST SENSITIVE COSMIC MONITORING EQUIPMENT IN THE SOLAR SYSTEM. WE USE IT TO KEEP TABS ON CHATTER FROM THE KREE, THE SKRULLS, THAT KIND OF THING.
YESTERDAY IT PICKED UP A MASSIVE SUPER-LUMINAL WAVE OF SPACE-TIME PASSING OVER THE EARTH AT THE EXACT MOMENT OF THE DISAPPEARANCES.
WE DON'T THINK THAT'S A COINCIDENCE.
THE EQUIPMENT WAS ABLE TO TRACK THE ORIGIN OF THIS WAVE TO WITHIN A FEW LIGHT YEARS OF THE GALACTIC CORE.
I DON'T HAVE TO TELL ANY OF YOU WHAT IT'S LIKE OUT THERE. WE NEED ANSWERS, WE NEED THEM NOW, AND WE PLAN TO FIND THEM--BY SENDING A TEAM TO INVESTIGATE THIS THING AT ITS SOURCE.
UH, 'SCUSE ME, INVISIBLE WOMAN.
TO THE CORE OF THE MILKY WAY GALAXY? THAT'S, LIKE, MILLIONS OF MILES AWAY.
A LITTLE OVER TWO HUNDRED THIRTY-FIVE QUADRILLION.
GEE, IS THAT ALL?

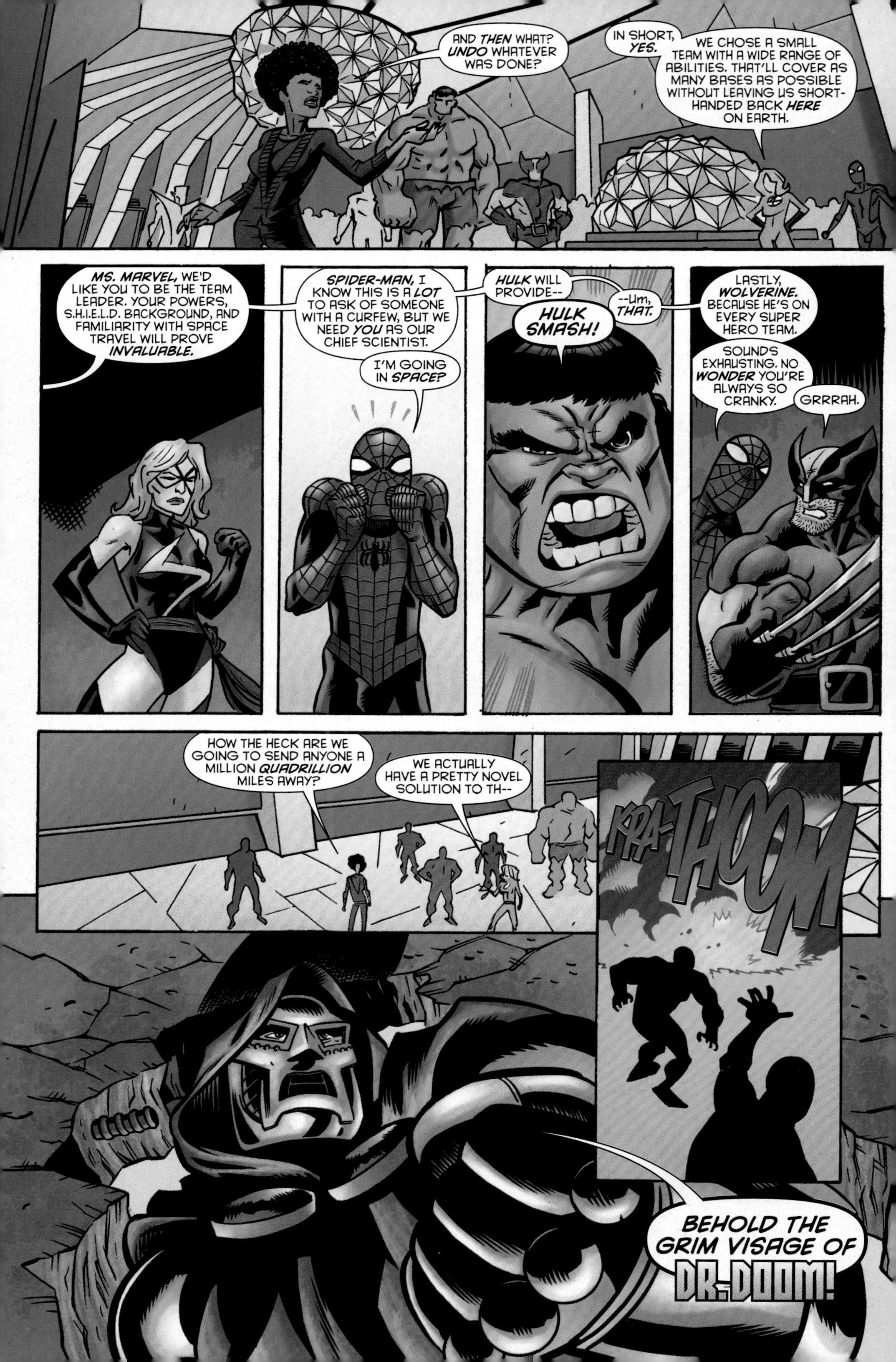
AND *THEN* WHAT? *UNDO* WHATEVER WAS DONE?
IN SHORT, *YES.*
WE CHOSE A SMALL TEAM WITH A WIDE RANGE OF ABILITIES. THAT'LL COVER AS MANY BASES AS POSSIBLE WITHOUT LEAVING US SHORT-HANDED BACK *HERE* ON EARTH.
MS. MARVEL, WE'D LIKE YOU TO BE THE TEAM LEADER. YOUR POWERS, S.H.I.E.L.D. BACKGROUND, AND FAMILIARITY WITH SPACE TRAVEL WILL PROVE *INVALUABLE.*
SPIDER-MAN, I KNOW THIS IS A *LOT* TO ASK OF SOMEONE WITH A CURFEW, BUT WE NEED *YOU* AS OUR CHIEF SCIENTIST.
I'M GOING IN *SPACE?*
HULK WILL PROVIDE--
--UM, *THAT.*
HULK SMASH!
LASTLY, *WOLVERINE.* BECAUSE HE'S ON EVERY SUPER HERO TEAM.
SOUNDS EXHAUSTING. NO *WONDER* YOU'RE ALWAYS SO CRANKY.
GRRRAH.
HOW THE HECK ARE WE GOING TO SEND ANYONE A MILLION *QUADRILLION* MILES AWAY?
WE ACTUALLY HAVE A PRETTY NOVEL SOLUTION TO TH--
KRA-THOOOM
BEHOLD THE GRIM VISAGE OF DR. DOOM!

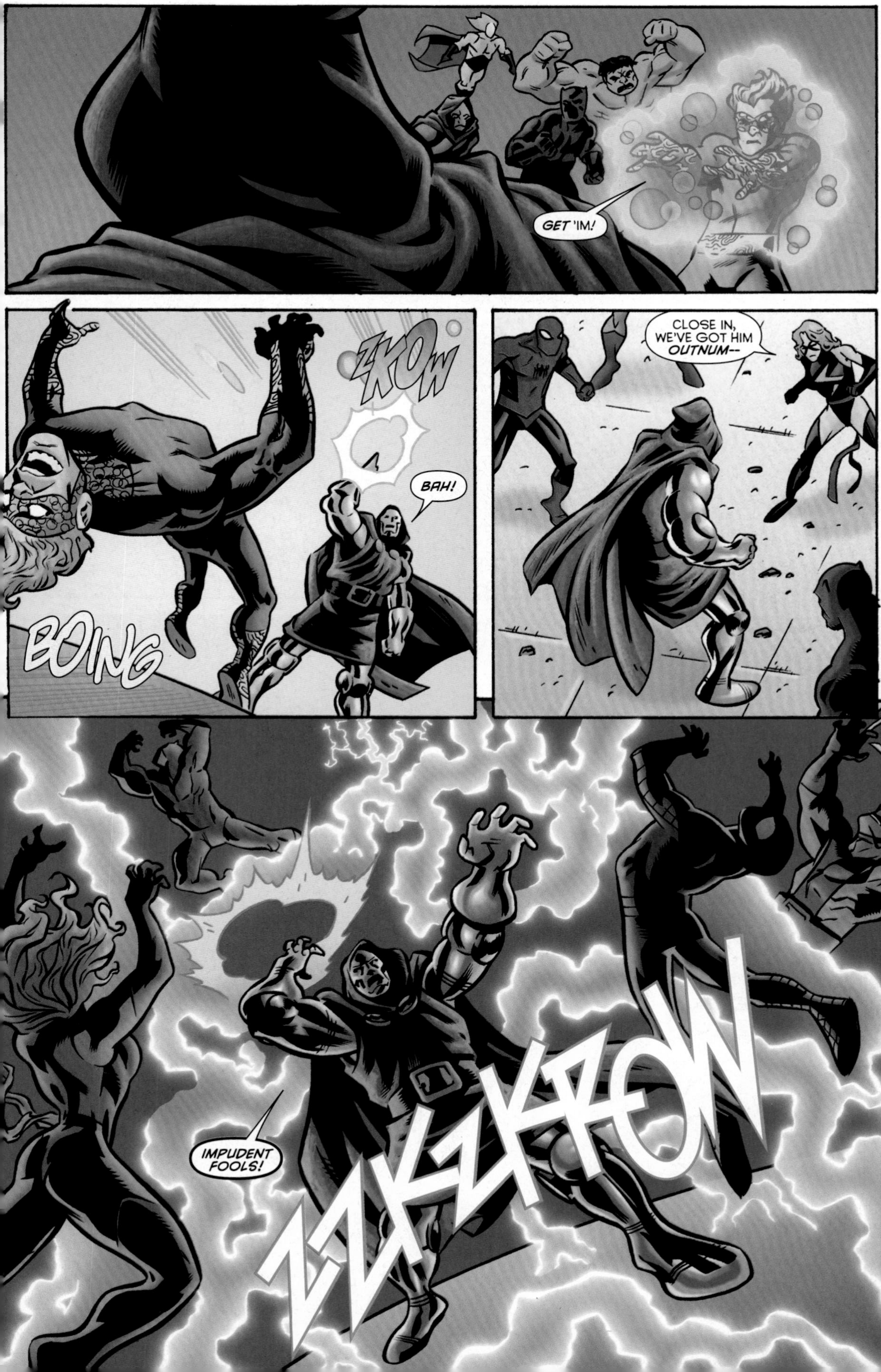
GET 'IM!
ZKOW
BAH!
BOING
CLOSE IN, WE'VE GOT HIM OUTNUM--
IMPUDENT FOOLS!
ZZKZZKROW

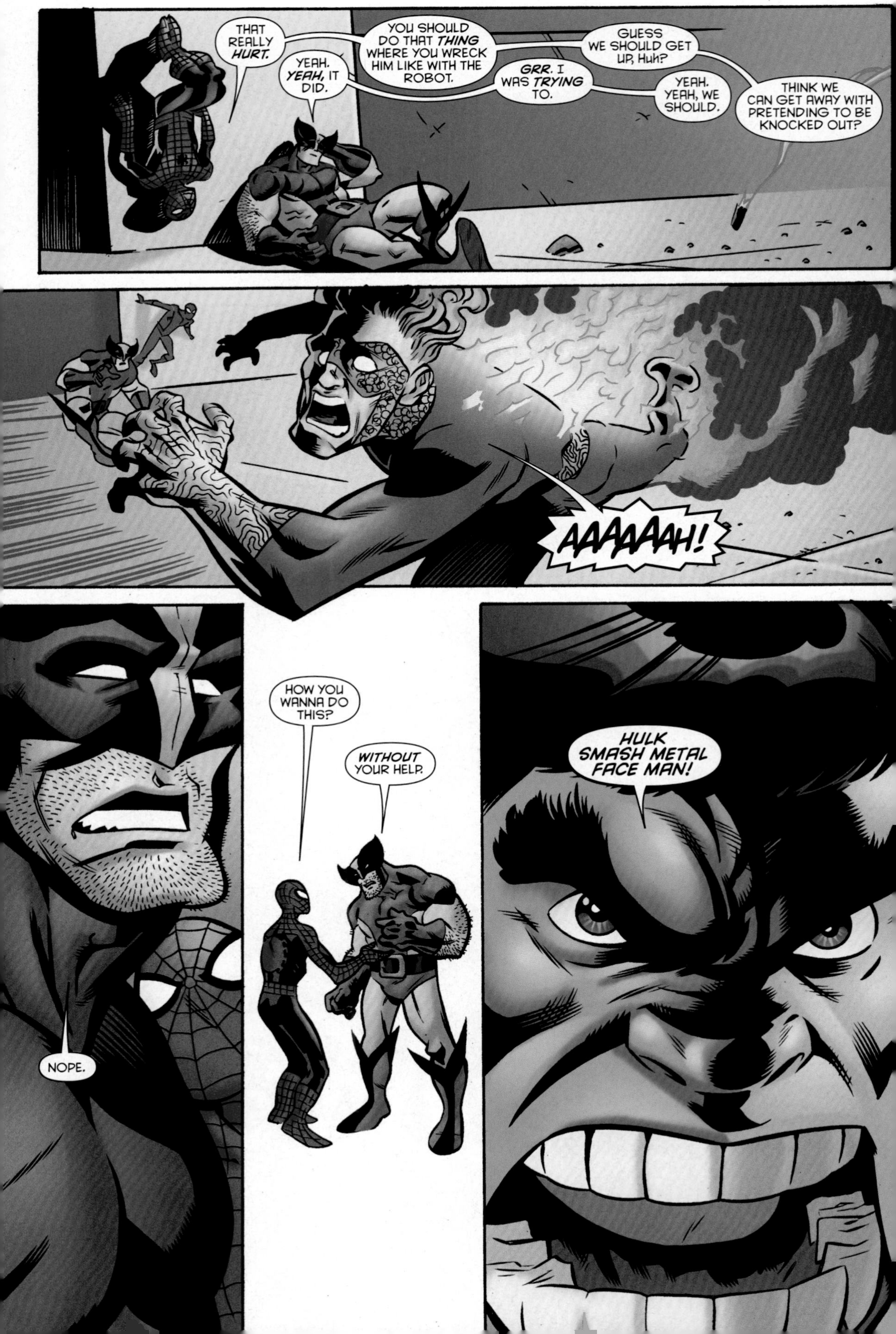

THAT REALLY *HURT.*
YEAH. *YEAH,* IT DID.
YOU SHOULD DO THAT *THING* WHERE YOU WRECK HIM LIKE WITH THE ROBOT.
GRR. I WAS *TRYING* TO.
GUESS WE SHOULD GET UP, HUH?
YEAH. YEAH, WE SHOULD.
THINK WE CAN GET AWAY WITH PRETENDING TO BE KNOCKED OUT?
AAAAAAH!
NOPE.
HOW YOU WANNA DO THIS?
WITHOUT YOUR HELP.
HULK SMASH METAL FACE MAN!

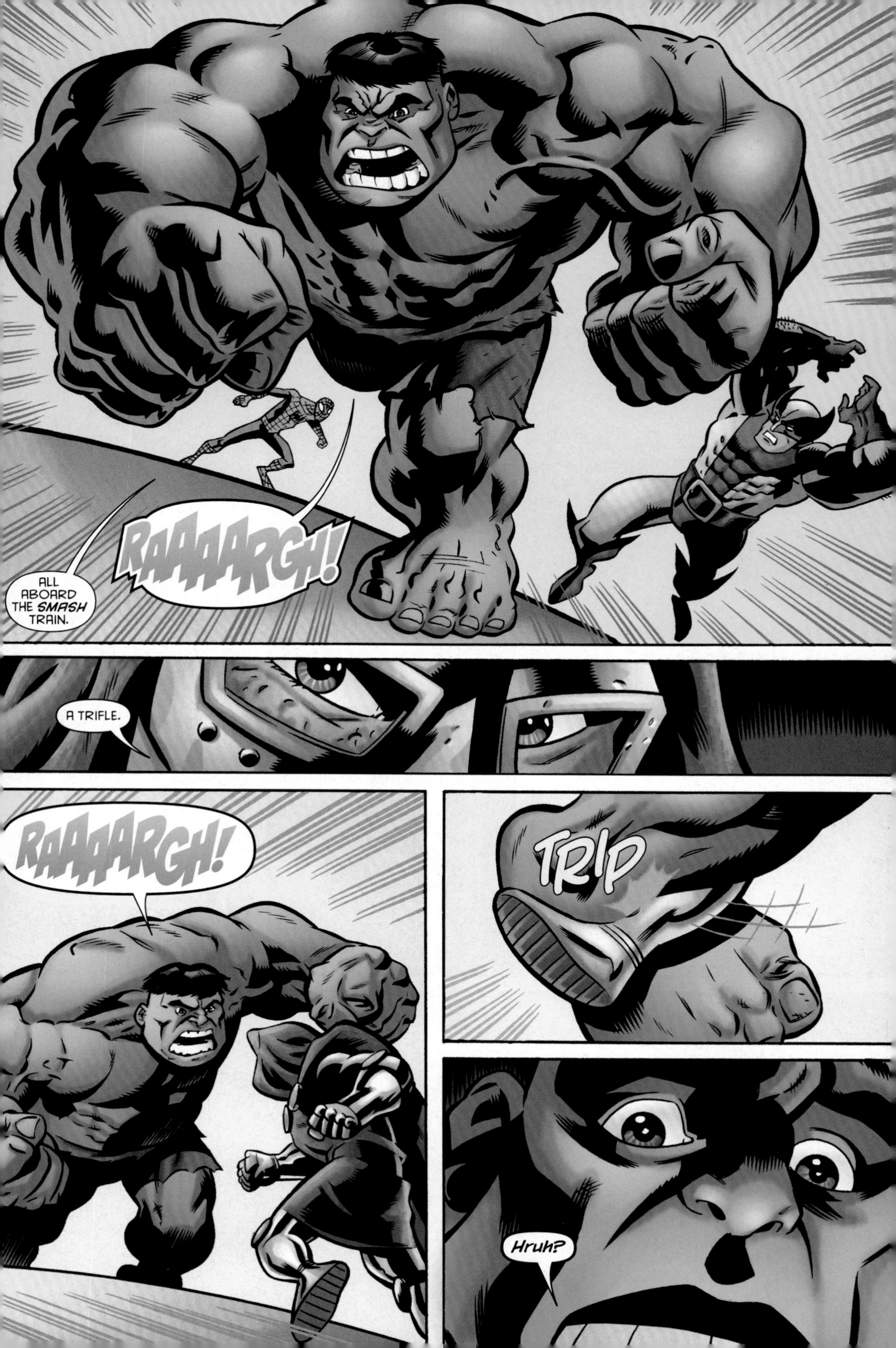

RAAAARGH!
ALL ABOARD THE SMASH TRAIN.
A TRIFLE.
RAAAARGH!
TRIP
Hruh?

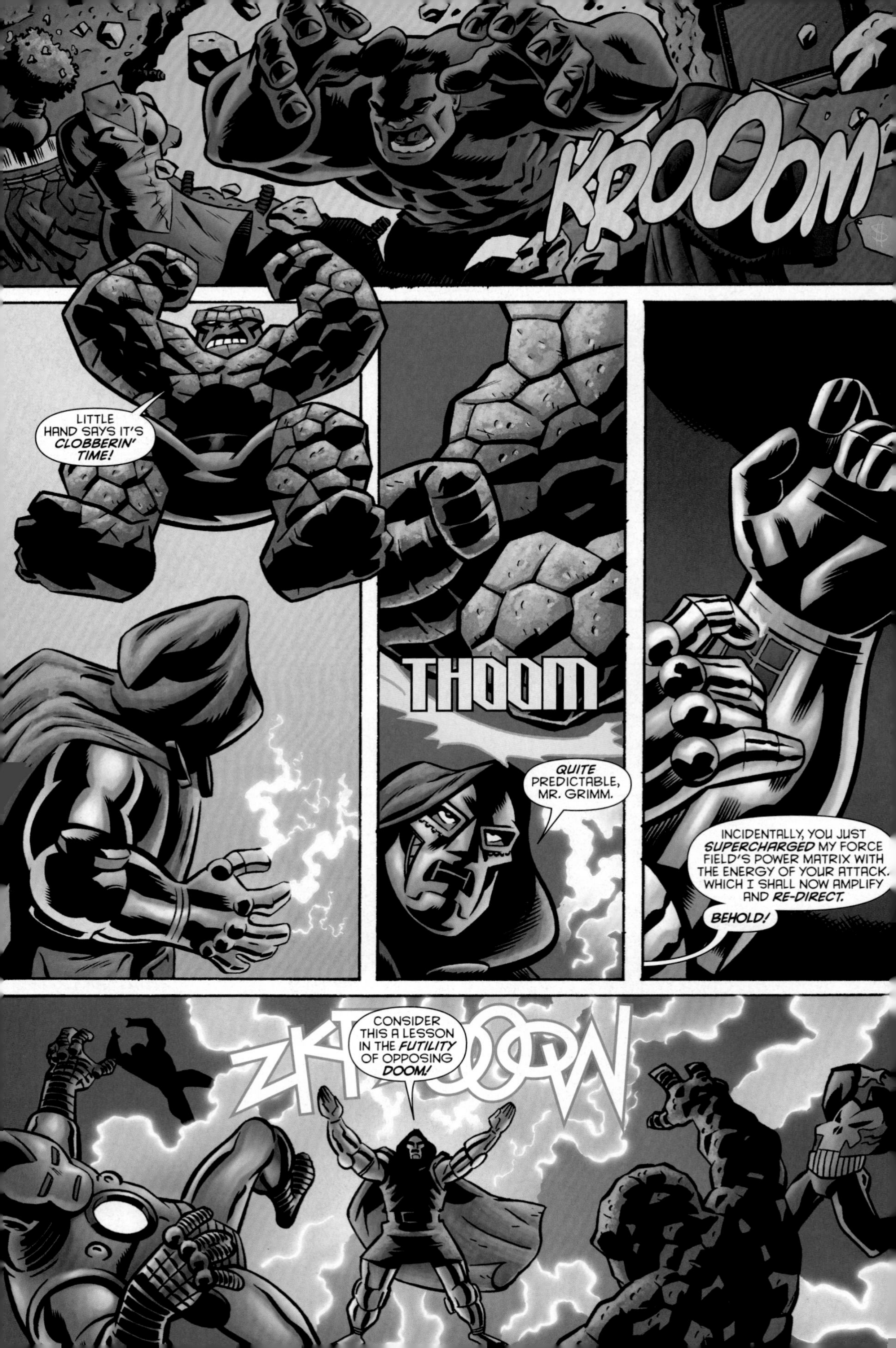
KROOOOM
LITTLE HAND SAYS IT'S CLOBBERIN' TIME!
THOOM
QUITE PREDICTABLE, MR. GRIMM.
INCIDENTALLY, YOU JUST SUPERCHARGED MY FORCE FIELD'S POWER MATRIX WITH THE ENERGY OF YOUR ATTACK. WHICH I SHALL NOW AMPLIFY AND RE-DIRECT.
BEHOLD!
CONSIDER THIS A LESSON IN THE FUTILITY OF OPPOSING DOOM!

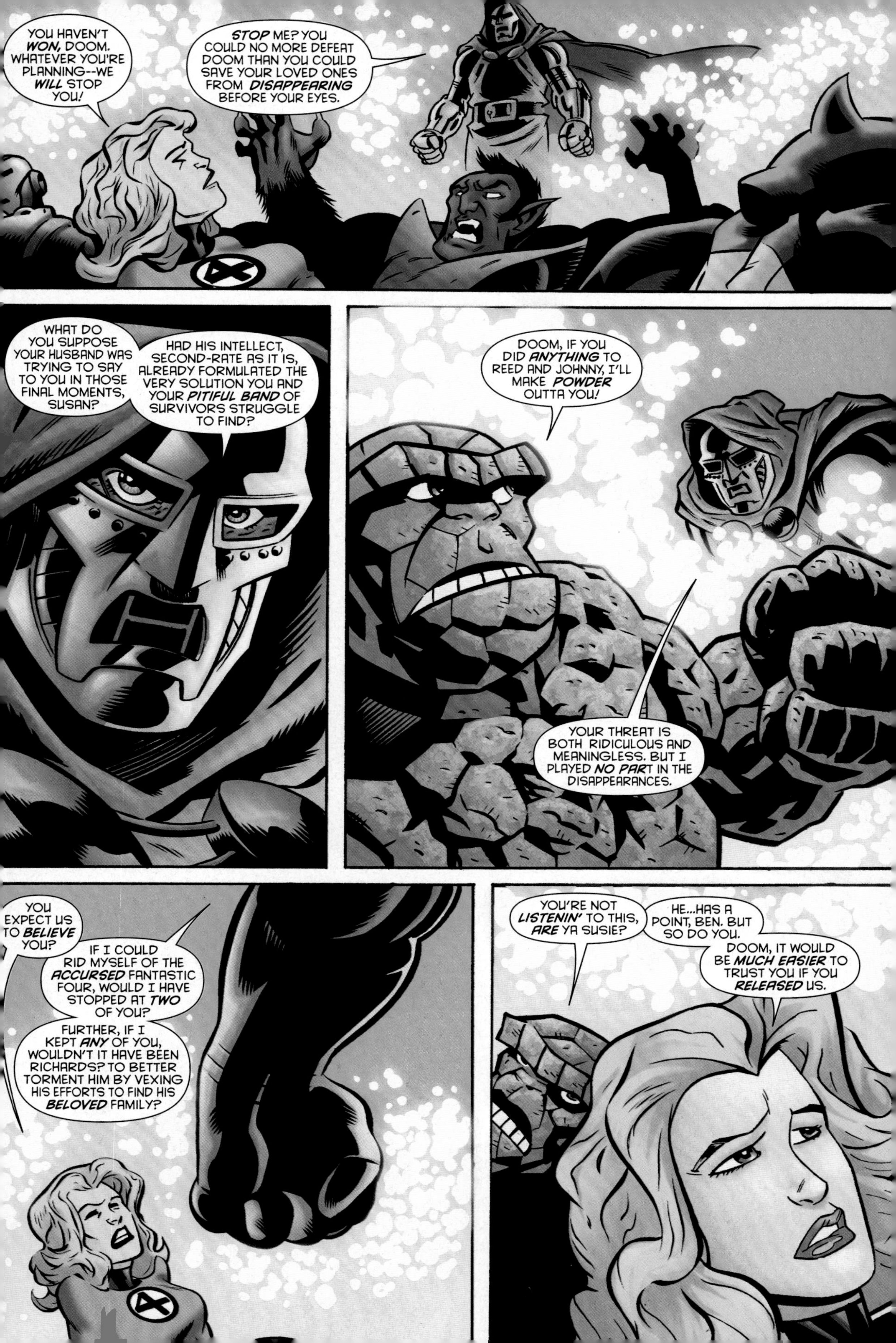
YOU HAVEN'T WON, DOOM. WHATEVER YOU'RE PLANNING--WE WILL STOP YOU!
STOP ME? YOU COULD NO MORE DEFEAT DOOM THAN YOU COULD SAVE YOUR LOVED ONES FROM DISAPPEARING BEFORE YOUR EYES.
WHAT DO YOU SUPPOSE YOUR HUSBAND WAS TRYING TO SAY TO YOU IN THOSE FINAL MOMENTS, SUSAN?
HAD HIS INTELLECT, SECOND-RATE AS IT IS, ALREADY FORMULATED THE VERY SOLUTION YOU AND YOUR PITIFUL BAND OF SURVIVORS STRUGGLE TO FIND?
DOOM, IF YOU DID ANYTHING TO REED AND JOHNNY, I'LL MAKE POWDER OUTTA YOU!
YOUR THREAT IS BOTH RIDICULOUS AND MEANINGLESS. BUT I PLAYED NO PART IN THE DISAPPEARANCES.
YOU EXPECT US TO BELIEVE YOU?
IF I COULD RID MYSELF OF THE ACCURSED FANTASTIC FOUR, WOULD I HAVE STOPPED AT TWO OF YOU?
FURTHER, IF I KEPT ANY OF YOU, WOULDN'T IT HAVE BEEN RICHARDS? TO BETTER TORMENT HIM BY VEXING HIS EFFORTS TO FIND HIS BELOVED FAMILY?
YOU'RE NOT LISTENIN' TO THIS, ARE YA SUSIE?
HE...HAS A POINT, BEN. BUT SO DO YOU.
DOOM, IT WOULD BE MUCH EASIER TO TRUST YOU IF YOU RELEASED US.

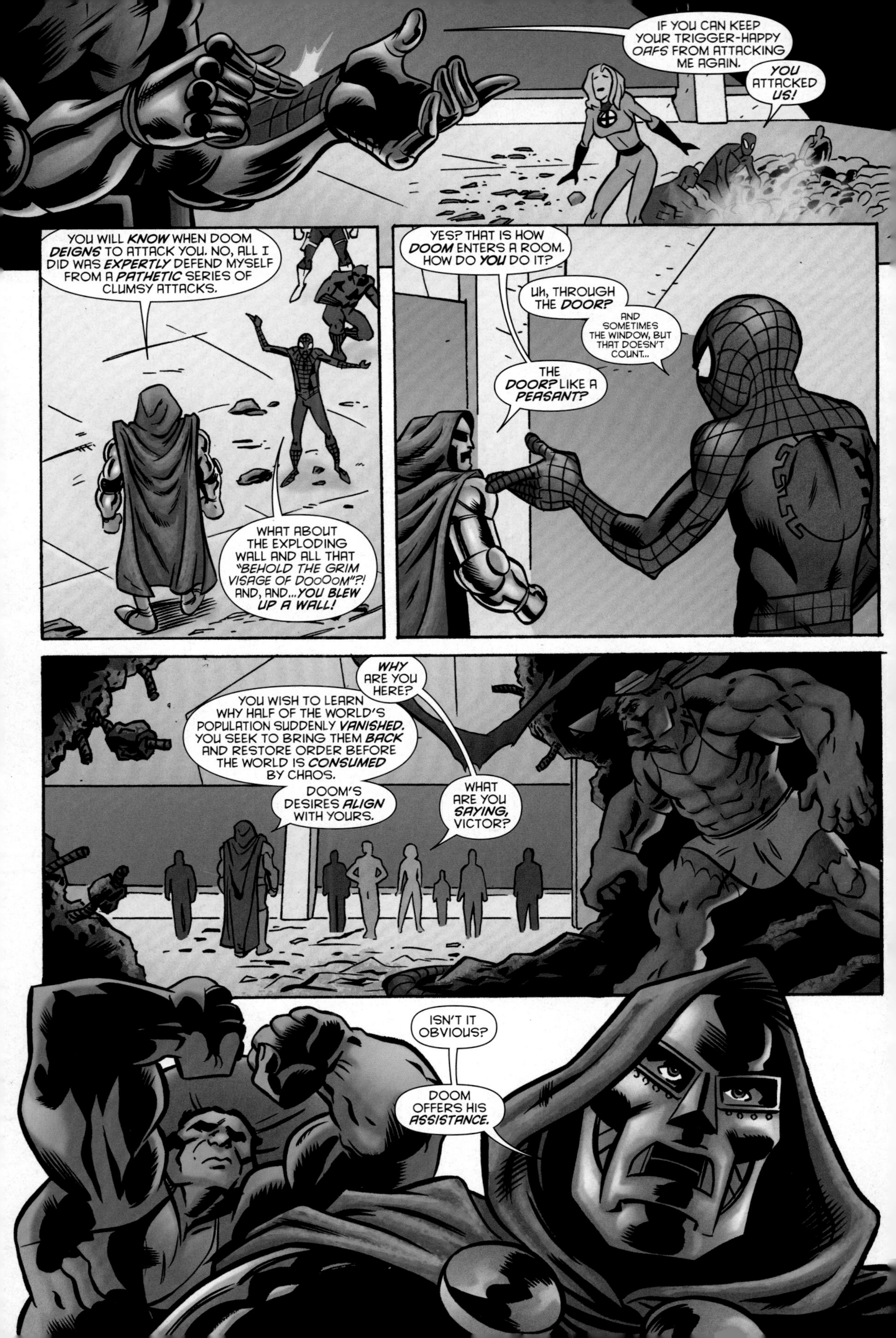
IF YOU CAN KEEP YOUR TRIGGER-HAPPY OAFS FROM ATTACKING ME AGAIN.
YOU ATTACKED US!
YOU WILL KNOW WHEN DOOM DEIGNS TO ATTACK YOU. NO, ALL I DID WAS EXPERTLY DEFEND MYSELF FROM A PATHETIC SERIES OF CLUMSY ATTACKS.
WHAT ABOUT THE EXPLODING WALL AND ALL THAT "BEHOLD THE GRIM VISAGE OF DOOOOM"?! AND, AND...YOU BLEW UP A WALL!
YES? THAT IS HOW DOOM ENTERS A ROOM. HOW DO YOU DO IT?
UH, THROUGH THE DOOR?
AND SOMETIMES THE WINDOW, BUT THAT DOESN'T COUNT...
THE DOOR? LIKE A PEASANT?
WHY ARE YOU HERE?
YOU WISH TO LEARN WHY HALF OF THE WORLD'S POPULATION SUDDENLY VANISHED. YOU SEEK TO BRING THEM BACK AND RESTORE ORDER BEFORE THE WORLD IS CONSUMED BY CHAOS.
DOOM'S DESIRES ALIGN WITH YOURS.
WHAT ARE YOU SAYING, VICTOR?
ISN'T IT OBVIOUS?
DOOM OFFERS HIS ASSISTANCE.

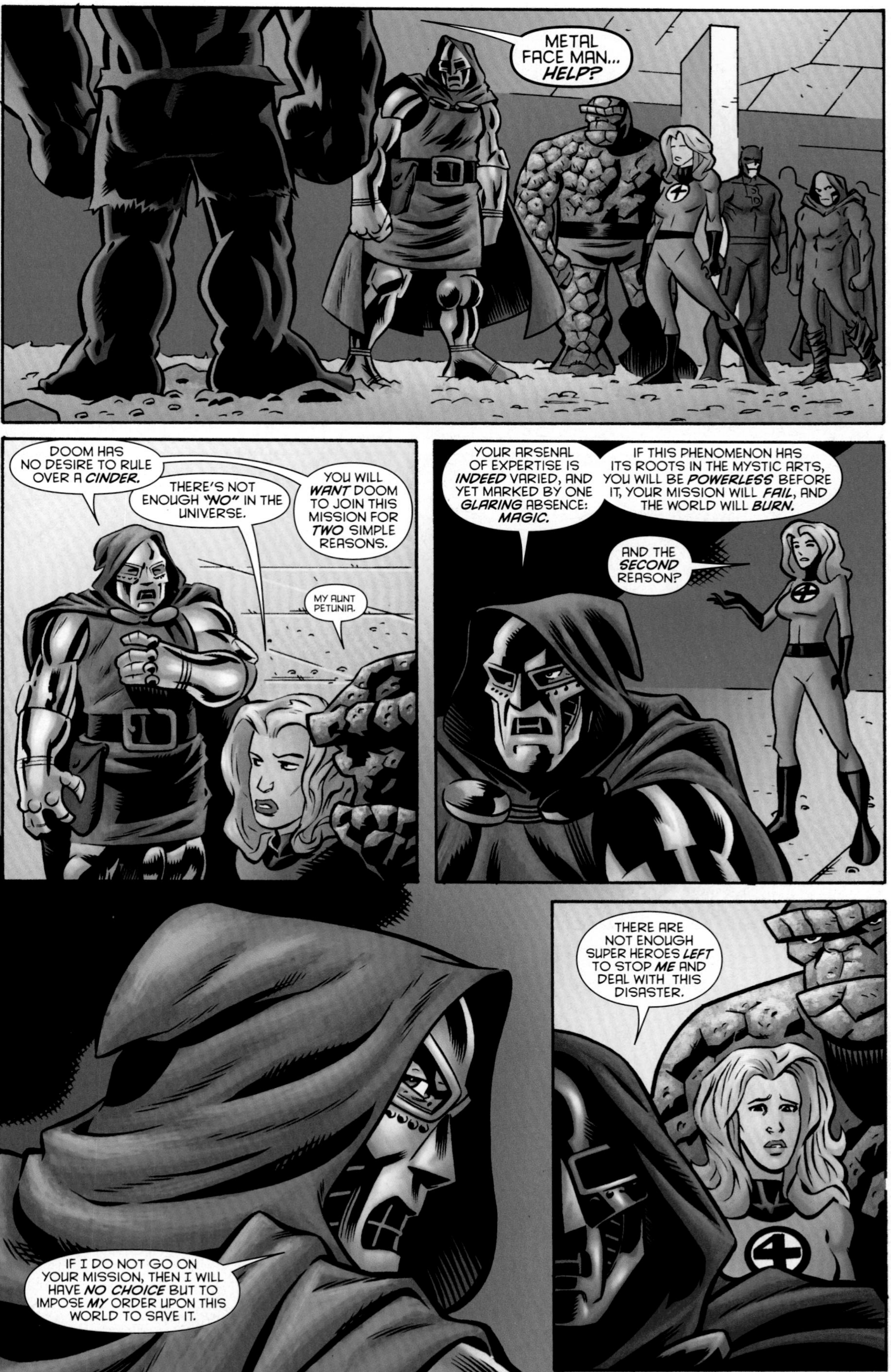
METAL FACE MAN... HELP?
DOOM HAS NO DESIRE TO RULE OVER A CINDER.
THERE'S NOT ENOUGH "NO" IN THE UNIVERSE.
YOU WILL WANT DOOM TO JOIN THIS MISSION FOR TWO SIMPLE REASONS.
MY AUNT PETUNIA.
YOUR ARSENAL OF EXPERTISE IS INDEED VARIED, AND YET MARKED BY ONE GLARING ABSENCE: MAGIC.
IF THIS PHENOMENON HAS ITS ROOTS IN THE MYSTIC ARTS, YOU WILL BE POWERLESS BEFORE IT, YOUR MISSION WILL FAIL, AND THE WORLD WILL BURN.
AND THE SECOND REASON?
IF I DO NOT GO ON YOUR MISSION, THEN I WILL HAVE NO CHOICE BUT TO IMPOSE MY ORDER UPON THIS WORLD TO SAVE IT.
THERE ARE NOT ENOUGH SUPER HEROES LEFT TO STOP ME AND DEAL WITH THIS DISASTER.

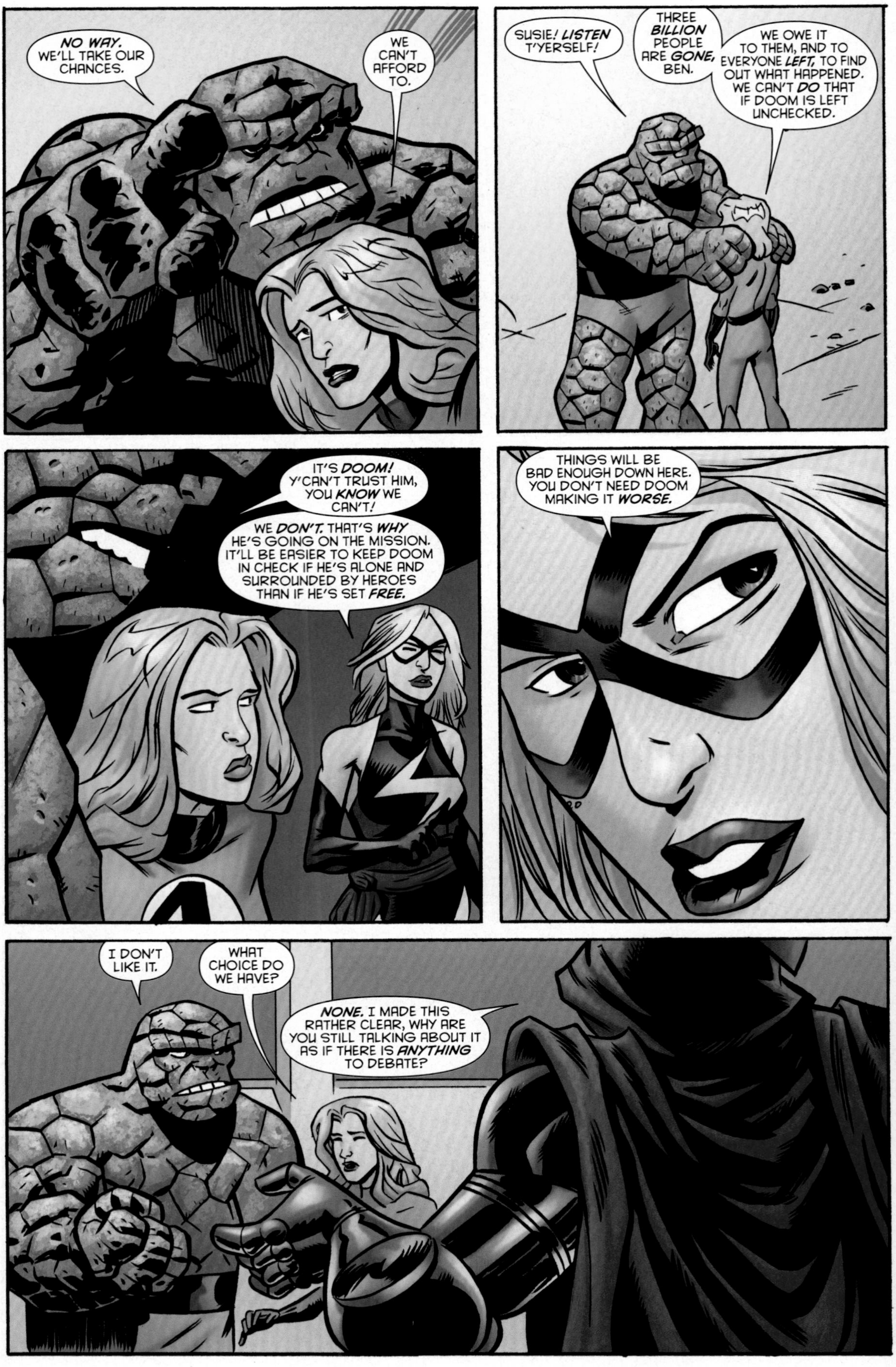
NO WAY. WE'LL TAKE OUR CHANCES.
WE CAN'T AFFORD TO.
SUSIE! LISTEN T'YERSELF!
THREE BILLION PEOPLE ARE GONE, BEN.
WE OWE IT TO THEM, AND TO EVERYONE LEFT, TO FIND OUT WHAT HAPPENED. WE CAN'T DO THAT IF DOOM IS LEFT UNCHECKED.
IT'S DOOM! Y'CAN'T TRUST HIM, YOU KNOW WE CAN'T!
WE DON'T. THAT'S WHY HE'S GOING ON THE MISSION. IT'LL BE EASIER TO KEEP DOOM IN CHECK IF HE'S ALONE AND SURROUNDED BY HEROES THAN IF HE'S SET FREE.
THINGS WILL BE BAD ENOUGH DOWN HERE. YOU DON'T NEED DOOM MAKING IT WORSE.
I DON'T LIKE IT.
WHAT CHOICE DO WE HAVE?
NONE. I MADE THIS RATHER CLEAR, WHY ARE YOU STILL TALKING ABOUT IT AS IF THERE IS ANYTHING TO DEBATE?

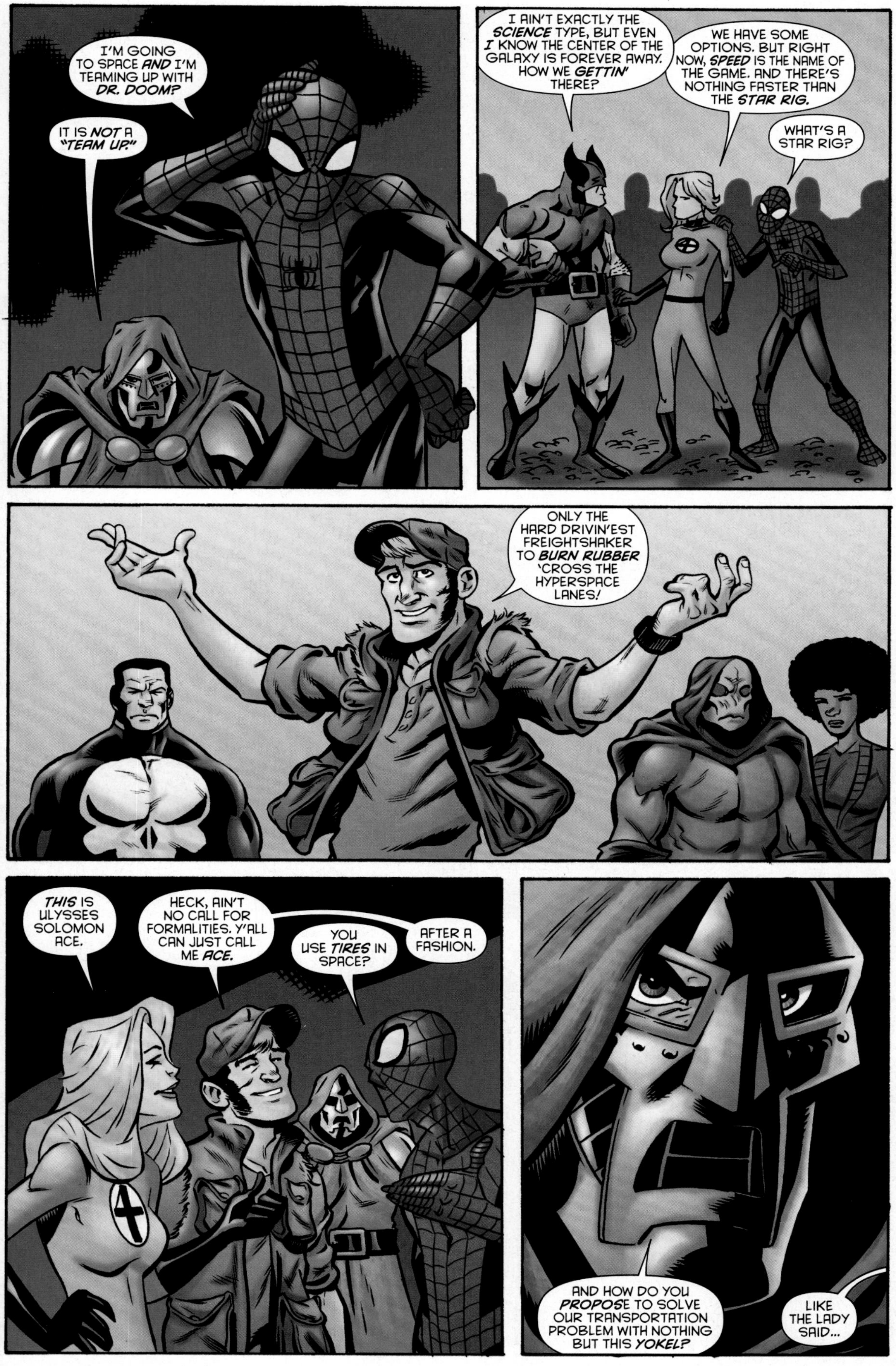
I'M GOING TO SPACE AND I'M TEAMING UP WITH DR. DOOM?
IT IS NOT A "TEAM UP."
I AIN'T EXACTLY THE SCIENCE TYPE, BUT EVEN I KNOW THE CENTER OF THE GALAXY IS FOREVER AWAY. HOW WE GETTIN' THERE?
WE HAVE SOME OPTIONS. BUT RIGHT NOW, SPEED IS THE NAME OF THE GAME. AND THERE'S NOTHING FASTER THAN THE STAR RIG.
WHAT'S A STAR RIG?
ONLY THE HARD DRIVIN'EST FREIGHTSHAKER TO BURN RUBBER 'CROSS THE HYPERSPACE LANES!
THIS IS ULYSSES SOLOMON ACE.
HECK, AIN'T NO CALL FOR FORMALITIES. Y'ALL CAN JUST CALL ME ACE.
YOU USE TIRES IN SPACE?
AFTER A FASHION.
AND HOW DO YOU PROPOSE TO SOLVE OUR TRANSPORTATION PROBLEM WITH NOTHING BUT THIS YOKEL?
LIKE THE LADY SAID...

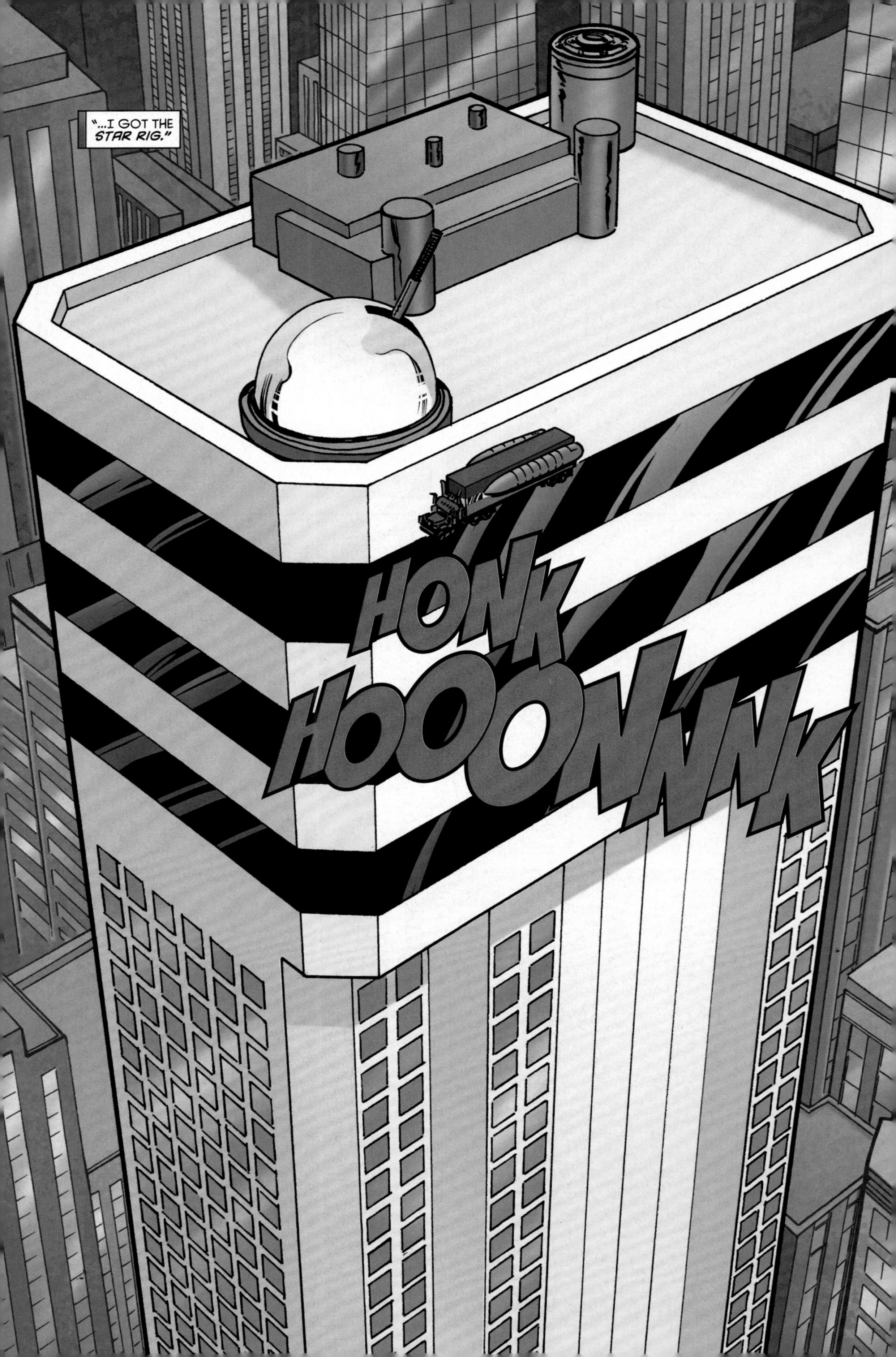
"...I GOT THE STAR RIG."
HONK
HOOONNNK

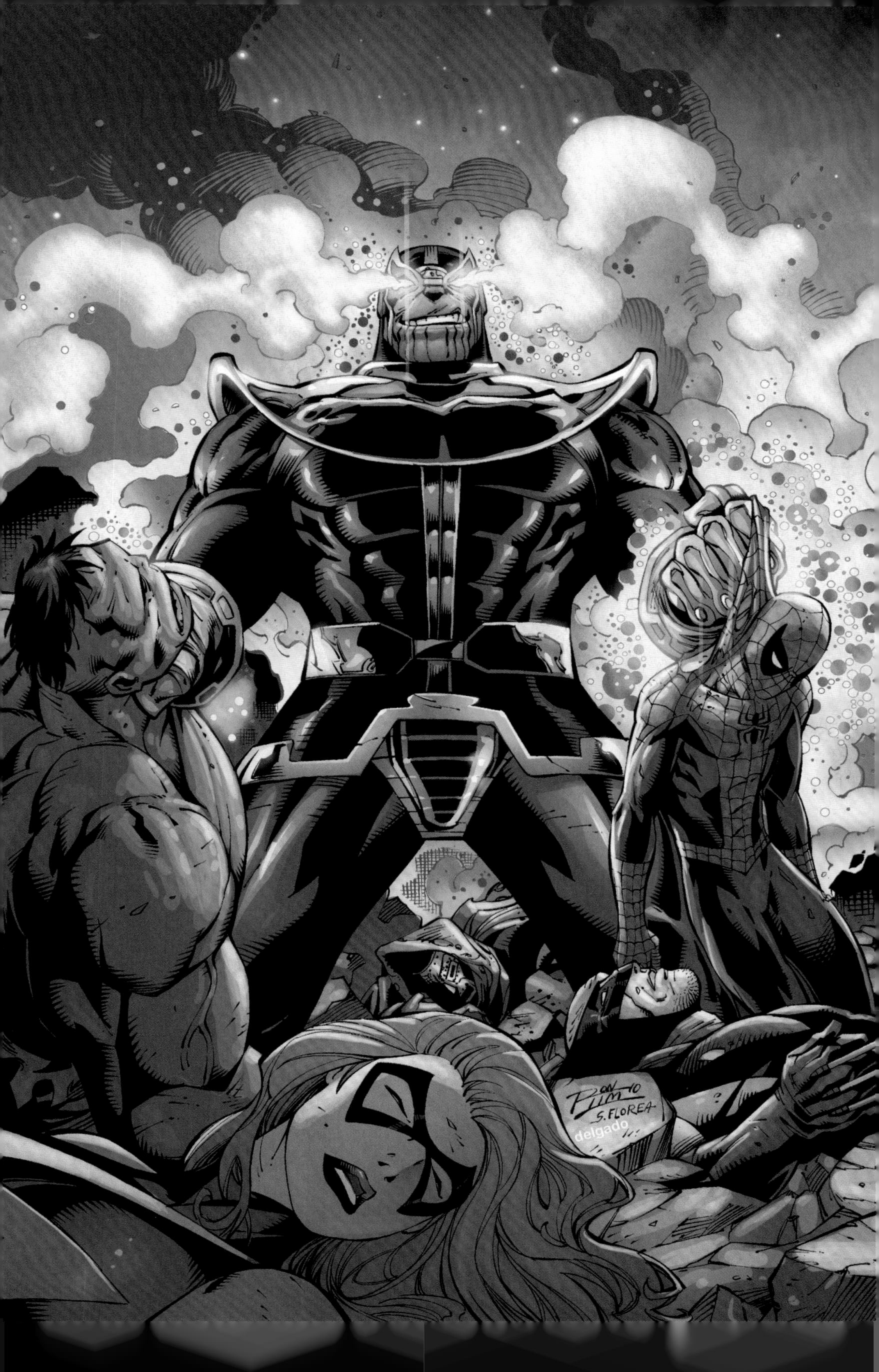
S.FLOREA
delgado

FOURTEEN HOURS AGO HALF OF THE WORLD'S POPULATION SIMPLY *DISAPPEARED.* THIS INCLUDED THE EARTH'S MIGHTIEST HEROES: *THE AVENGERS.*

POLICE AND SUPER HEROES ALL OVER THE GLOBE ARE STRETCHED TO THEIR LIMITS TO PROVIDE AID TO A PANICKED AND DESPERATE GLOBAL CITIZENRY.

SUE STORM, THE INVISIBLE WOMAN OF THE FANTASTIC FOUR, DISCOVERED THAT A DISTURBANCE NEAR THE CENTER OF THE MILKY WAY GALAXY SEEMS TO BE THE CAUSE OF THE DISAPPEARANCE.

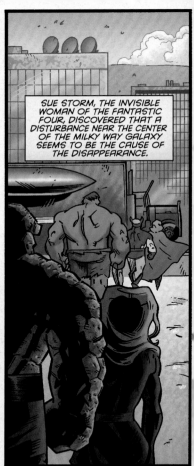

SHE ASSEMBLED A SPECIAL TASK FORCE TO INVESTIGATE: *THE NEW AVENGERS.*

NO ONE KNOWS IF THEY'LL COME BACK.

PETER PARKER, *SPIDER-MAN:* SCIENTIST.

BRUCE BANNER, *HULK:* SMASH.

LOGAN, *WOLVERINE:* SCOUT.

VICTOR VON DOOM, *DOCTOR DOOM:* EVIL WIZARD.

CAROL DANVERS, *MS. MARVEL:* TEAM LEADER.

THEY ARE THE ONLY HOPE FOR HUMANKIND...

I'M GOING TO *SPACE!*

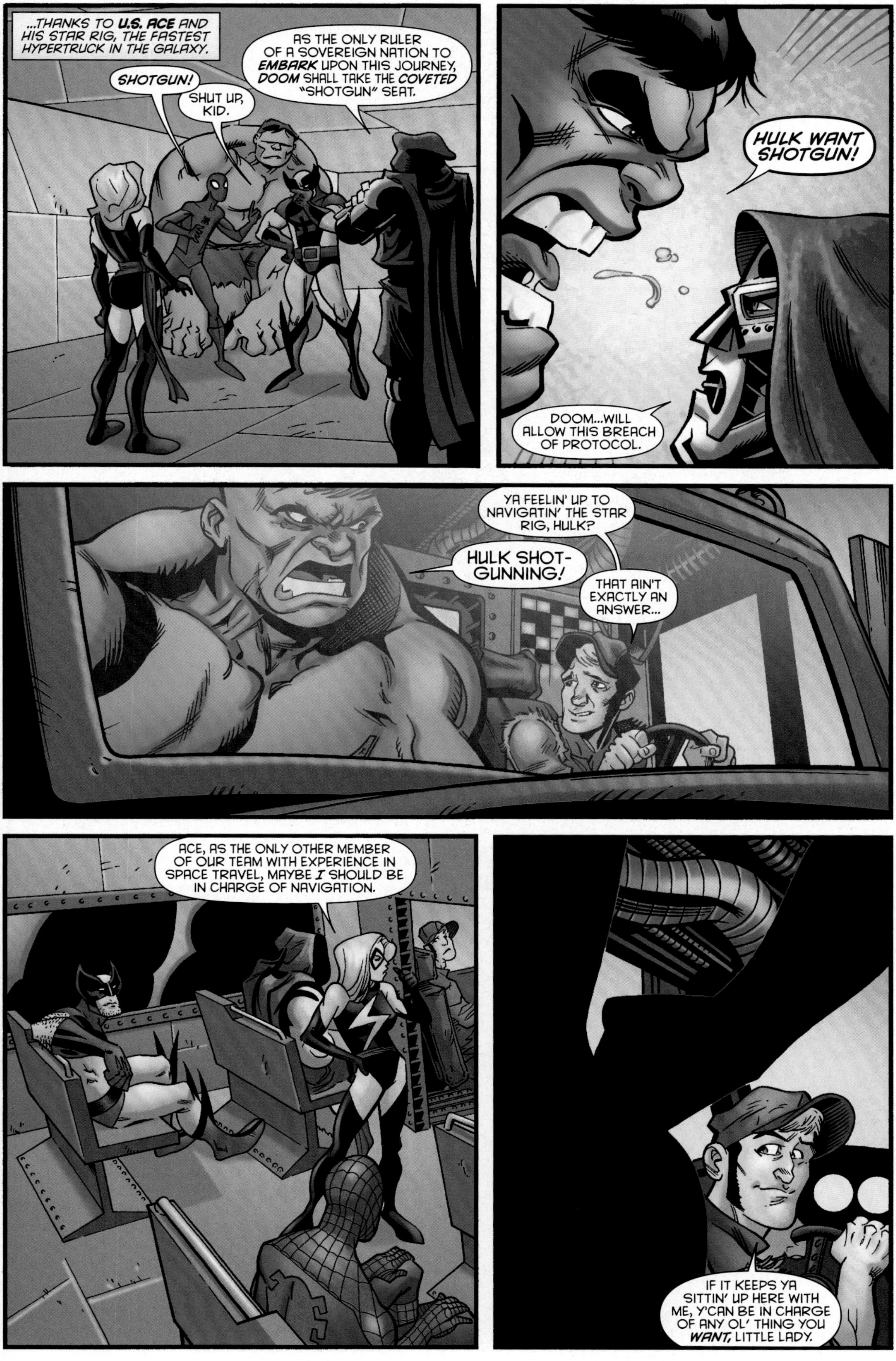
...THANKS TO U.S. ACE AND HIS STAR RIG, THE FASTEST HYPERTRUCK IN THE GALAXY.
AS THE ONLY RULER OF A SOVEREIGN NATION TO EMBARK UPON THIS JOURNEY, DOOM SHALL TAKE THE COVETED "SHOTGUN" SEAT.
SHOTGUN!
SHUT UP, KID.
HULK WANT SHOTGUN!
DOOM...WILL ALLOW THIS BREACH OF PROTOCOL.
YA FEELIN' UP TO NAVIGATIN' THE STAR RIG, HULK?
HULK SHOT-GUNNING!
THAT AIN'T EXACTLY AN ANSWER...
ACE, AS THE ONLY OTHER MEMBER OF OUR TEAM WITH EXPERIENCE IN SPACE TRAVEL, MAYBE I SHOULD BE IN CHARGE OF NAVIGATION.
IF IT KEEPS YA SITTIN' UP HERE WITH ME, Y'CAN BE IN CHARGE OF ANY OL' THING YOU WANT, LITTLE LADY.

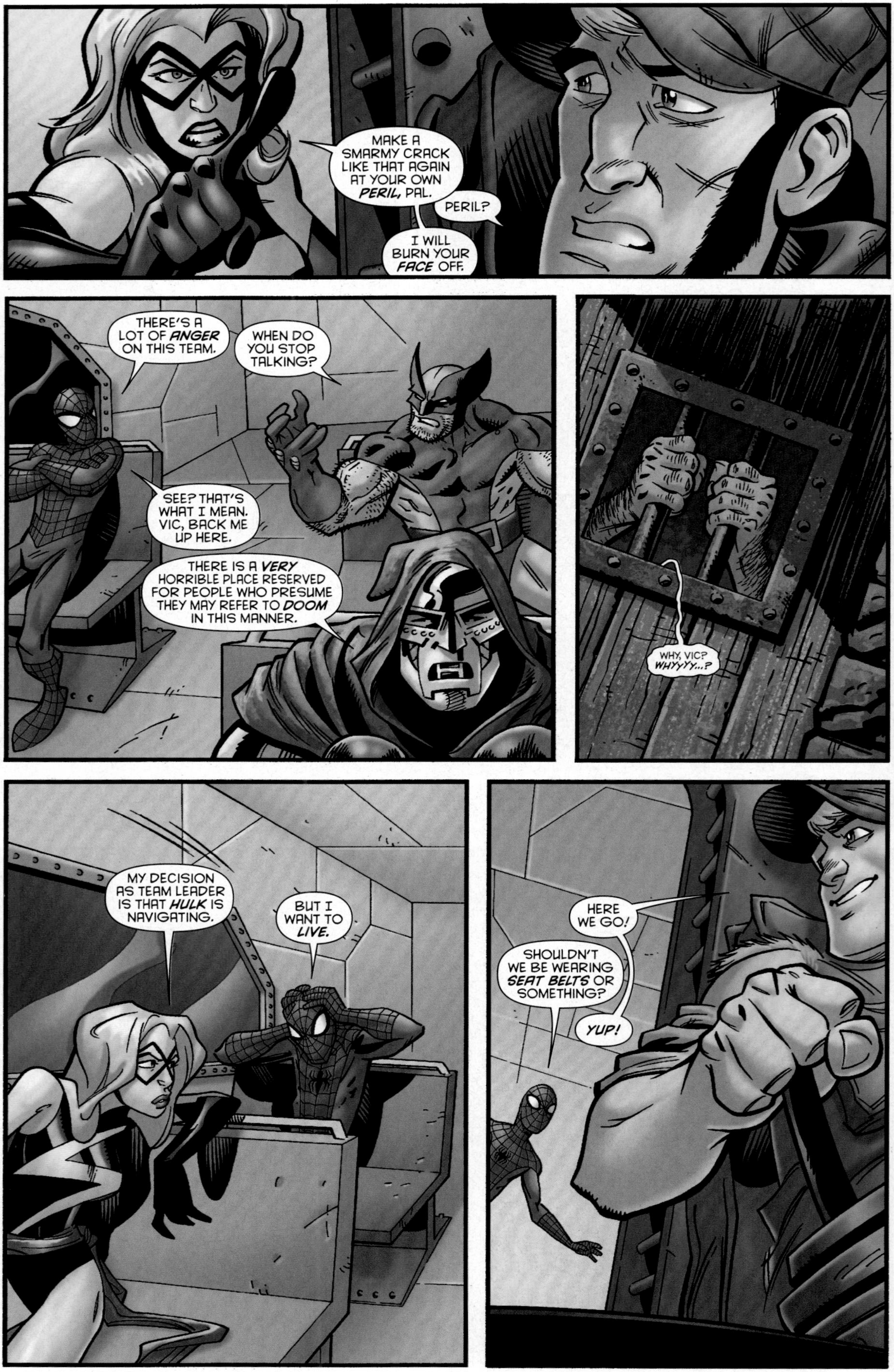
MAKE A SMARMY CRACK LIKE THAT AGAIN AT YOUR OWN *PERIL,* PAL.
PERIL?
I WILL BURN YOUR *FACE* OFF.
THERE'S A LOT OF *ANGER* ON THIS TEAM.
WHEN DO YOU STOP TALKING?
SEE? THAT'S WHAT I MEAN. VIC, BACK ME UP HERE.
THERE IS A *VERY* HORRIBLE PLACE RESERVED FOR PEOPLE WHO PRESUME THEY MAY REFER TO *DOOM* IN THIS MANNER.
WHY, VIC? *WHYYYY...?*
MY DECISION AS TEAM LEADER IS THAT *HULK* IS NAVIGATING.
BUT I WANT TO *LIVE.*
HERE WE GO!
SHOULDN'T WE BE WEARING *SEAT BELTS* OR SOMETHING?
YUP!

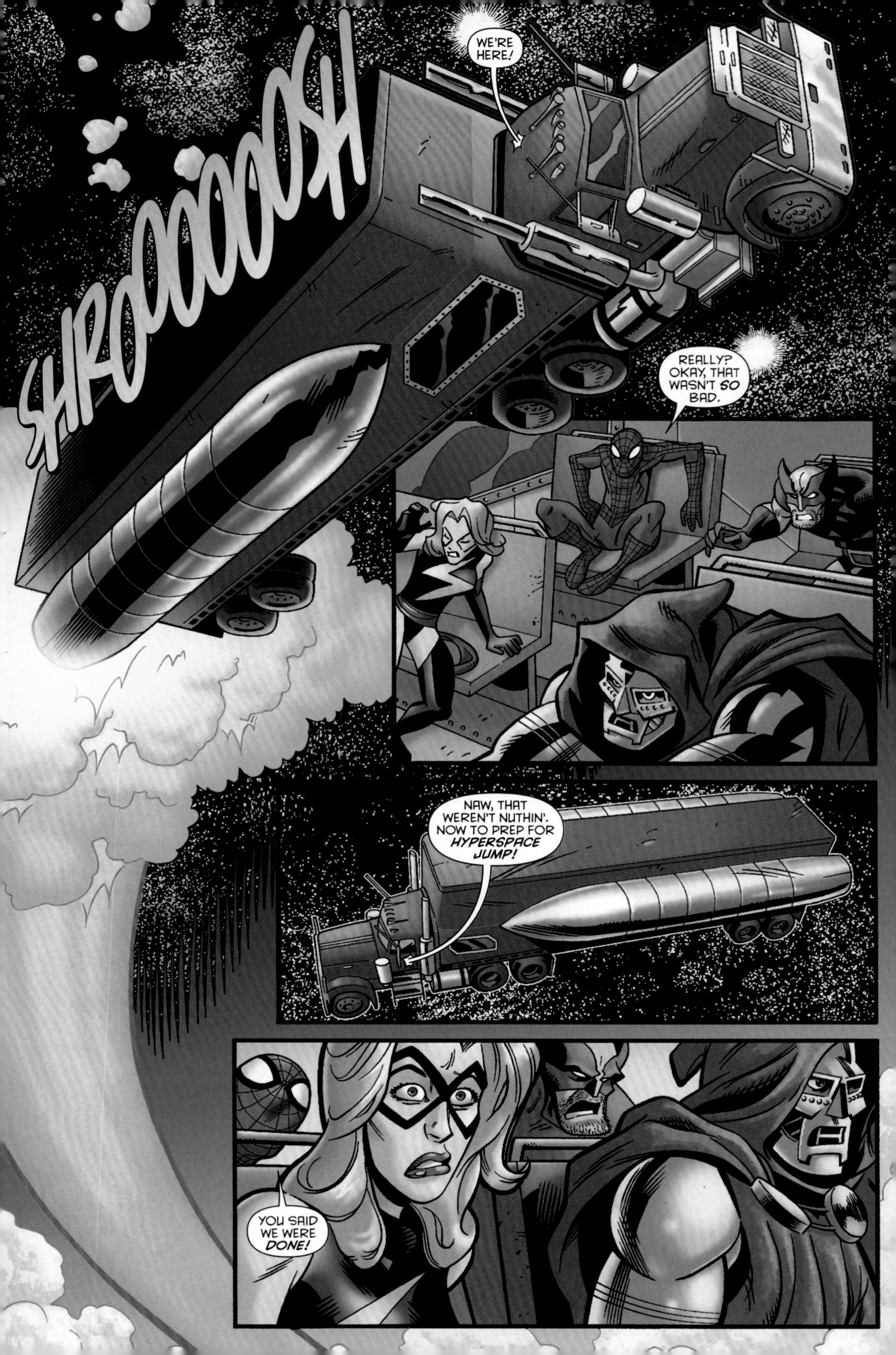
SHROOOOOOSH
WE'RE HERE!
REALLY? OKAY, THAT WASN'T *SO* BAD.
NAW, THAT WEREN'T NUTHIN'. NOW TO PREP FOR *HYPERSPACE JUMP!*
YOU SAID WE WERE *DONE!*

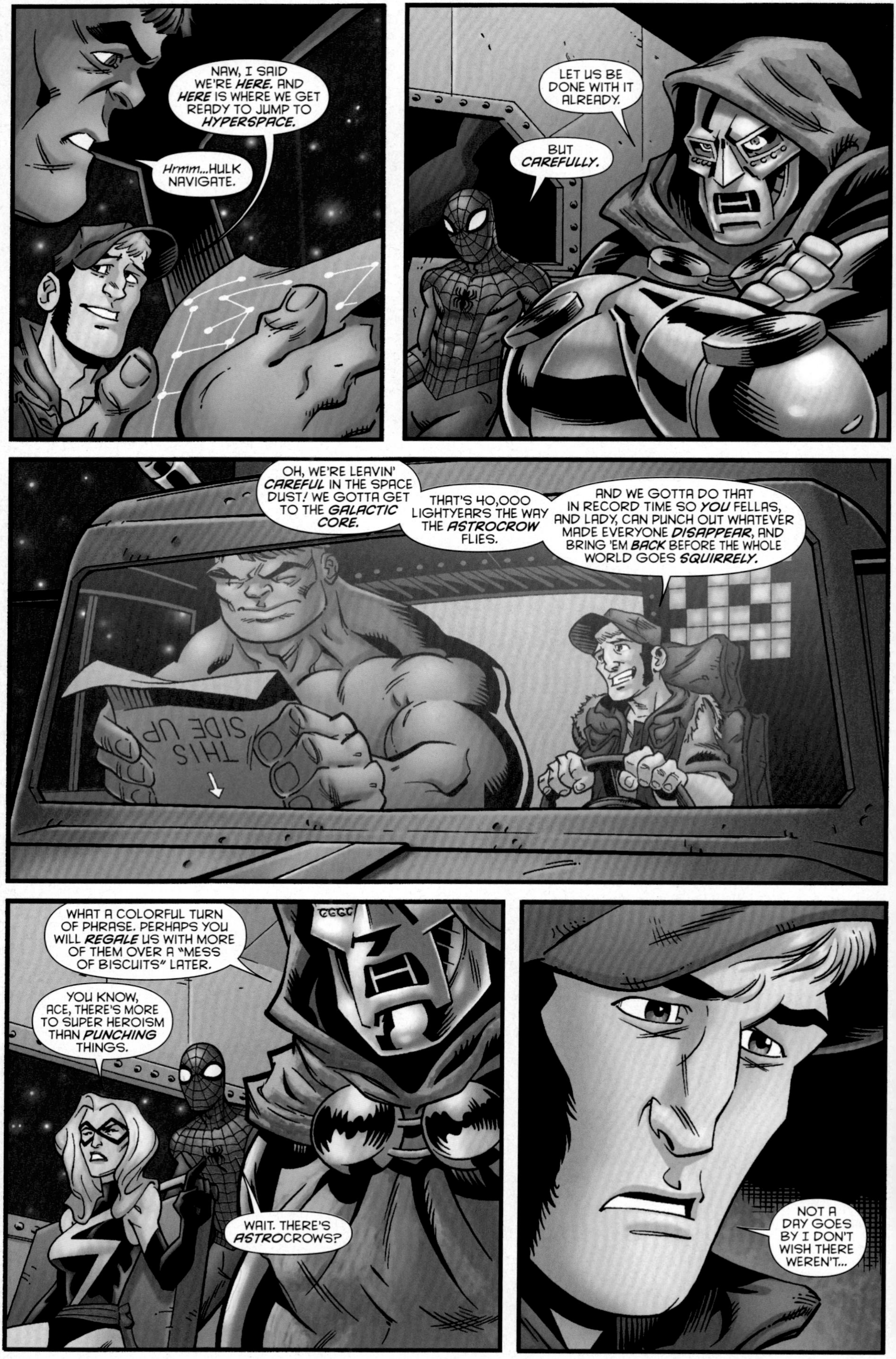
NAW, I SAID WE'RE *HERE*. AND *HERE* IS WHERE WE GET READY TO JUMP TO *HYPERSPACE*.
Hrmm...HULK NAVIGATE.
LET US BE DONE WITH IT ALREADY.
BUT *CAREFULLY*.
OH, WE'RE LEAVIN' *CAREFUL* IN THE SPACE DUST! WE GOTTA GET TO THE *GALACTIC CORE*.
THAT'S 40,000 LIGHTYEAR'S THE WAY THE *ASTROCROW* FLIES.
AND WE GOTTA DO THAT IN RECORD TIME SO *YOU* FELLAS, AND LADY, CAN PUNCH OUT WHATEVER MADE EVERYONE *DISAPPEAR*, AND BRING 'EM *BACK* BEFORE THE WHOLE WORLD GOES *SQUIRRELY*.
THIS SIDE UP
WHAT A COLORFUL TURN OF PHRASE. PERHAPS YOU WILL *REGALE* US WITH MORE OF THEM OVER A "MESS OF BISCUITS" LATER.
YOU KNOW, ACE, THERE'S MORE TO SUPER HEROISM THAN *PUNCHING* THINGS.
WAIT. THERE'S *ASTRO*CROWS?
NOT A DAY GOES BY I DON'T WISH THERE WEREN'T...

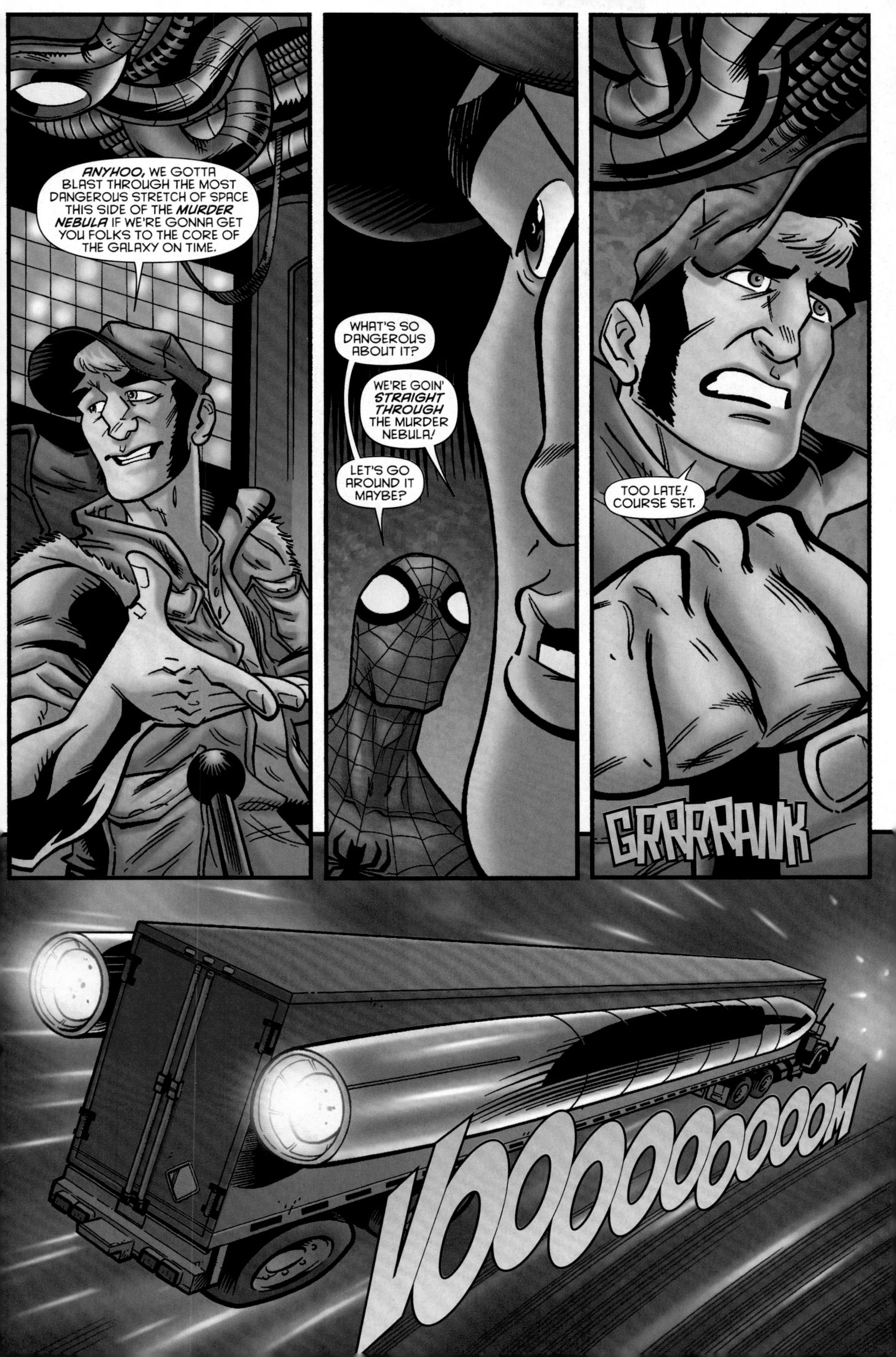

ANYHOO, WE GOTTA BLAST THROUGH THE MOST DANGEROUS STRETCH OF SPACE THIS SIDE OF THE MURDER NEBULA IF WE'RE GONNA GET YOU FOLKS TO THE CORE OF THE GALAXY ON TIME.
WHAT'S SO DANGEROUS ABOUT IT?
WE'RE GOIN' STRAIGHT THROUGH THE MURDER NEBULA!
LET'S GO AROUND IT MAYBE?
TOO LATE! COURSE SET.
GRRRRANK
VOOOOOOOOOM

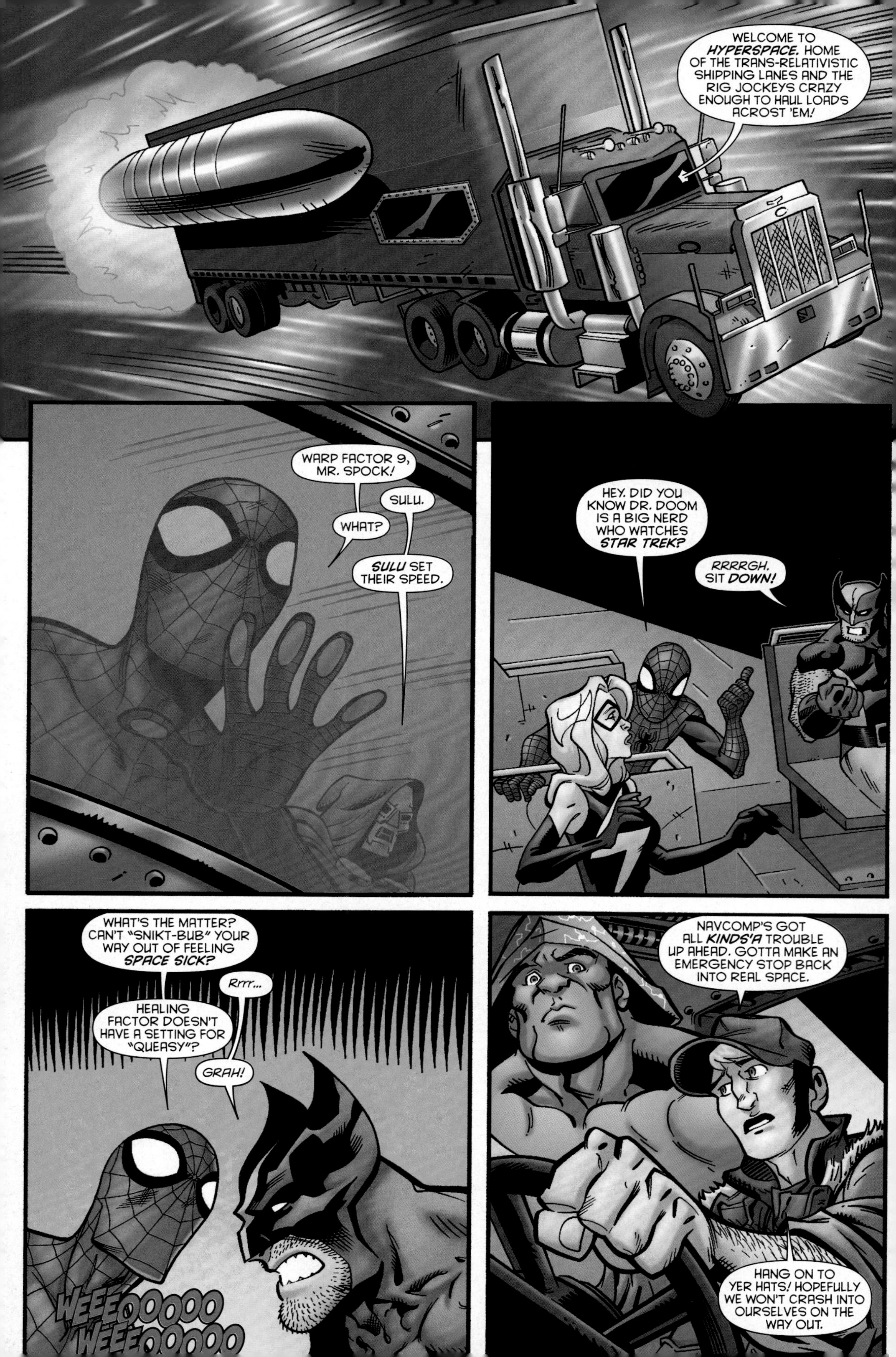
WELCOME TO HYPERSPACE. HOME OF THE TRANS-RELATIVISTIC SHIPPING LANES AND THE RIG JOCKEYS CRAZY ENOUGH TO HAUL LOADS ACROST 'EM!
WARP FACTOR 9, MR. SPOCK!
SULU.
WHAT?
SULU SET THEIR SPEED.
HEY. DID YOU KNOW DR. DOOM IS A BIG NERD WHO WATCHES STAR TREK?
RRRRGH. SIT DOWN!
WHAT'S THE MATTER? CAN'T "SNIKT-BUB" YOUR WAY OUT OF FEELING SPACE SICK?
Rrrr...
HEALING FACTOR DOESN'T HAVE A SETTING FOR "QUEASY"?
GRAH!
WEEEOOOOO
WEEEOOOOO
NAVCOMP'S GOT ALL KINDS'A TROUBLE UP AHEAD. GOTTA MAKE AN EMERGENCY STOP BACK INTO REAL SPACE.
HANG ON TO YER HATS! HOPEFULLY WE WON'T CRASH INTO OURSELVES ON THE WAY OUT.

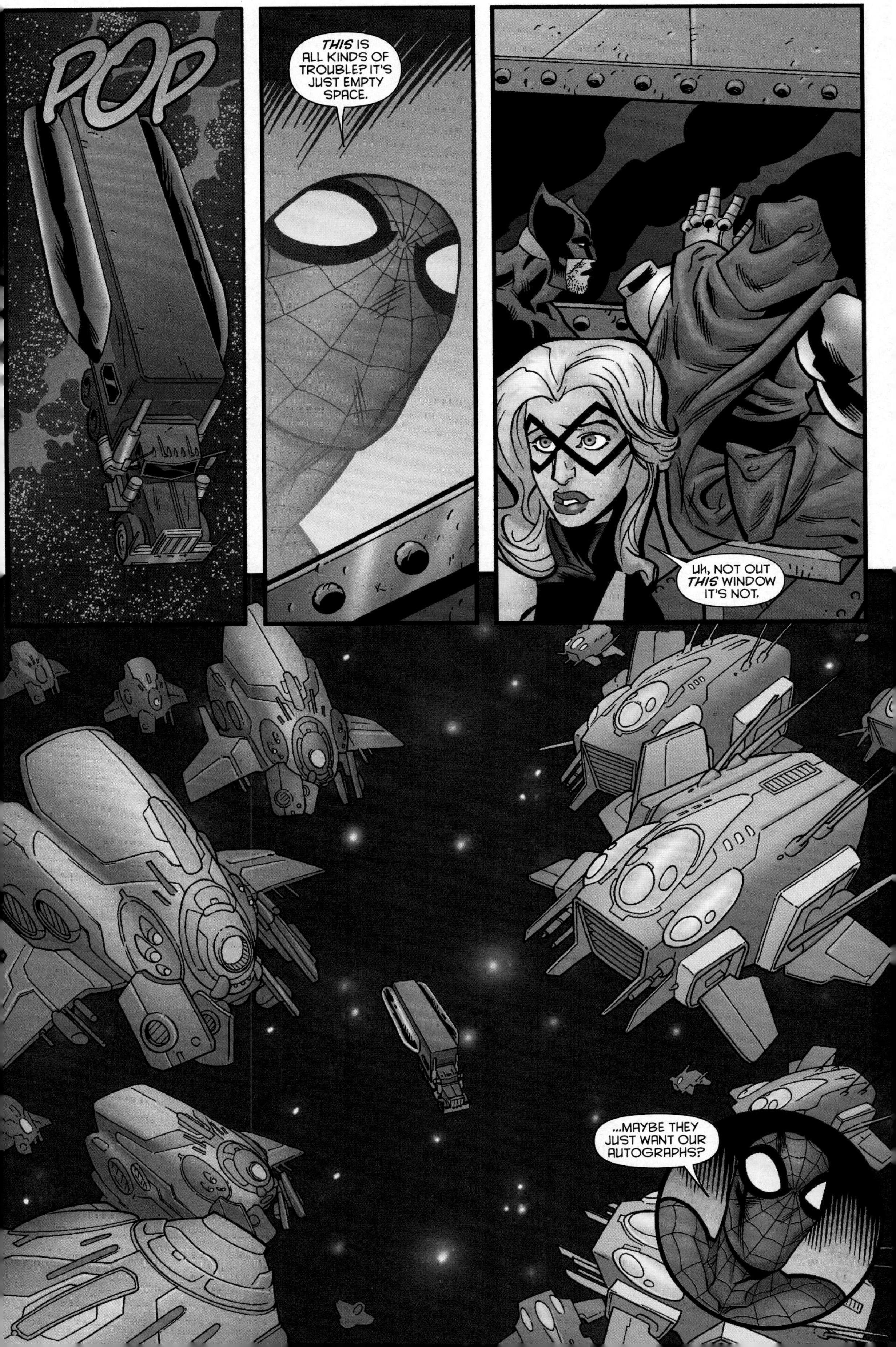
POP
THIS IS ALL KINDS OF TROUBLE? IT'S JUST EMPTY SPACE.
UH, NOT OUT THIS WINDOW IT'S NOT.
...MAYBE THEY JUST WANT OUR AUTOGRAPHS?

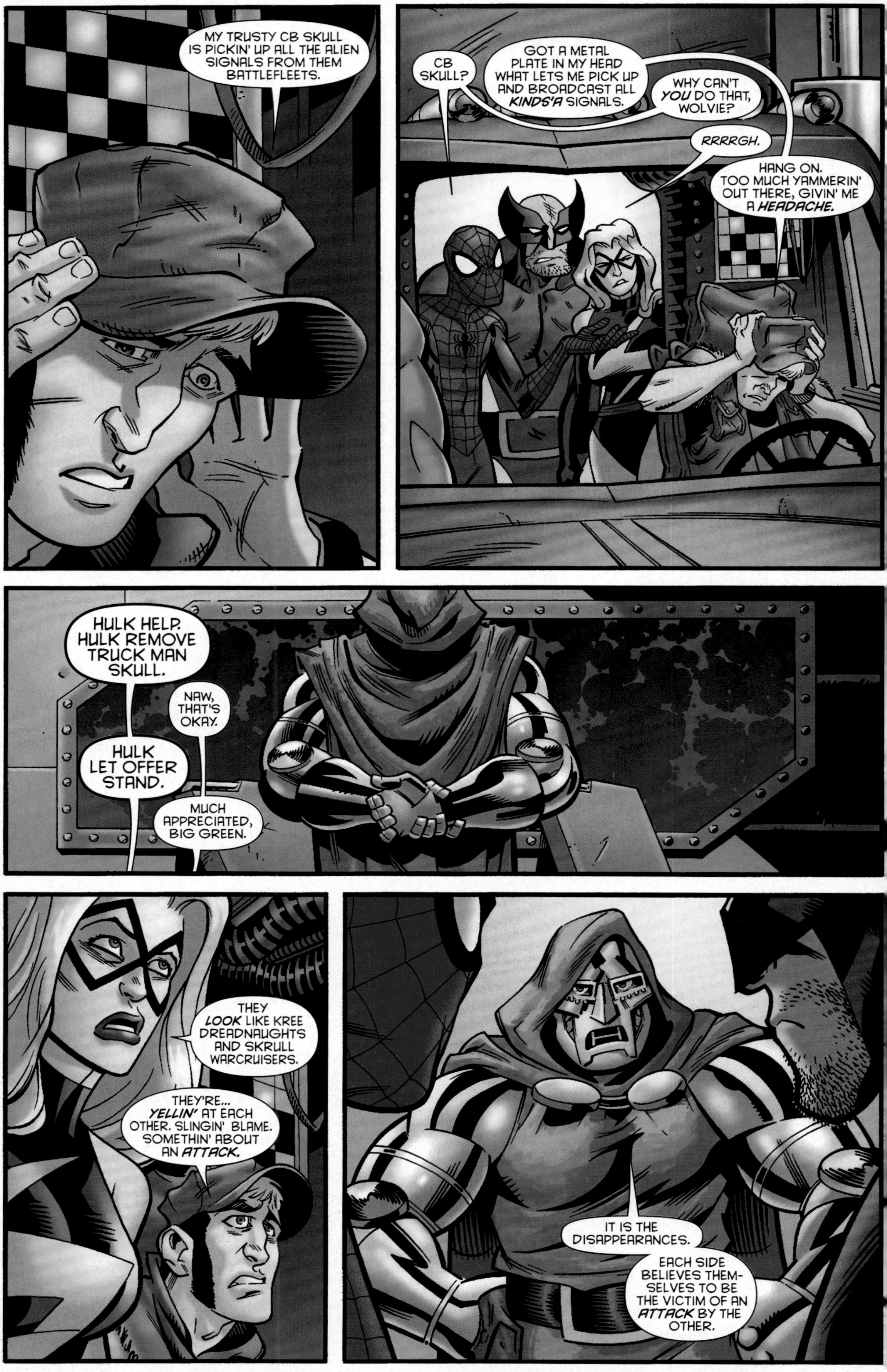
MY TRUSTY CB SKULL IS PICKIN' UP ALL THE ALIEN SIGNALS FROM THEM BATTLEFLEETS.
CB SKULL?
GOT A METAL PLATE IN MY HEAD WHAT LETS ME PICK UP AND BROADCAST ALL KINDS'A SIGNALS.
WHY CAN'T YOU DO THAT, WOLVIE?
RRRRGH.
HANG ON. TOO MUCH YAMMERIN' OUT THERE, GIVIN' ME A HEADACHE.
HULK HELP. HULK REMOVE TRUCK MAN SKULL.
NAW, THAT'S OKAY.
HULK LET OFFER STAND.
MUCH APPRECIATED, BIG GREEN.
THEY LOOK LIKE KREE DREADNAUGHTS AND SKRULL WARCRUISERS.
THEY'RE... YELLIN' AT EACH OTHER. SLINGIN' BLAME. SOMETHIN' ABOUT AN ATTACK.
IT IS THE DISAPPEARANCES.
EACH SIDE BELIEVES THEM-SELVES TO BE THE VICTIM OF AN ATTACK BY THE OTHER.

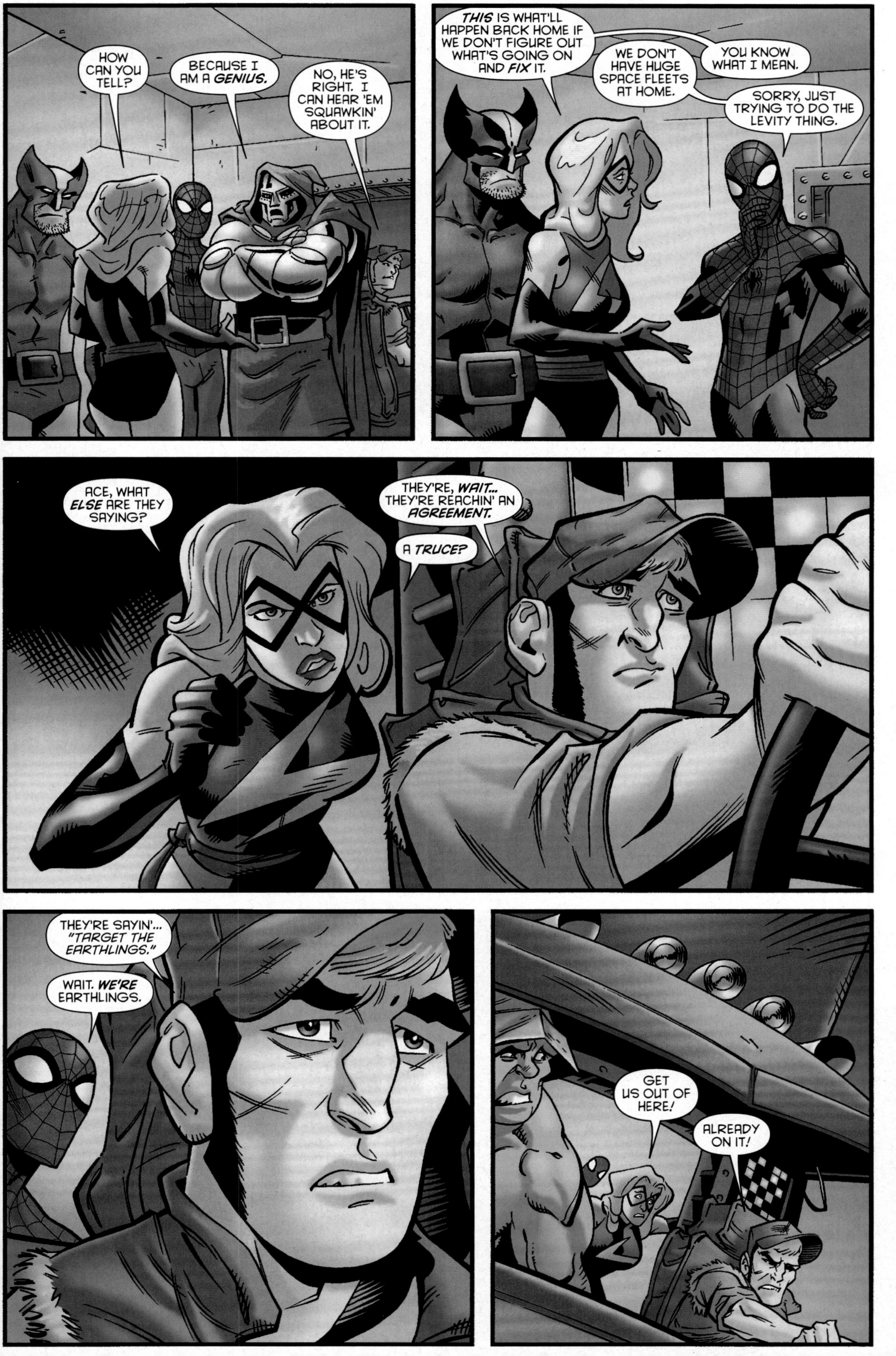
HOW CAN YOU TELL?
BECAUSE I AM A GENIUS.
NO, HE'S RIGHT. I CAN HEAR 'EM SQUAWKIN' ABOUT IT.
THIS IS WHAT'LL HAPPEN BACK HOME IF WE DON'T FIGURE OUT WHAT'S GOING ON AND FIX IT.
WE DON'T HAVE HUGE SPACE FLEETS AT HOME.
YOU KNOW WHAT I MEAN.
SORRY, JUST TRYING TO DO THE LEVITY THING.
ACE, WHAT ELSE ARE THEY SAYING?
THEY'RE, WAIT... THEY'RE REACHIN' AN AGREEMENT.
A TRUCE?
THEY'RE SAYIN'... "TARGET THE EARTHLINGS."
WAIT. WE'RE EARTHLINGS.
GET US OUT OF HERE!
ALREADY ON IT!

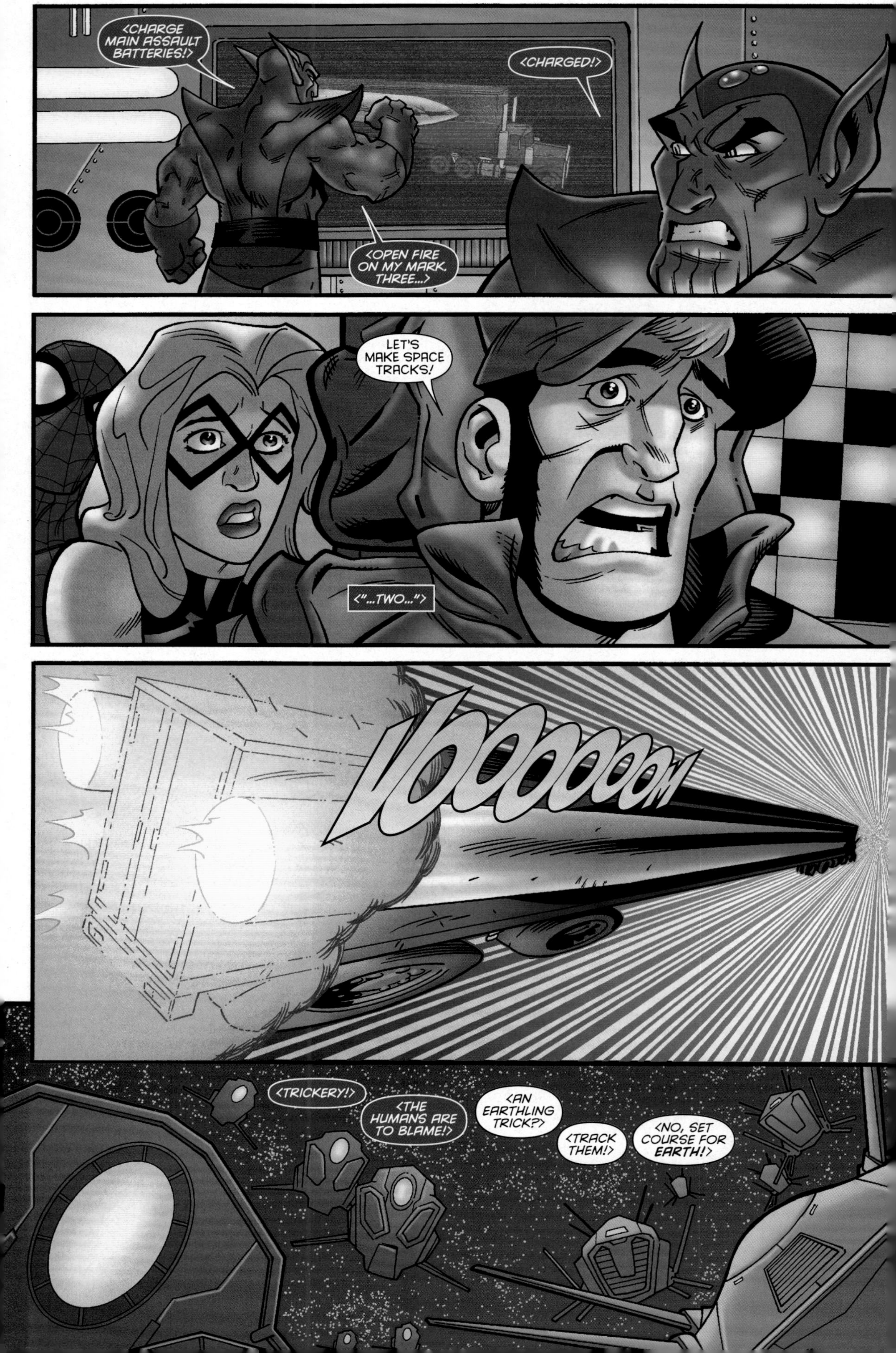
<CHARGE MAIN ASSAULT BATTERIES!>
<CHARGED!>
<OPEN FIRE ON MY MARK. THREE...>
LET'S MAKE SPACE TRACKS!
<"...TWO...">
VOOOOOOM
<TRICKERY!>
<THE HUMANS ARE TO BLAME!>
<AN EARTHLING TRICK?>
<TRACK THEM!>
<NO, SET COURSE FOR EARTH!>

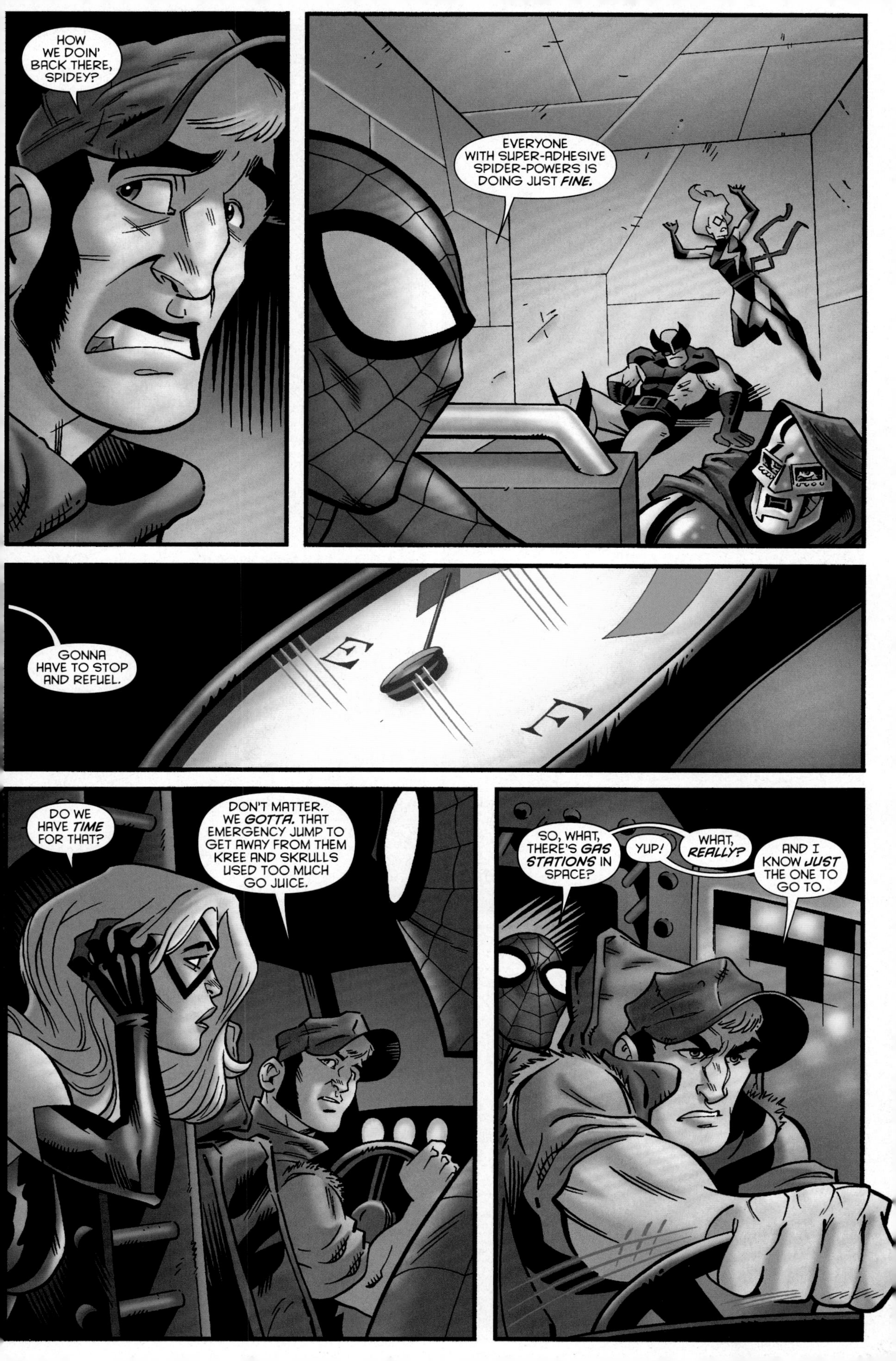

HOW WE DOIN' BACK THERE, SPIDEY?
EVERYONE WITH SUPER-ADHESIVE SPIDER-POWERS IS DOING JUST *FINE.*
GONNA HAVE TO STOP AND REFUEL.
E
F
DO WE HAVE *TIME* FOR THAT?
DON'T MATTER. WE *GOTTA.* THAT EMERGENCY JUMP TO GET AWAY FROM THEM KREE AND SKRULLS USED TOO MUCH GO JUICE.
SO, WHAT, THERE'S *GAS STATIONS* IN SPACE?
YUP!
WHAT, *REALLY?*
AND I KNOW *JUST* THE ONE TO GO TO.

WE'RE HERE.

VOOP

WELCOME TO THE STAR STOP!

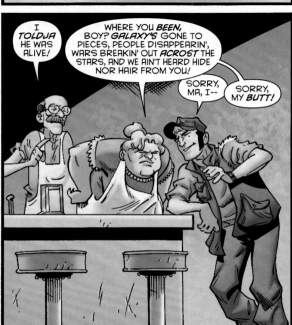

I TOLDJA HE WAS ALIVE!

WHERE YOU BEEN, BOY? GALAXY'S GONE TO PIECES, PEOPLE DISAPPEARIN', WARS BREAKIN' OUT ACROST THE STARS, AND WE AIN'T HEARD HIDE NOR HAIR FROM YOU!

SORRY, MA, I--

SORRY, MY BUTT!

"MA"?

THERE ARE MORE OF THEM. HOW HORRID.

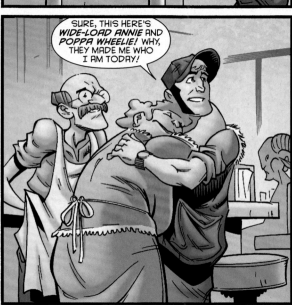

SURE, THIS HERE'S WIDE-LOAD ANNIE AND POPPA WHEELIE! WHY, THEY MADE ME WHO I AM TODAY!

NOW WE KNOW WHO TO BLAME.

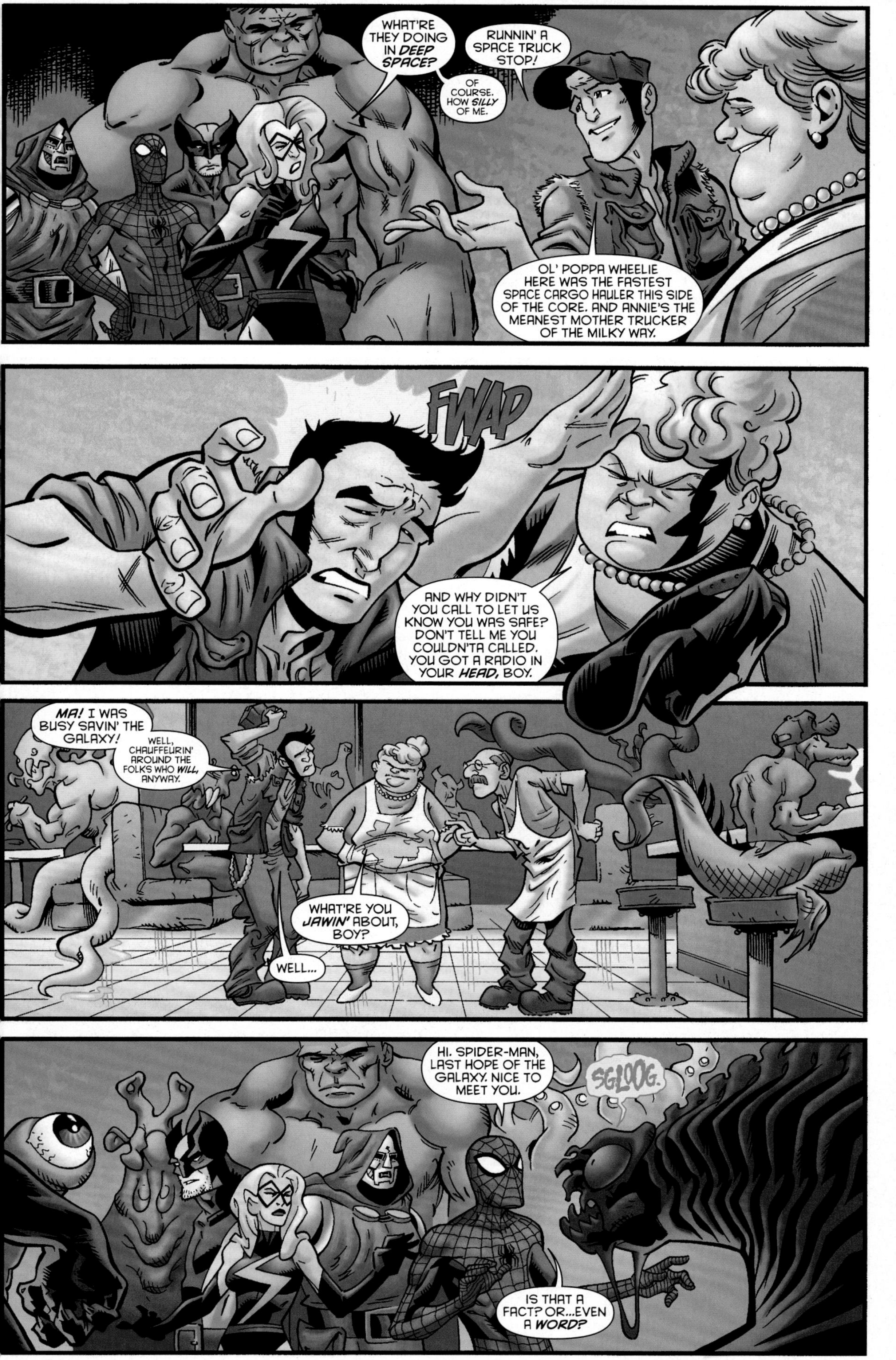
WHAT'RE THEY DOING IN DEEP SPACE?
RUNNIN' A SPACE TRUCK STOP!
OF COURSE. HOW SILLY OF ME.
OL' POPPA WHEELIE HERE WAS THE FASTEST SPACE CARGO HAULER THIS SIDE OF THE CORE. AND ANNIE'S THE MEANEST MOTHER TRUCKER OF THE MILKY WAY.
FWAP
AND WHY DIDN'T YOU CALL TO LET US KNOW YOU WAS SAFE? DON'T TELL ME YOU COULDN'TA CALLED. YOU GOT A RADIO IN YOUR HEAD, BOY.
MA! I WAS BUSY SAVIN' THE GALAXY!
WELL, CHAUFFEURIN' AROUND THE FOLKS WHO WILL, ANYWAY.
WHAT'RE YOU JAWIN' ABOUT, BOY?
WELL...
HI. SPIDER-MAN, LAST HOPE OF THE GALAXY. NICE TO MEET YOU.
SGLOOG.
IS THAT A FACT? OR...EVEN A WORD?

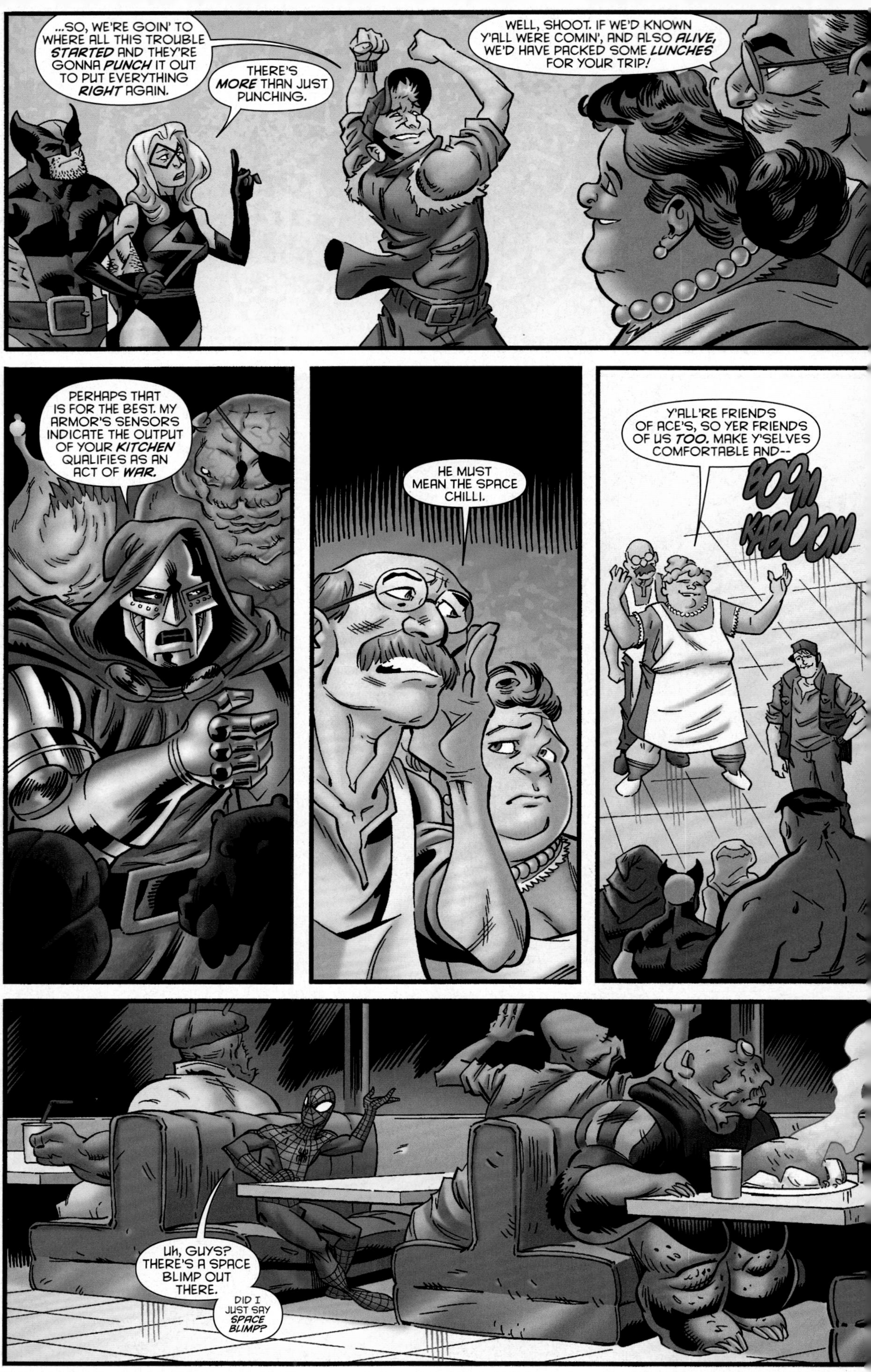
...SO, WE'RE GOIN' TO WHERE ALL THIS TROUBLE STARTED AND THEY'RE GONNA PUNCH IT OUT TO PUT EVERYTHING RIGHT AGAIN.
THERE'S MORE THAN JUST PUNCHING.
WELL, SHOOT. IF WE'D KNOWN Y'ALL WERE COMIN', AND ALSO ALIVE, WE'D HAVE PACKED SOME LUNCHES FOR YOUR TRIP!
PERHAPS THAT IS FOR THE BEST. MY ARMOR'S SENSORS INDICATE THE OUTPUT OF YOUR KITCHEN QUALIFIES AS AN ACT OF WAR.
HE MUST MEAN THE SPACE CHILLI.
Y'ALL'RE FRIENDS OF ACE'S, SO YER FRIENDS OF US TOO. MAKE Y'SELVES COMFORTABLE AND--
BOOM KABOOM
UH, GUYS? THERE'S A SPACE BLIMP OUT THERE.
DID I JUST SAY SPACE BLIMP?

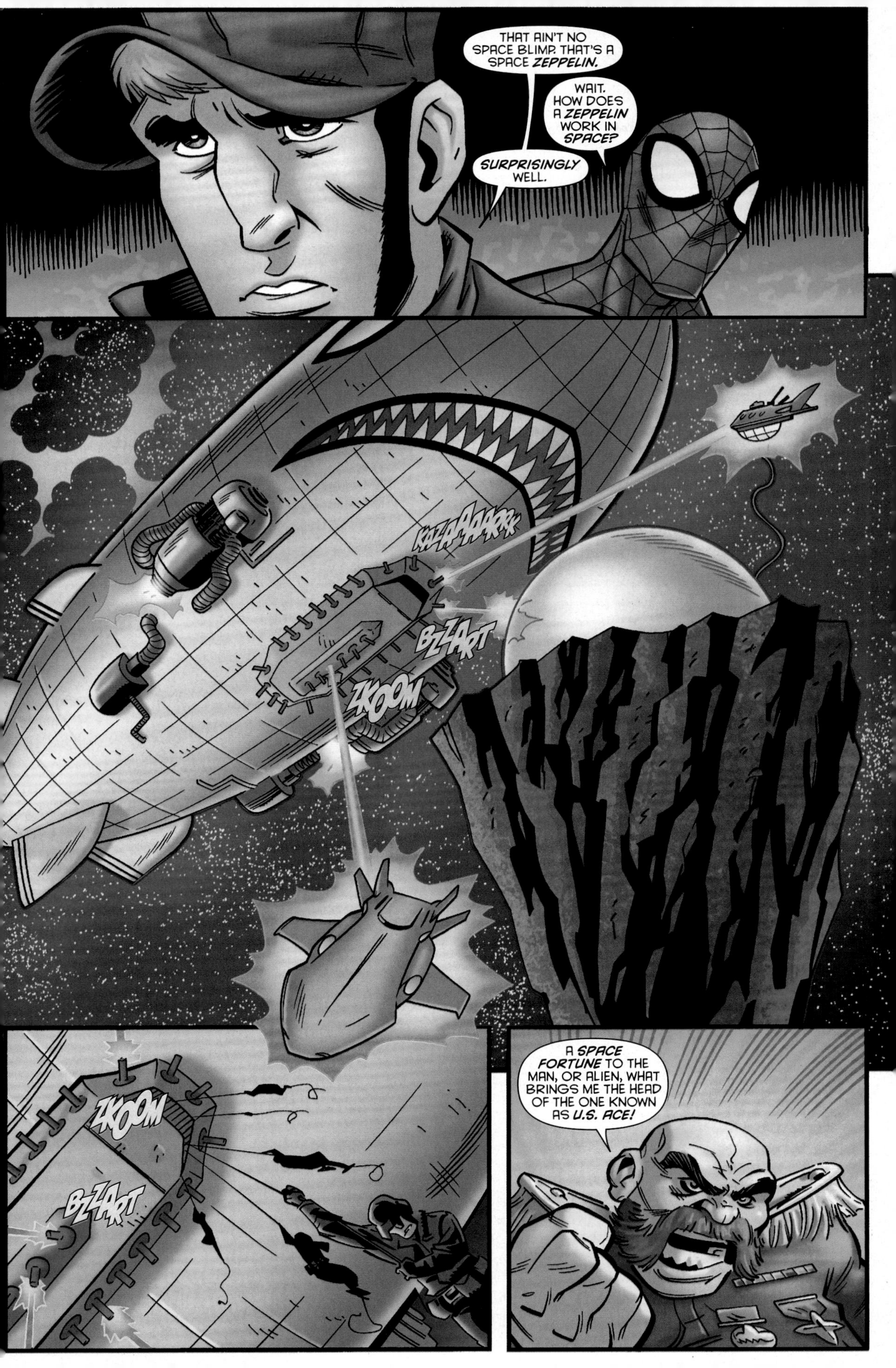
THAT AIN'T NO SPACE BLIMP. THAT'S A SPACE ZEPPELIN.
WAIT. HOW DOES A ZEPPELIN WORK IN SPACE?
SURPRISINGLY WELL.
KAZAAAAARRK
BZZART
ZKOOM
ZKOOM
BZZART
A SPACE FORTUNE TO THE MAN, OR ALIEN, WHAT BRINGS ME THE HEAD OF THE ONE KNOWN AS U.S. ACE!

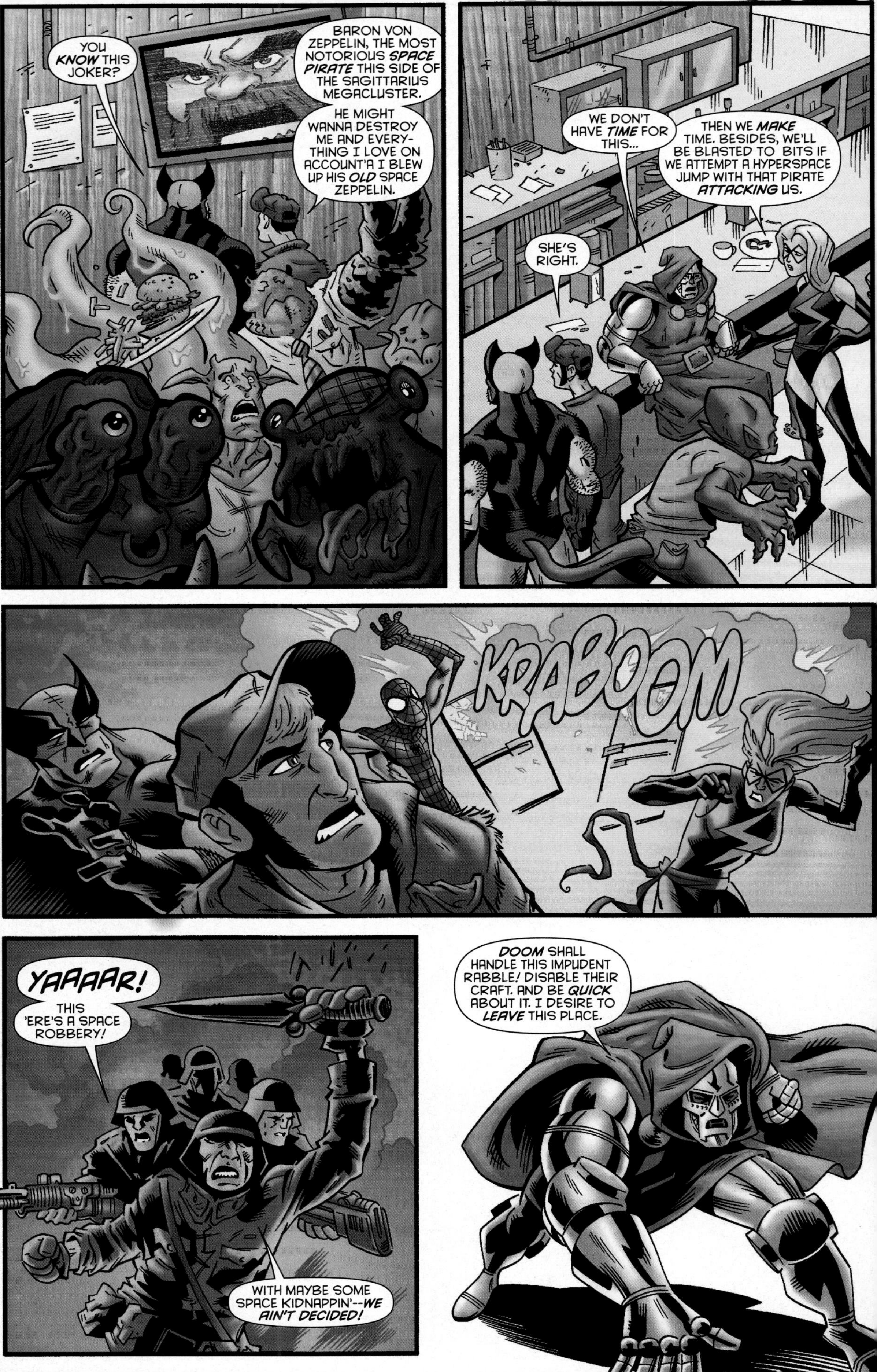
YOU KNOW THIS JOKER?
BARON VON ZEPPELIN, THE MOST NOTORIOUS SPACE PIRATE THIS SIDE OF THE SAGITTARIUS MEGACLUSTER.
HE MIGHT WANNA DESTROY ME AND EVERYTHING I LOVE ON ACCOUNT'A I BLEW UP HIS OLD SPACE ZEPPELIN.
WE DON'T HAVE TIME FOR THIS...
THEN WE MAKE TIME. BESIDES, WE'LL BE BLASTED TO BITS IF WE ATTEMPT A HYPERSPACE JUMP WITH THAT PIRATE ATTACKING US.
SHE'S RIGHT.
KRABOOM
YAAAAR!
THIS 'ERE'S A SPACE ROBBERY!
WITH MAYBE SOME SPACE KIDNAPPIN'--WE AIN'T DECIDED!
DOOM SHALL HANDLE THIS IMPUDENT RABBLE! DISABLE THEIR CRAFT. AND BE QUICK ABOUT IT. I DESIRE TO LEAVE THIS PLACE.

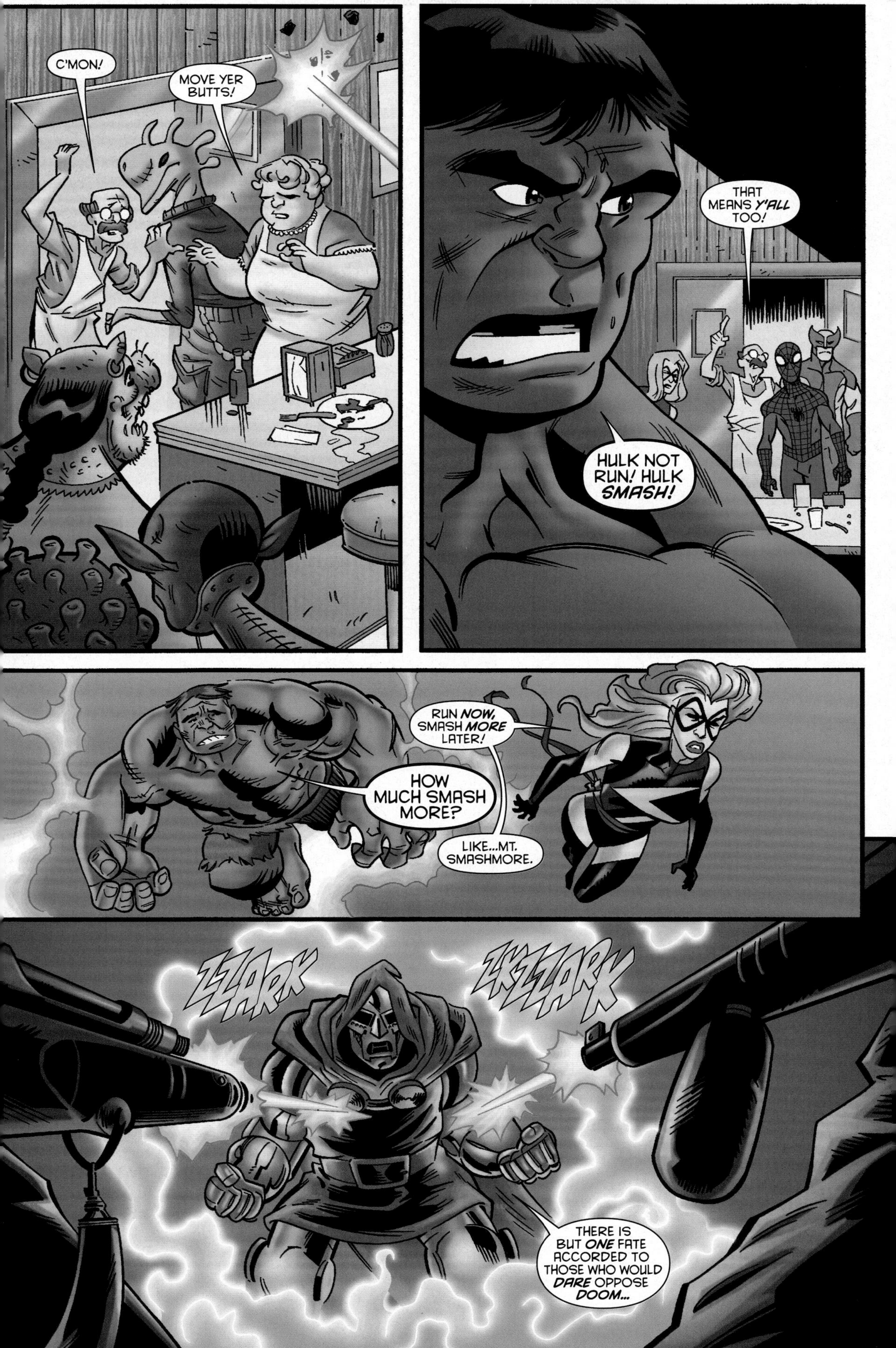
C'MON!
MOVE YER BUTTS!
THAT MEANS *Y'ALL* TOO!
HULK NOT RUN! HULK *SMASH!*
RUN *NOW,* SMASH *MORE* LATER!
HOW MUCH SMASH MORE?
LIKE...MT. SMASHMORE.
ZZARK
ZKZZARK
THERE IS BUT *ONE* FATE ACCORDED TO THOSE WHO WOULD *DARE* OPPOSE *DOOM...*

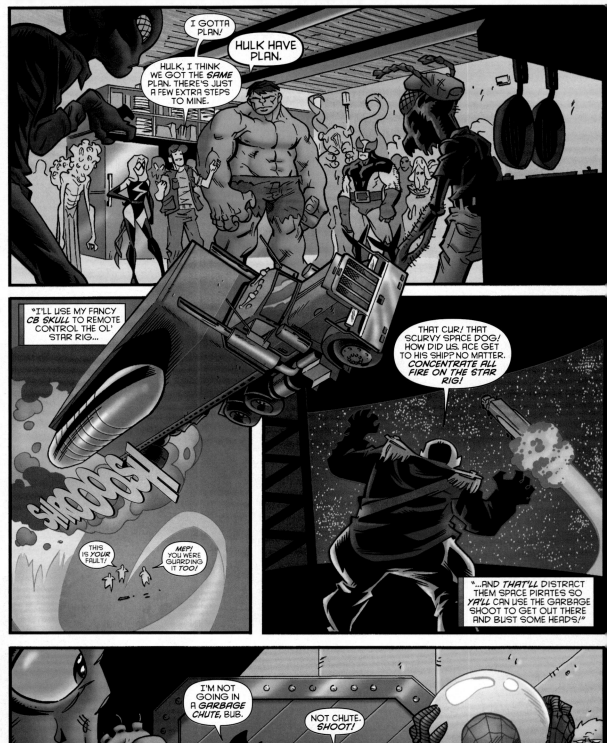

I GOTTA PLAN!

HULK HAVE PLAN.

HULK, I THINK WE GOT THE *SAME* PLAN. THERE'S JUST A FEW EXTRA STEPS TO MINE.

"I'LL USE MY FANCY *CB SKULL* TO REMOTE CONTROL THE OL' STAR RIG...

SHROOOSH!

THIS IS *YOUR* FAULT!

MEP! YOU WERE GUARDING IT *TOO*!

THAT CUR! THAT SCURVY SPACE DOG! HOW DID US. ACE GET TO HIS SHIP? NO MATTER. *CONCENTRATE ALL FIRE ON THE STAR RIG!*

"...AND *THAT'LL* DISTRACT THEM SPACE PIRATES SO *YA'LL* CAN USE THE GARBAGE SHOOT TO GET OUT THERE AND BUST SOME HEADS!"

I'M NOT GOING IN A *GARBAGE CHUTE*, BUB.

NOT CHUTE. *SHOOT!*

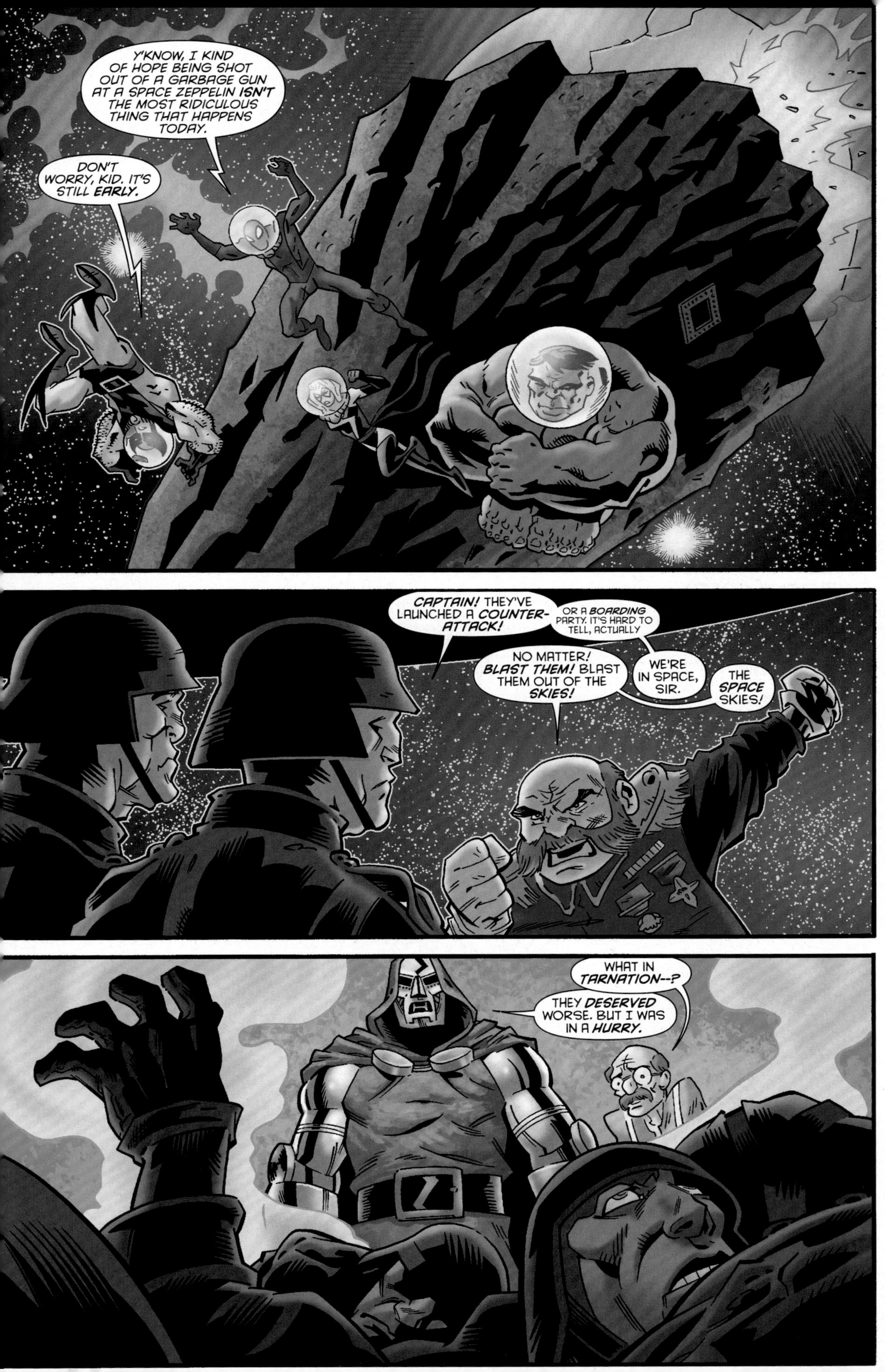
Y'KNOW, I KIND OF HOPE BEING SHOT OUT OF A GARBAGE GUN AT A SPACE ZEPPELIN ISN'T THE MOST RIDICULOUS THING THAT HAPPENS TODAY.
DON'T WORRY, KID. IT'S STILL EARLY.
CAPTAIN! THEY'VE LAUNCHED A COUNTER-ATTACK!
OR A BOARDING PARTY. IT'S HARD TO TELL, ACTUALLY
NO MATTER! BLAST THEM! BLAST THEM OUT OF THE SKIES!
WE'RE IN SPACE, SIR.
THE SPACE SKIES!
WHAT IN TARNATION--?
THEY DESERVED WORSE. BUT I WAS IN A HURRY.

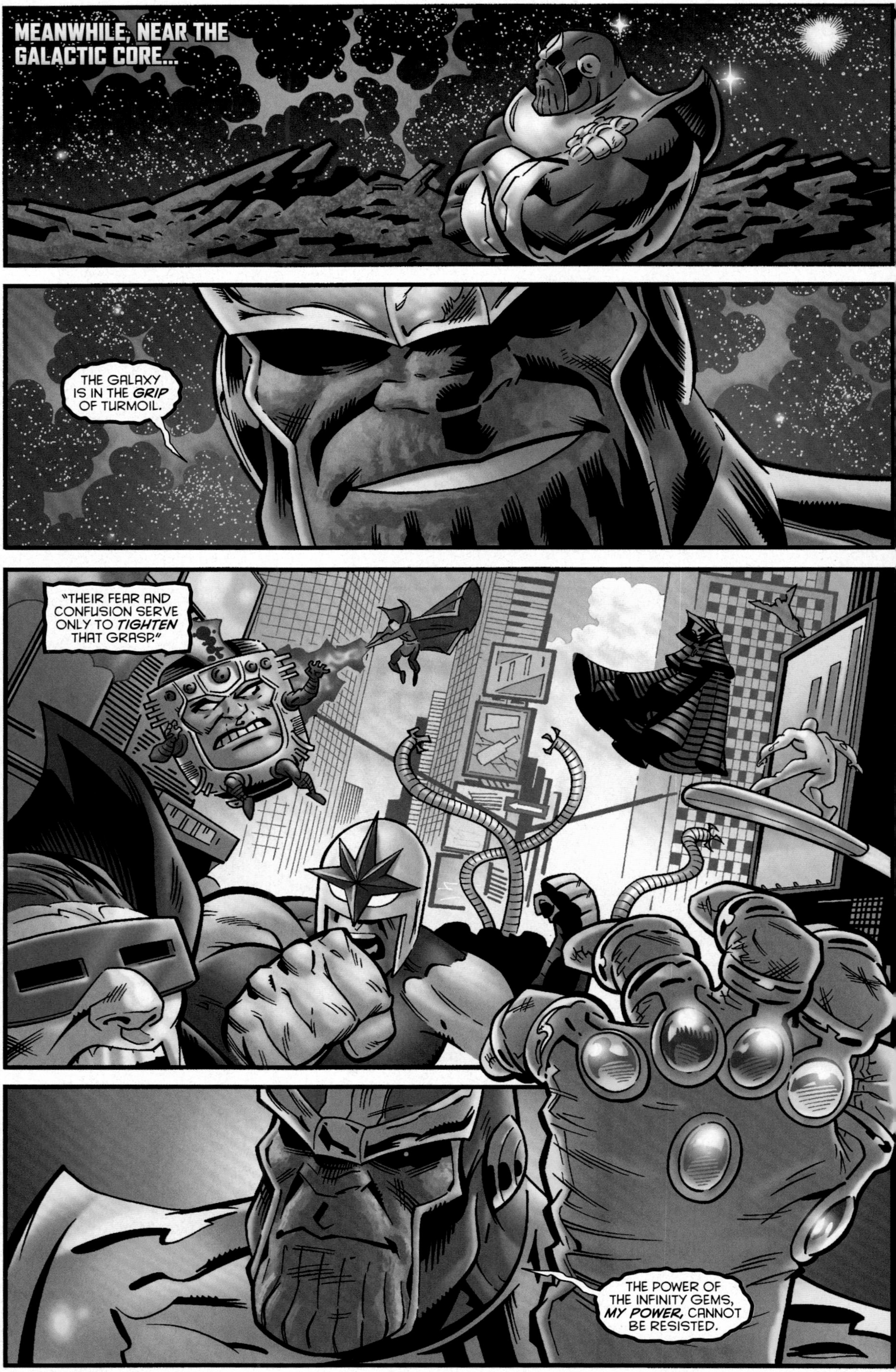
MEANWHILE, NEAR THE GALACTIC CORE...
THE GALAXY IS IN THE *GRIP* OF TURMOIL.
"THEIR FEAR AND CONFUSION SERVE ONLY TO *TIGHTEN* THAT GRASP."
THE POWER OF THE INFINITY GEMS, *MY POWER,* CANNOT BE RESISTED.

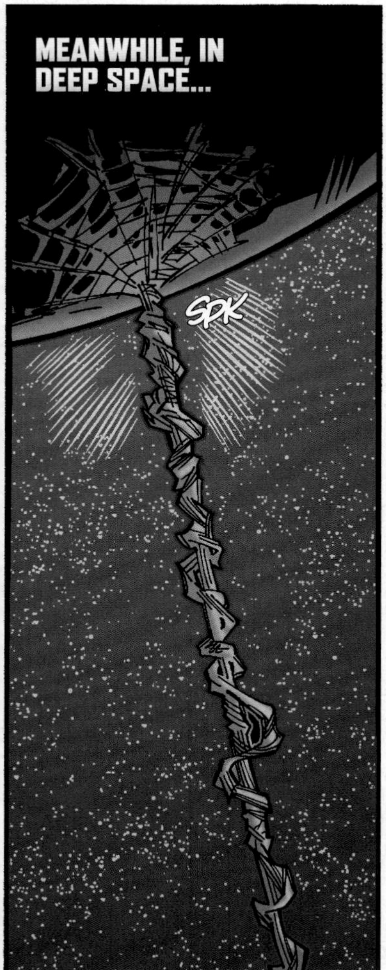
MEANWHILE, IN DEEP SPACE...
SPK

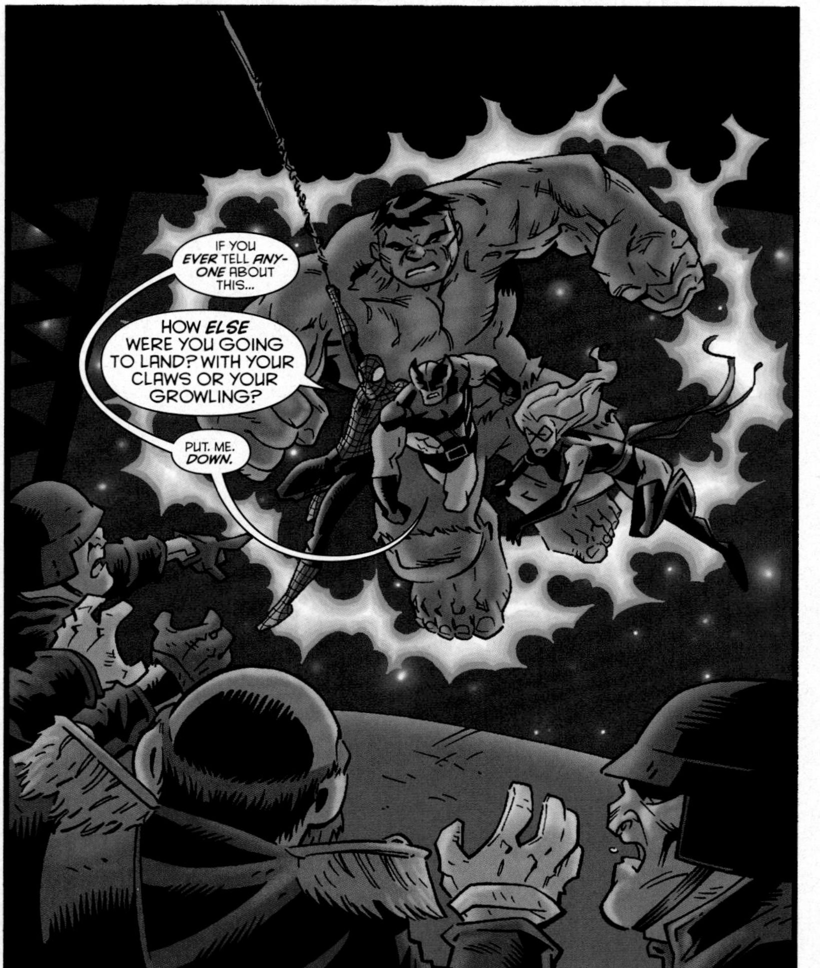
IF YOU EVER TELL ANY-ONE ABOUT THIS...
HOW ELSE WERE YOU GOING TO LAND? WITH YOUR CLAWS OR YOUR GROWLING?
PUT. ME. DOWN.

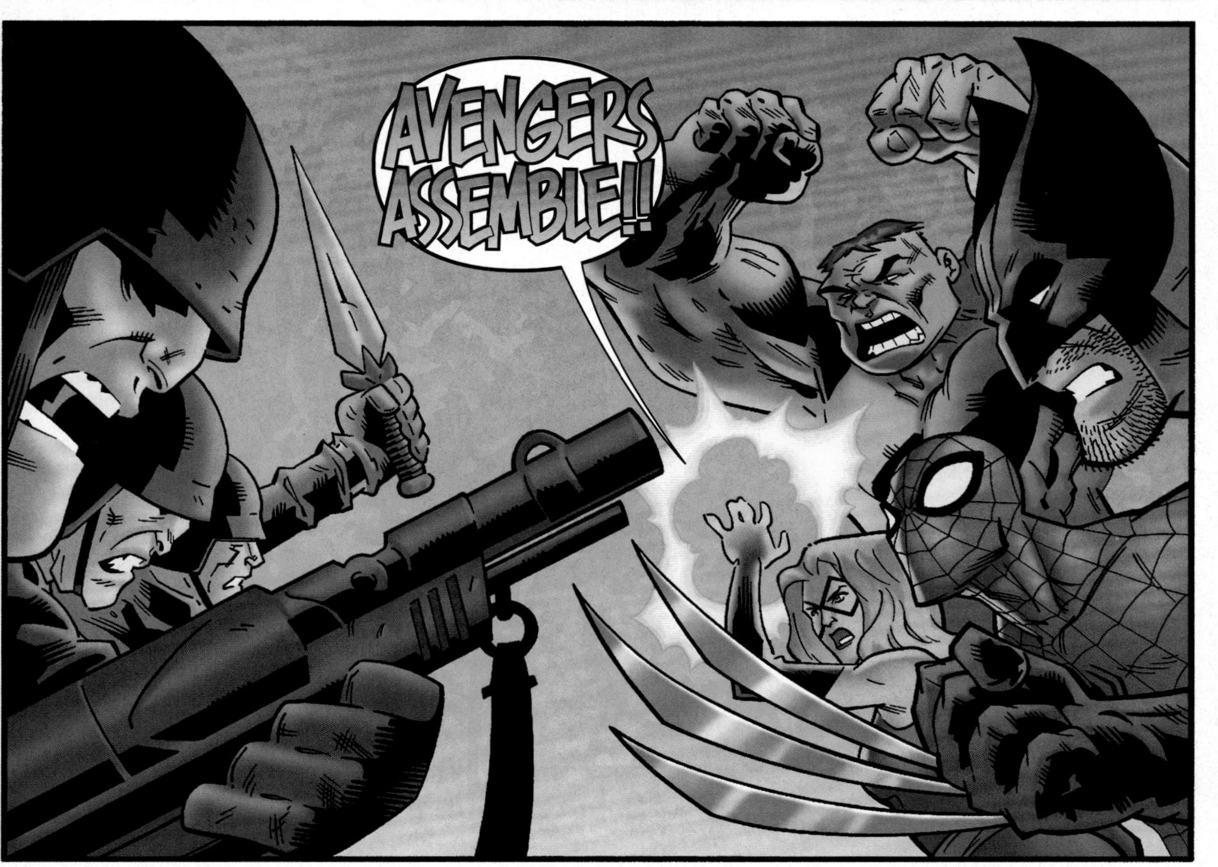
AVENGERS ASSEMBLE!!

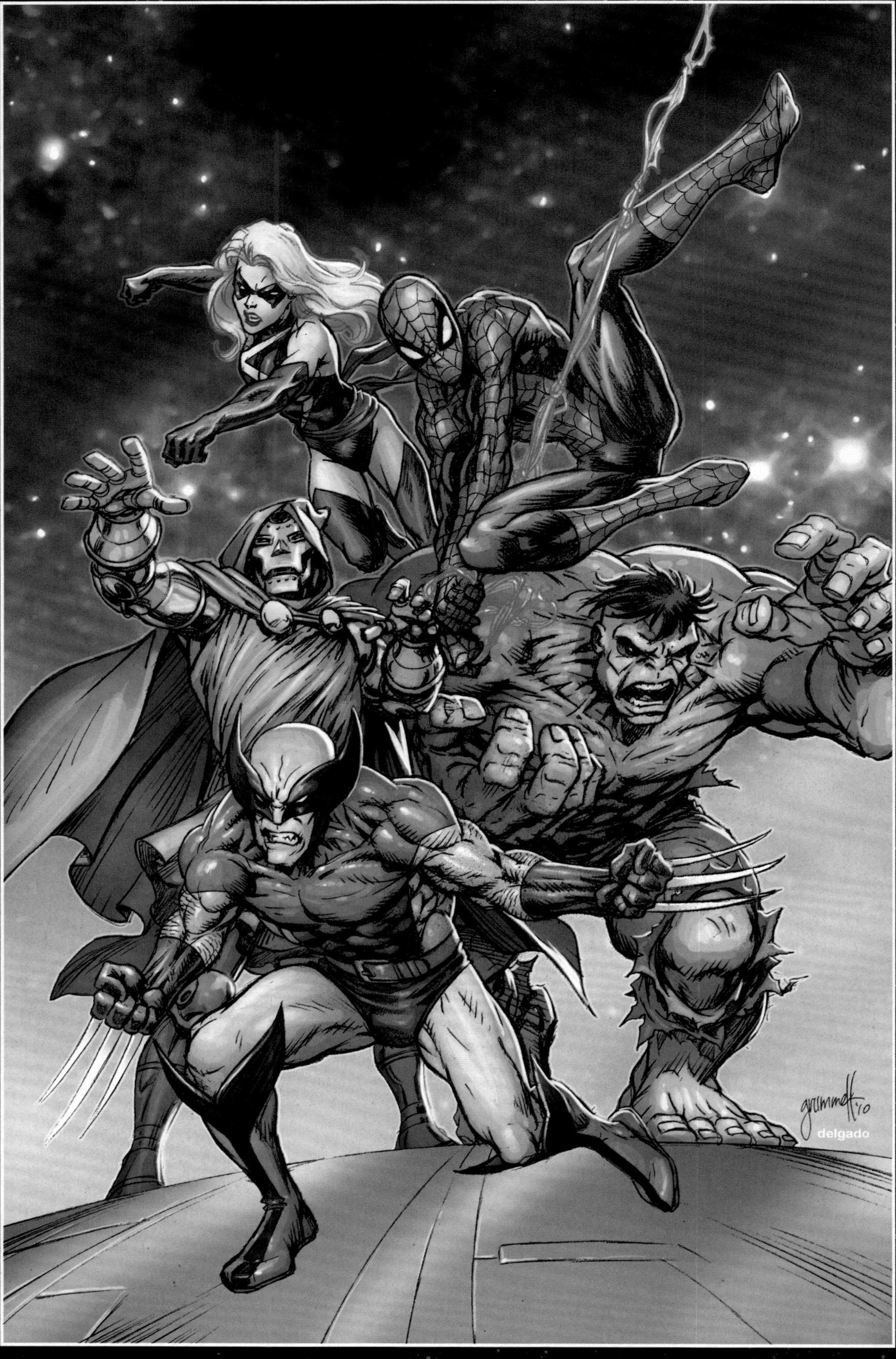
grummett '10
delgado

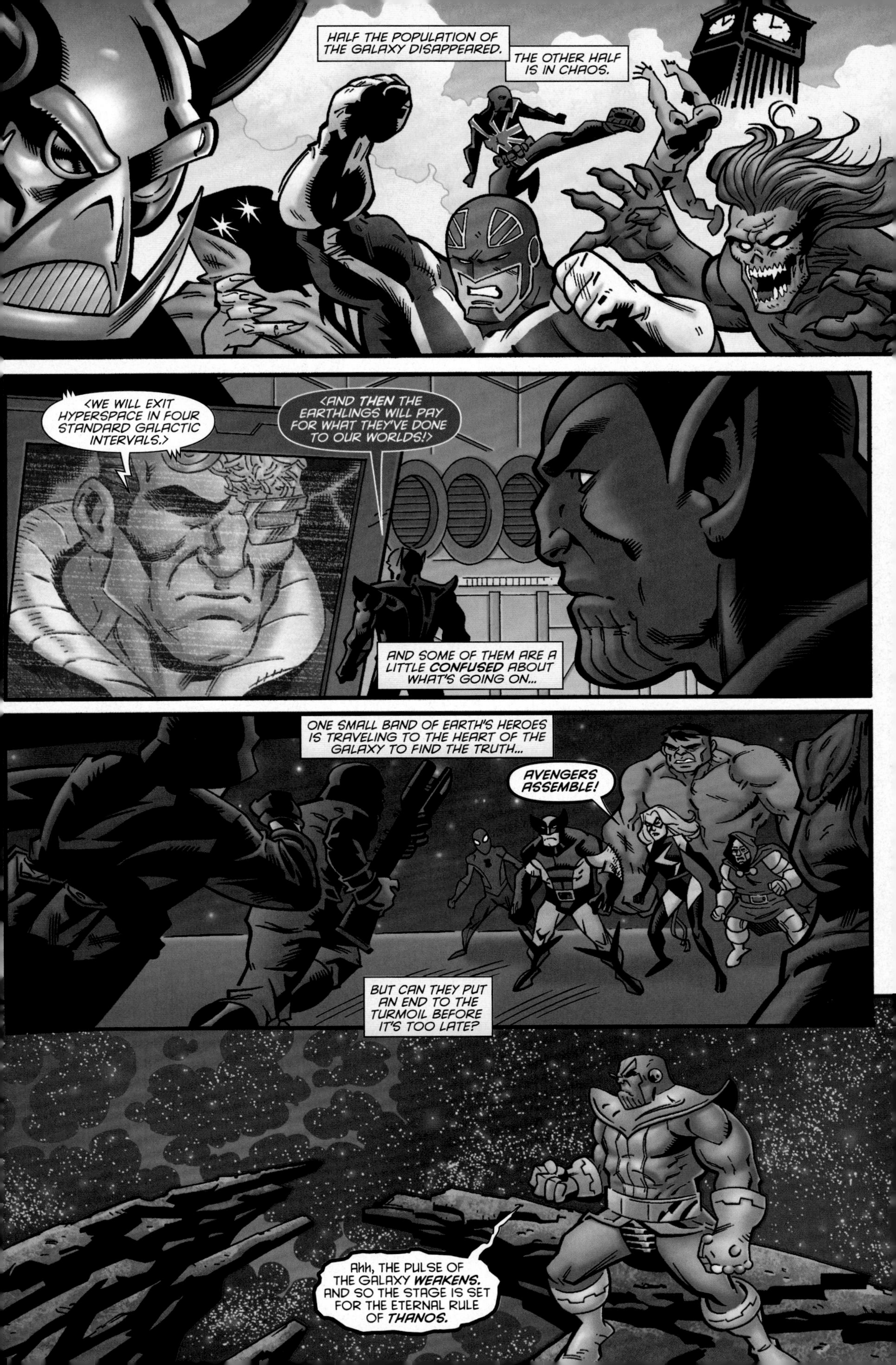
HALF THE POPULATION OF THE GALAXY DISAPPEARED.
THE OTHER HALF IS IN CHAOS.
<WE WILL EXIT HYPERSPACE IN FOUR STANDARD GALACTIC INTERVALS.>
<AND THEN THE EARTHLINGS WILL PAY FOR WHAT THEY'VE DONE TO OUR WORLDS!>
AND SOME OF THEM ARE A LITTLE CONFUSED ABOUT WHAT'S GOING ON...
ONE SMALL BAND OF EARTH'S HEROES IS TRAVELING TO THE HEART OF THE GALAXY TO FIND THE TRUTH...
AVENGERS ASSEMBLE!
BUT CAN THEY PUT AN END TO THE TURMOIL BEFORE IT'S TOO LATE?
AHH, THE PULSE OF THE GALAXY WEAKENS. AND SO THE STAGE IS SET FOR THE ETERNAL RULE OF THANOS.

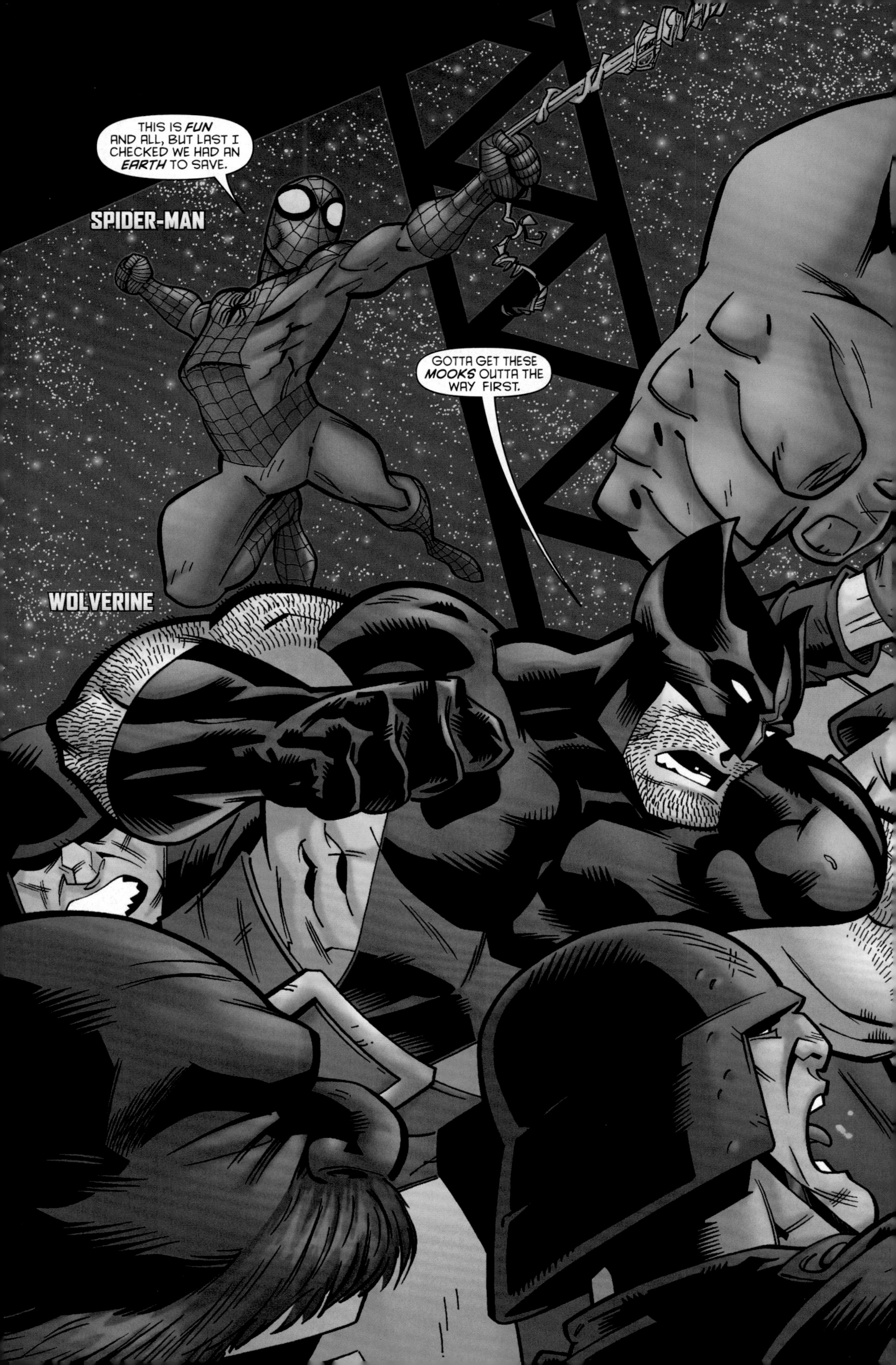

THIS IS FUN AND ALL, BUT LAST I CHECKED WE HAD AN EARTH TO SAVE.
SPIDER-MAN
GOTTA GET THESE MOOKS OUTTA THE WAY FIRST.
WOLVERINE

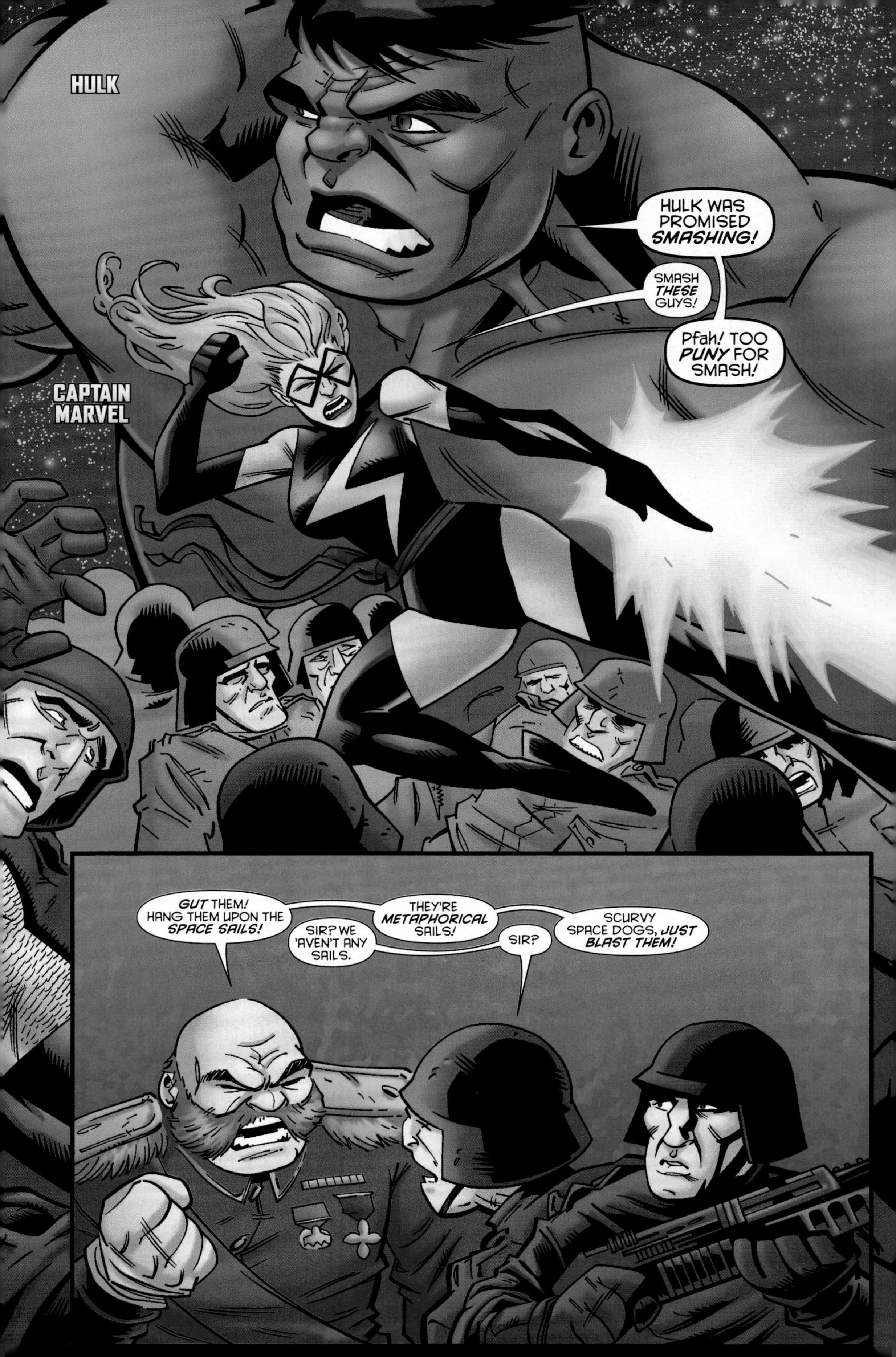
HULK
HULK WAS PROMISED SMASHING!
SMASH THESE GUYS!
Pfah! TOO PUNY FOR SMASH!
CAPTAIN MARVEL
GUT THEM! HANG THEM UPON THE SPACE SAILS!
SIR? WE 'AVEN'T ANY SAILS.
THEY'RE METAPHORICAL SAILS!
SIR?
SCURVY SPACE DOGS, JUST BLAST THEM!

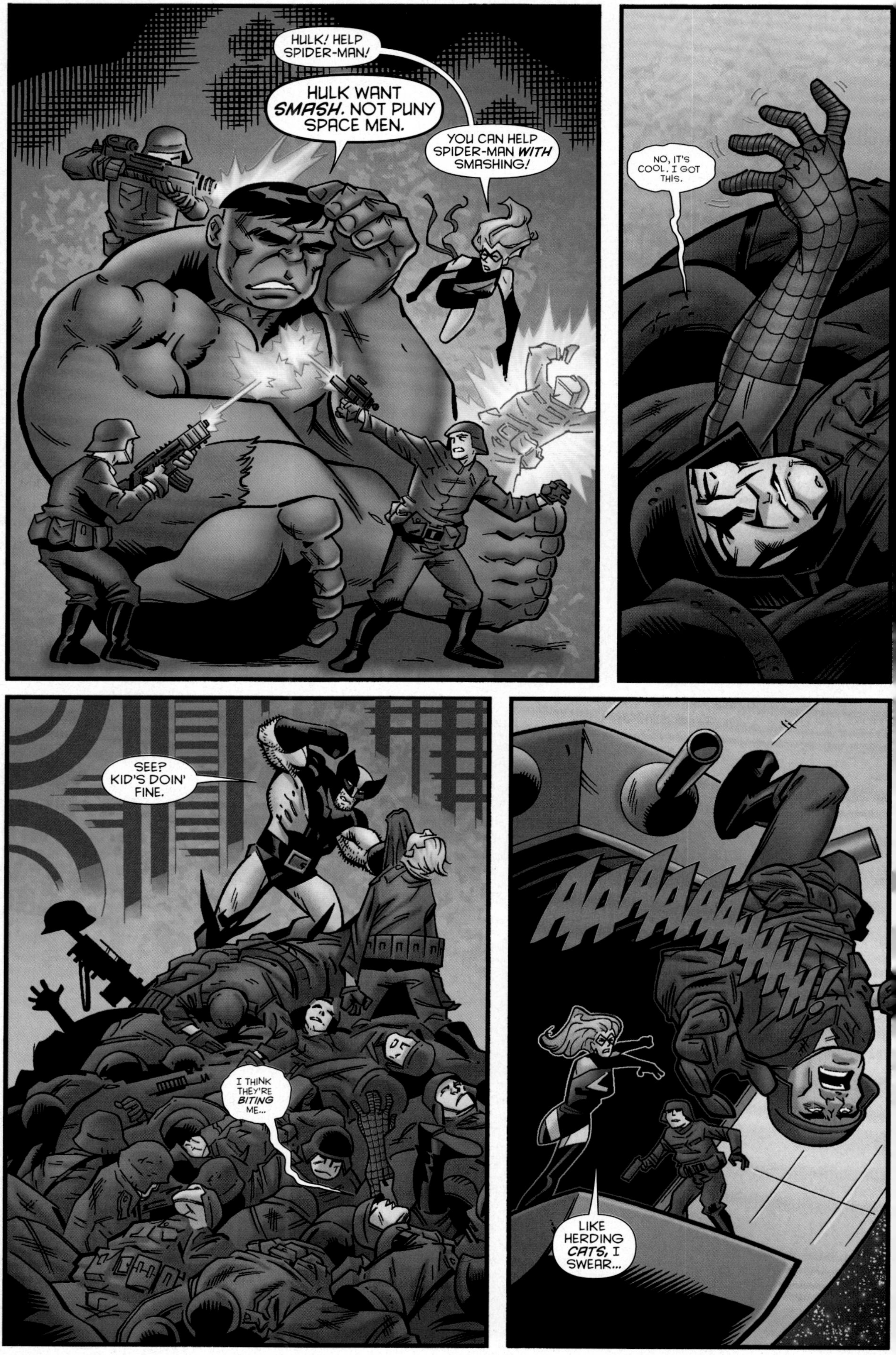

HULK! HELP SPIDER-MAN!
HULK WANT SMASH. NOT PUNY SPACE MEN.
YOU CAN HELP SPIDER-MAN WITH SMASHING!
NO, IT'S COOL. I GOT THIS.
SEE? KID'S DOIN' FINE.
I THINK THEY'RE BITING ME...
AAAAAAAHHH!
LIKE HERDING CATS, I SWEAR...

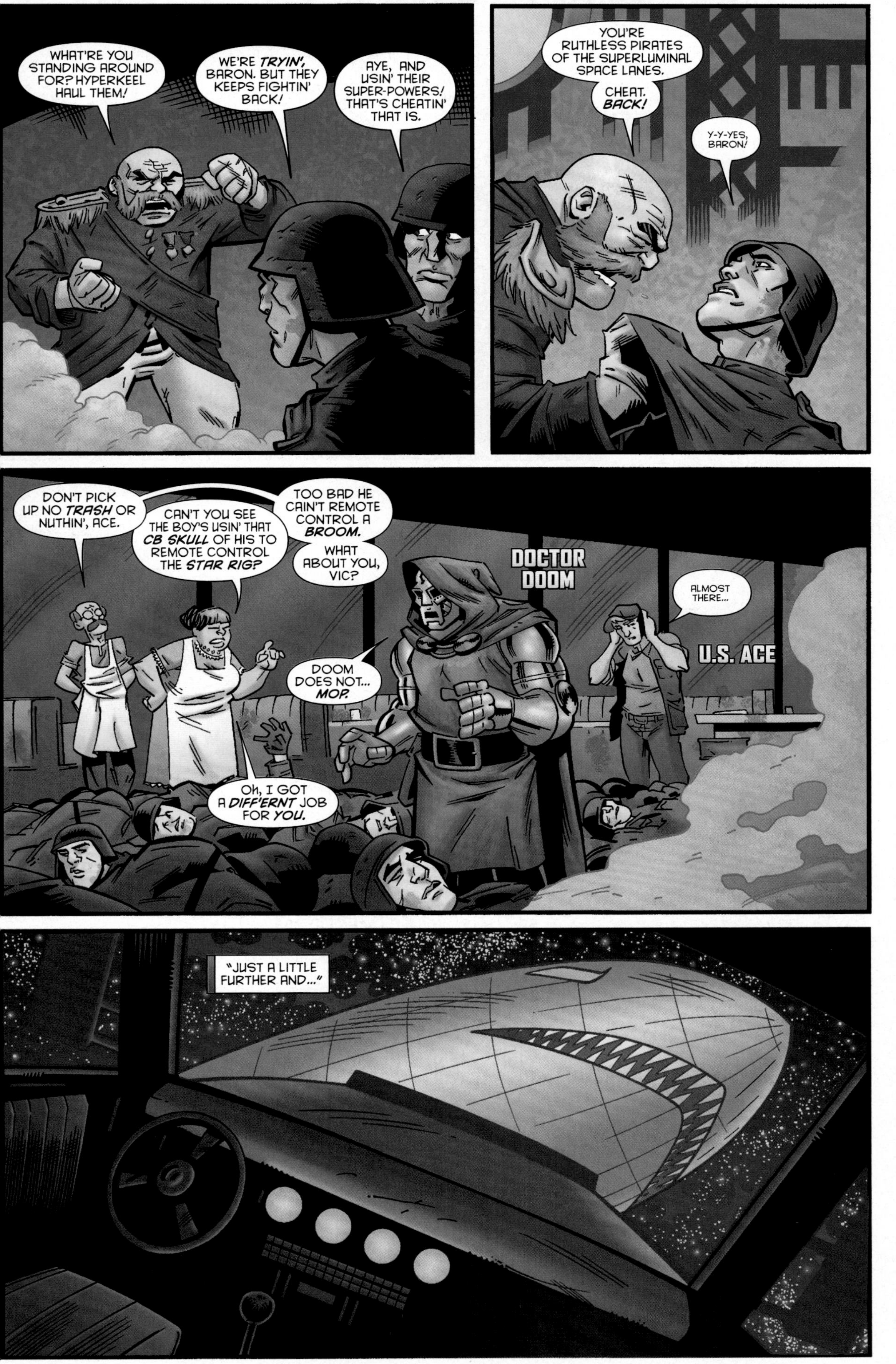
WHAT'RE YOU STANDING AROUND FOR? HYPERKEEL HAUL THEM!
WE'RE TRYIN', BARON. BUT THEY KEEPS FIGHTIN' BACK!
AYE, AND USIN' THEIR SUPER-POWERS! THAT'S CHEATIN' THAT IS.
YOU'RE RUTHLESS PIRATES OF THE SUPERLUMINAL SPACE LANES.
CHEAT. BACK!
Y-Y-YES, BARON!
DON'T PICK UP NO TRASH OR NUTHIN', ACE.
CAN'T YOU SEE THE BOY'S USIN' THAT CB SKULL OF HIS TO REMOTE CONTROL THE STAR RIG?
TOO BAD HE CAIN'T REMOTE CONTROL A BROOM.
WHAT ABOUT YOU, VIC?
DOCTOR DOOM
ALMOST THERE...
U.S. ACE
DOOM DOES NOT... MOP.
Oh, I GOT A DIFF'ERNT JOB FOR YOU.
"JUST A LITTLE FURTHER AND..."

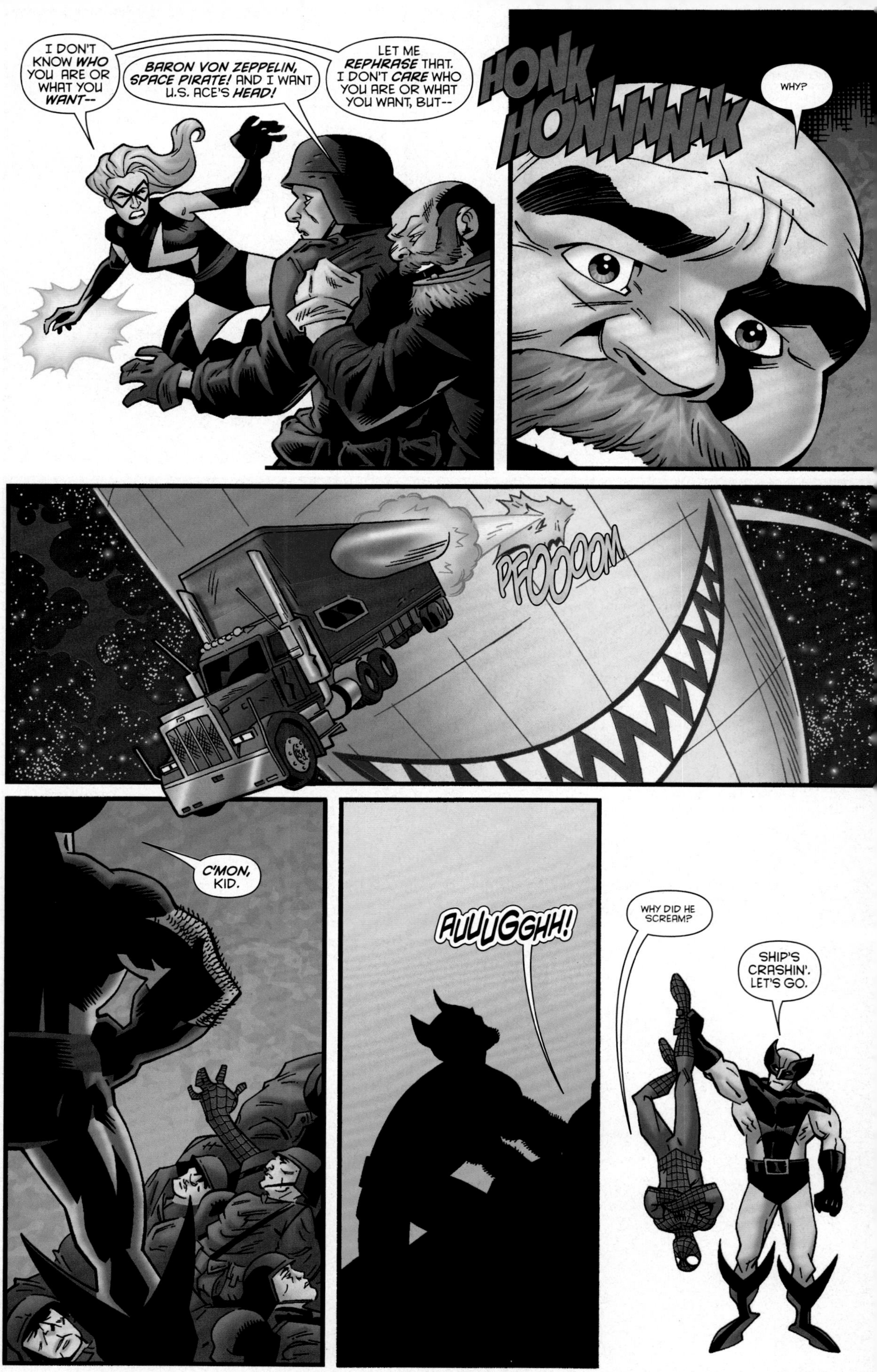
I DON'T KNOW *WHO* YOU ARE OR WHAT YOU *WANT*--
BARON VON ZEPPELIN, SPACE PIRATE! AND I WANT U.S. ACE'S *HEAD!*
LET ME *REPHRASE* THAT. I DON'T *CARE* WHO YOU ARE OR WHAT YOU WANT, BUT--
HONK HONNNNNK
WHY?
PFOOOOM
C'MON, KID.
AUUUGGHH!
WHY DID HE SCREAM?
SHIP'S CRASHIN'. LET'S GO.

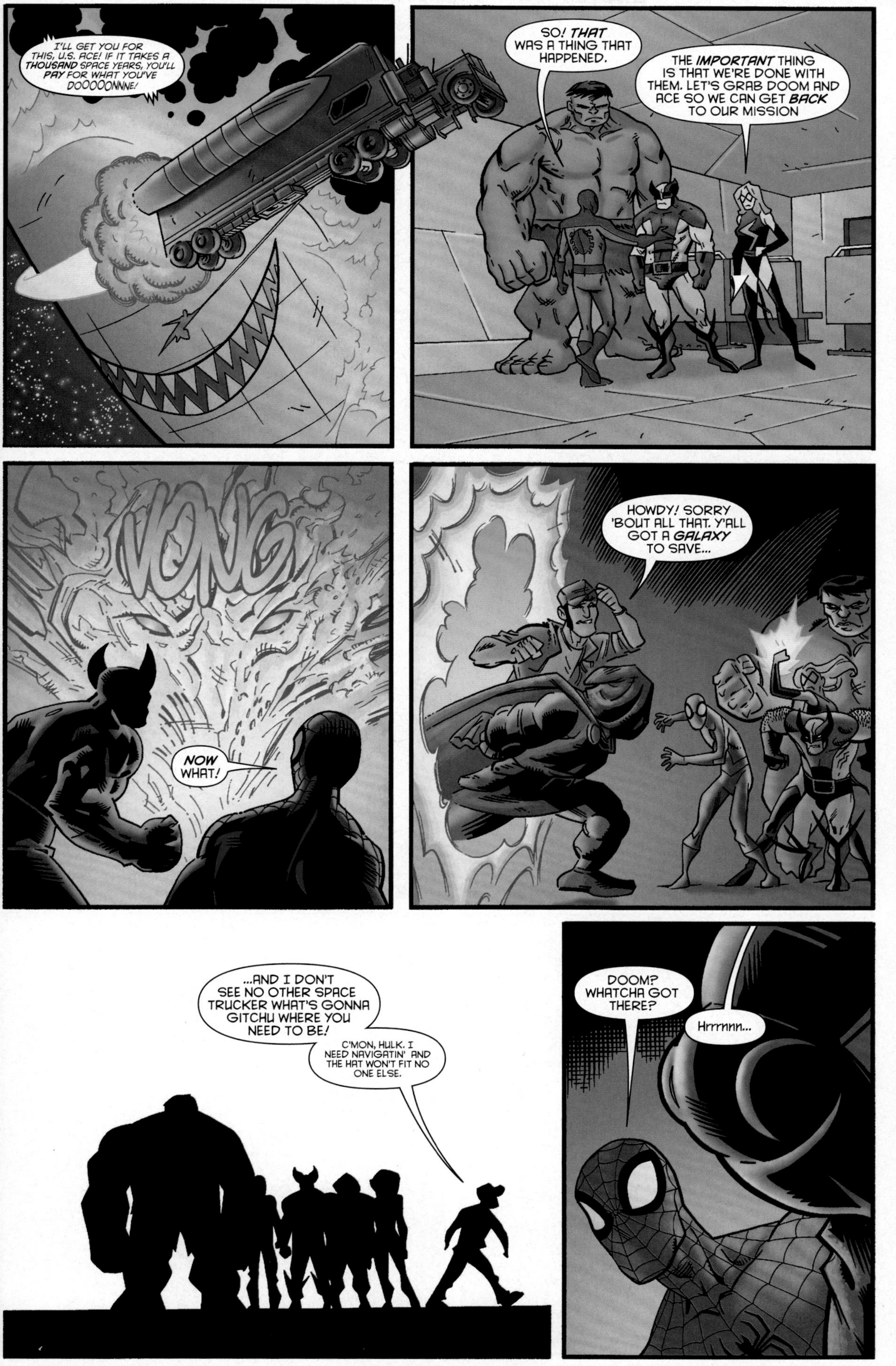
I'LL GET YOU FOR THIS, U.S. ACE! IF IT TAKES A THOUSAND SPACE YEARS, YOU'LL PAY FOR WHAT YOU'VE DOOOOONNNE!
SO! THAT WAS A THING THAT HAPPENED.
THE IMPORTANT THING IS THAT WE'RE DONE WITH THEM. LET'S GRAB DOOM AND ACE SO WE CAN GET BACK TO OUR MISSION
VONG
NOW WHAT!
HOWDY! SORRY 'BOUT ALL THAT. Y'ALL GOT A GALAXY TO SAVE...
...AND I DON'T SEE NO OTHER SPACE TRUCKER WHAT'S GONNA GITCHU WHERE YOU NEED TO BE!
C'MON, HULK. I NEED NAVIGATIN' AND THE HAT WON'T FIT NO ONE ELSE.
DOOM? WHATCHA GOT THERE?
Hrrrnnn...

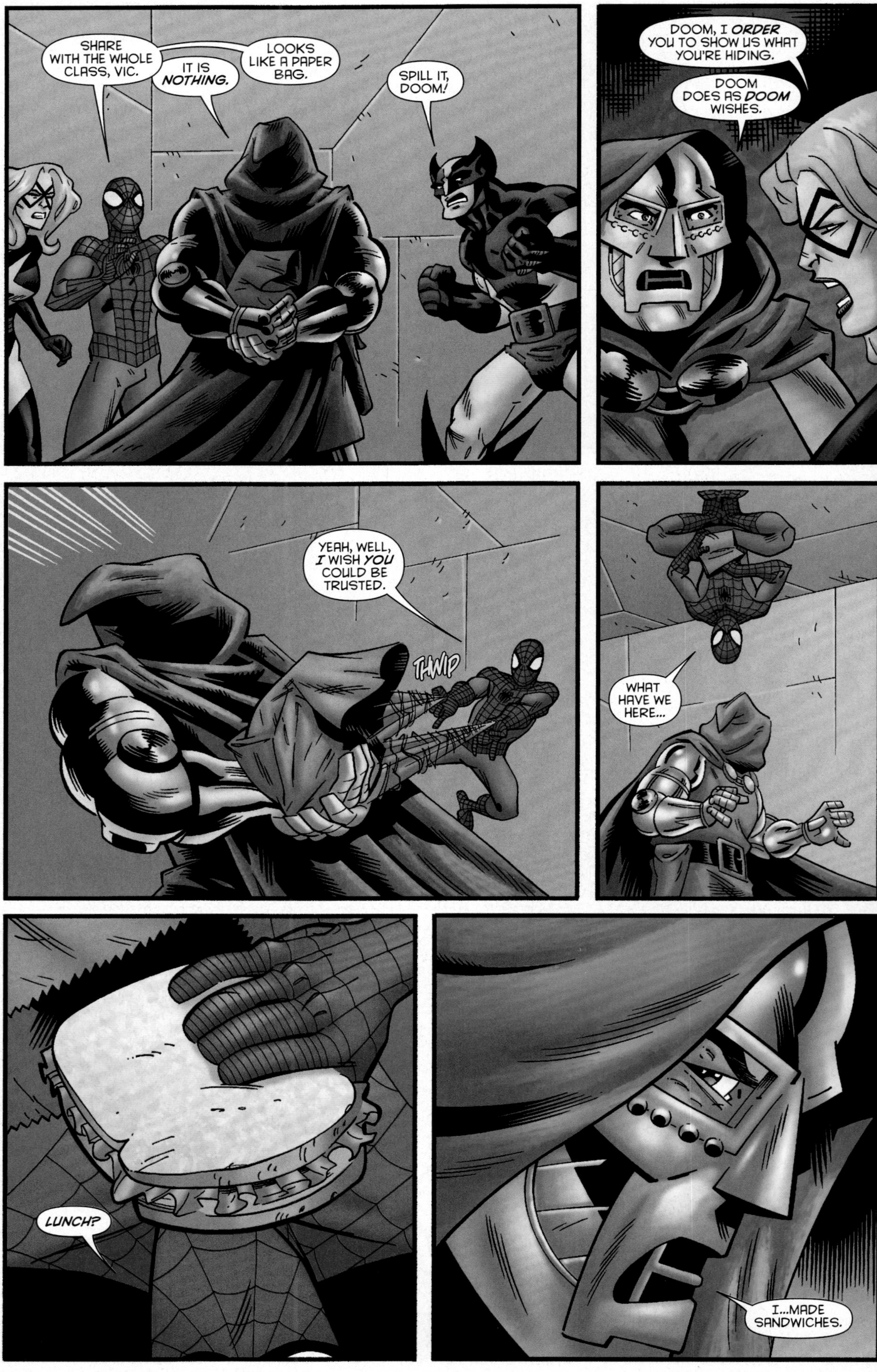
SHARE WITH THE WHOLE CLASS, VIC.
IT IS *NOTHING.*
LOOKS LIKE A PAPER BAG.
SPILL IT, DOOM!
DOOM, I *ORDER* YOU TO SHOW US WHAT YOU'RE HIDING.
DOOM DOES AS *DOOM* WISHES.
YEAH, WELL, *I* WISH *YOU* COULD BE TRUSTED.
THWIP
WHAT HAVE WE HERE...
LUNCH?
I...MADE SANDWICHES.

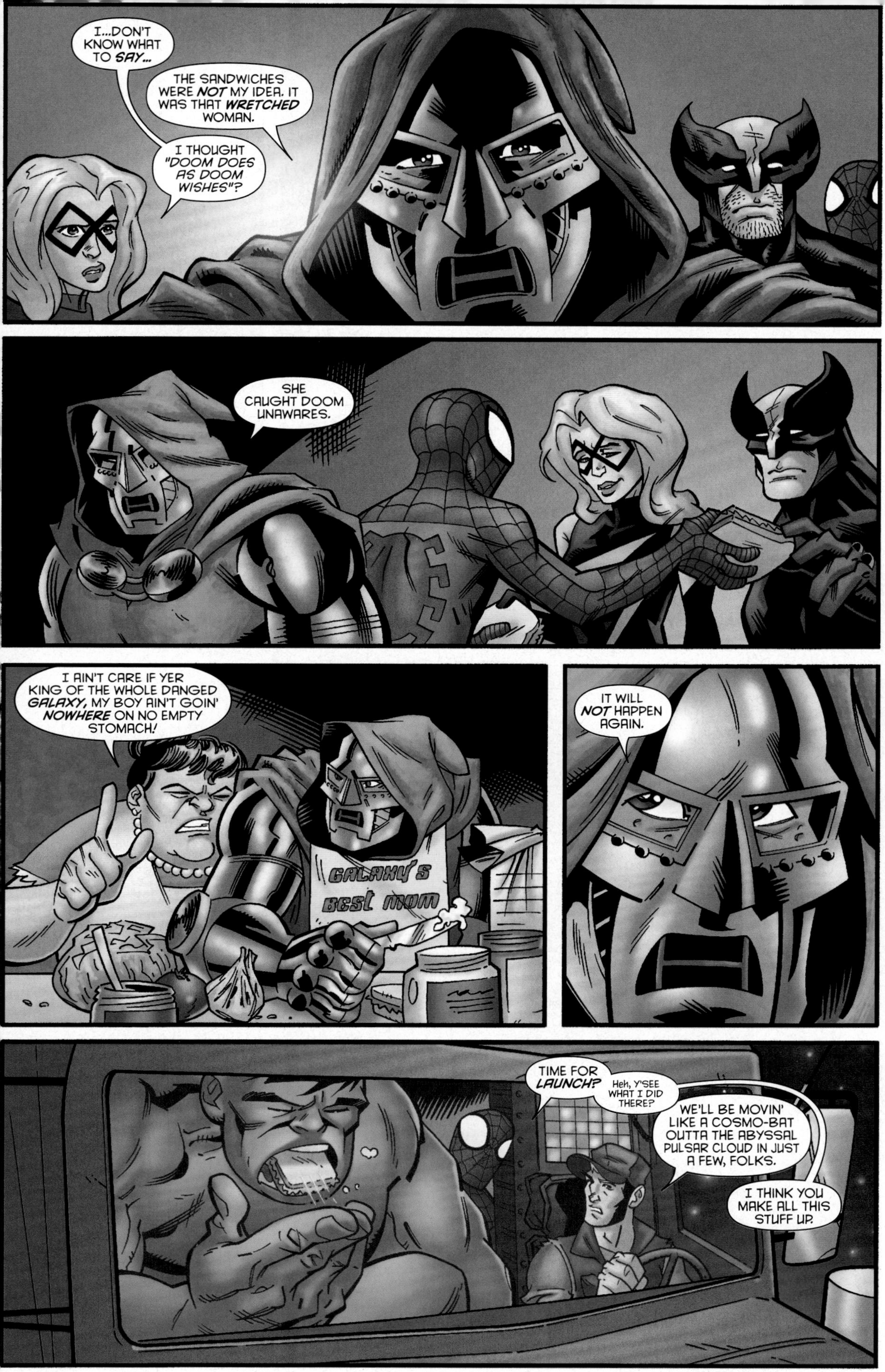

I...DON'T KNOW WHAT TO SAY...
THE SANDWICHES WERE NOT MY IDEA. IT WAS THAT WRETCHED WOMAN.
I THOUGHT "DOOM DOES AS DOOM WISHES"?
SHE CAUGHT DOOM UNAWARES.
I AIN'T CARE IF YER KING OF THE WHOLE DANGED GALAXY, MY BOY AIN'T GOIN' NOWHERE ON NO EMPTY STOMACH!
GALAXY'S BEST MOM
IT WILL NOT HAPPEN AGAIN.
TIME FOR LAUNCH?
Heh, Y'SEE WHAT I DID THERE?
WE'LL BE MOVIN' LIKE A COSMO-BAT OUTTA THE ABYSSAL PULSAR CLOUD IN JUST A FEW, FOLKS.
I THINK YOU MAKE ALL THIS STUFF UP.

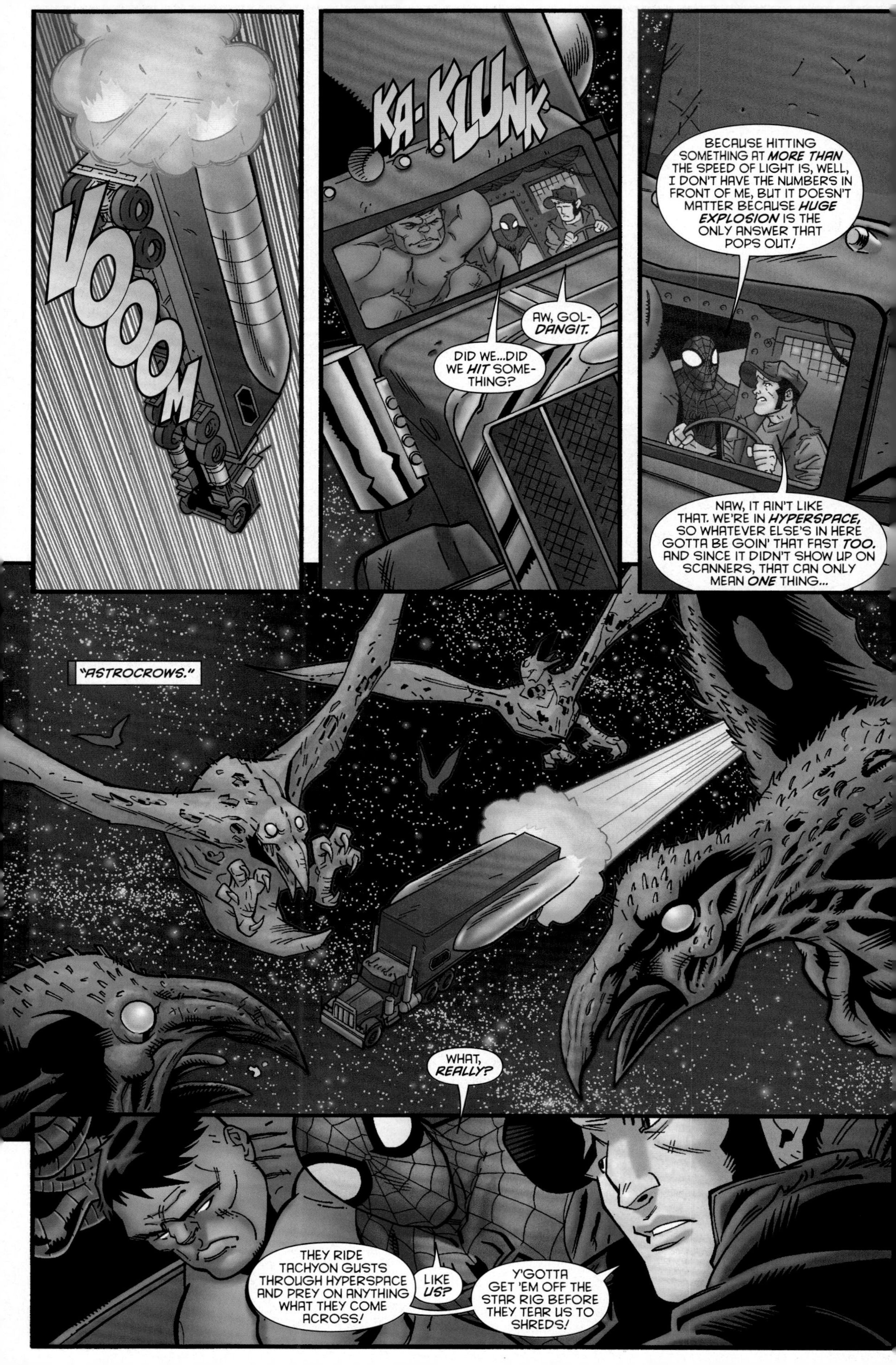
VOOOOM
KA-KLUNK
DID WE...DID WE HIT SOMETHING?
AW, GOL-DANGIT.
BECAUSE HITTING SOMETHING AT MORE THAN THE SPEED OF LIGHT IS, WELL, I DON'T HAVE THE NUMBERS IN FRONT OF ME, BUT IT DOESN'T MATTER BECAUSE HUGE EXPLOSION IS THE ONLY ANSWER THAT POPS OUT!
NAW, IT AIN'T LIKE THAT. WE'RE IN HYPERSPACE, SO WHATEVER ELSE'S IN HERE GOTTA BE GOIN' THAT FAST TOO. AND SINCE IT DIDN'T SHOW UP ON SCANNERS, THAT CAN ONLY MEAN ONE THING...
"ASTROCROWS."
WHAT, REALLY?
THEY RIDE TACHYON GUSTS THROUGH HYPERSPACE AND PREY ON ANYTHING WHAT THEY COME ACROSS!
LIKE US?
Y'GOTTA GET 'EM OFF THE STAR RIG BEFORE THEY TEAR US TO SHREDS!

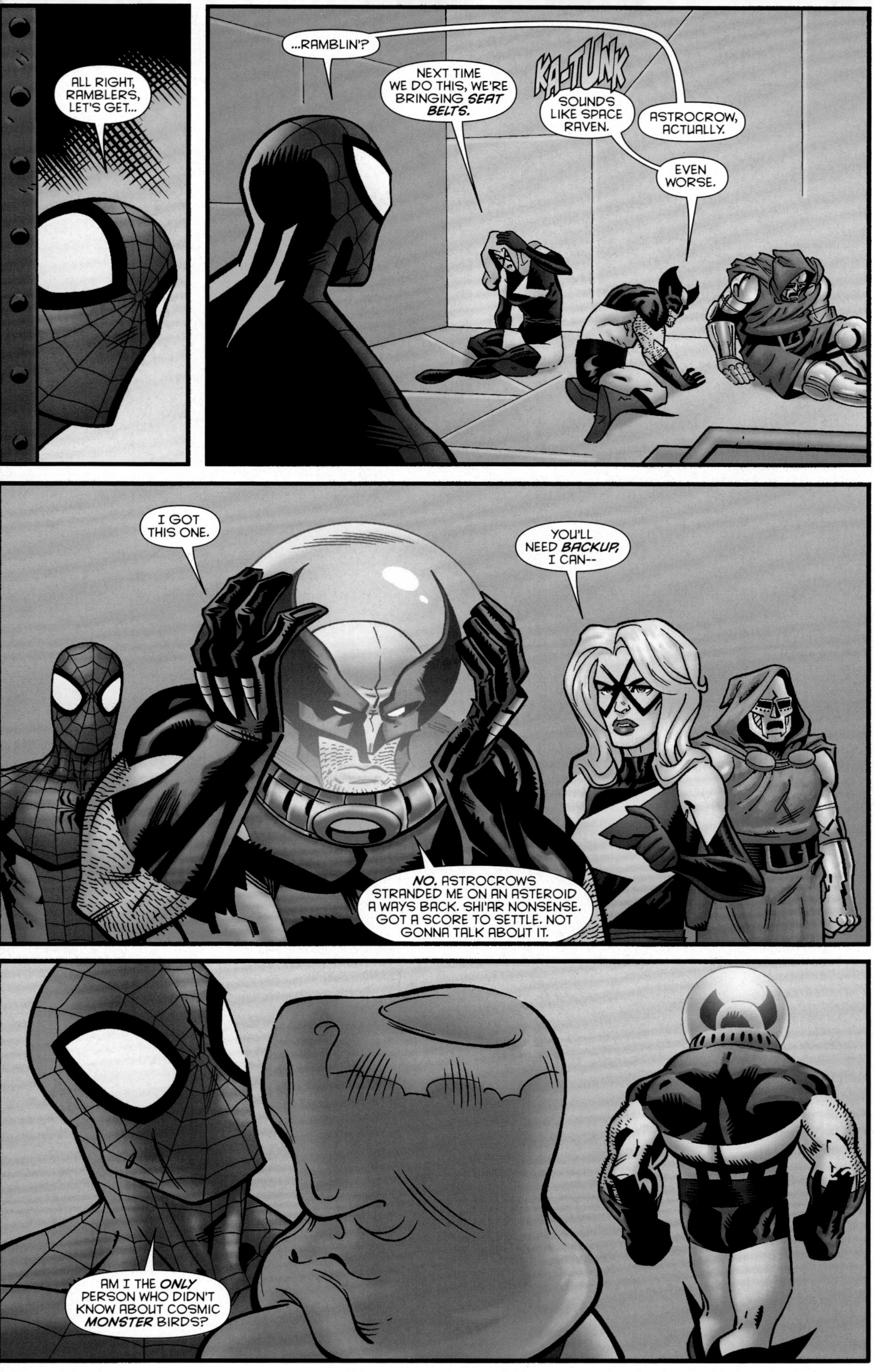
ALL RIGHT, RAMBLERS, LET'S GET...
...RAMBLIN'?
NEXT TIME WE DO THIS, WE'RE BRINGING SEAT BELTS.
KA-TUNK
SOUNDS LIKE SPACE RAVEN.
ASTROCROW, ACTUALLY.
EVEN WORSE.
I GOT THIS ONE.
YOU'LL NEED BACKUP. I CAN--
NO. ASTROCROWS STRANDED ME ON AN ASTEROID A WAYS BACK. SHI'AR NONSENSE. GOT A SCORE TO SETTLE. NOT GONNA TALK ABOUT IT.
AM I THE ONLY PERSON WHO DIDN'T KNOW ABOUT COSMIC MONSTER BIRDS?

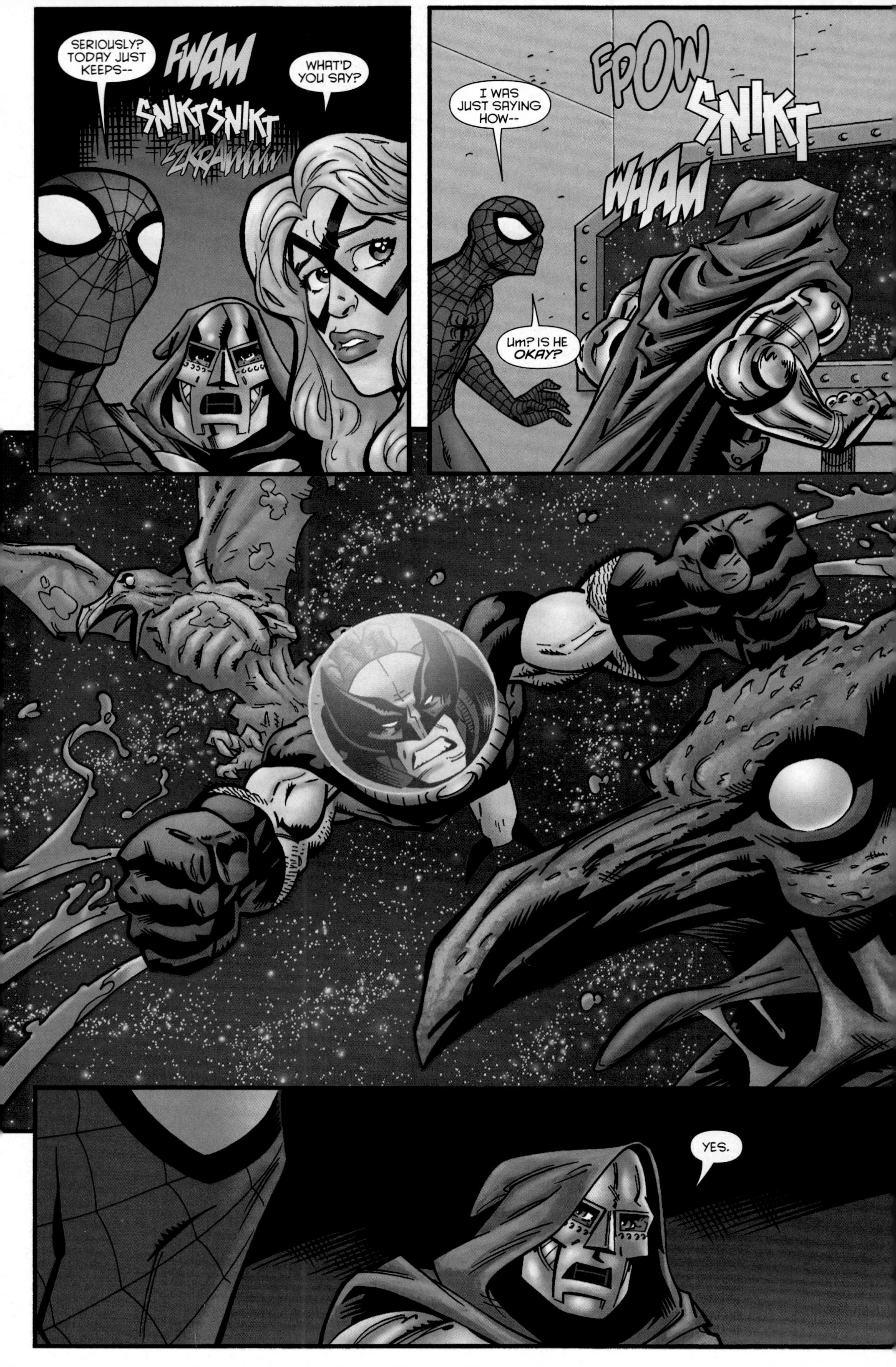
SERIOUSLY? TODAY JUST KEEPS--
FWAM
SNIKT SNIKT
ZZKRAW
WHAT'D YOU SAY?
I WAS JUST SAYING HOW--
FPOW
SNIKT
WHAM
UM? IS HE OKAY?
YES.

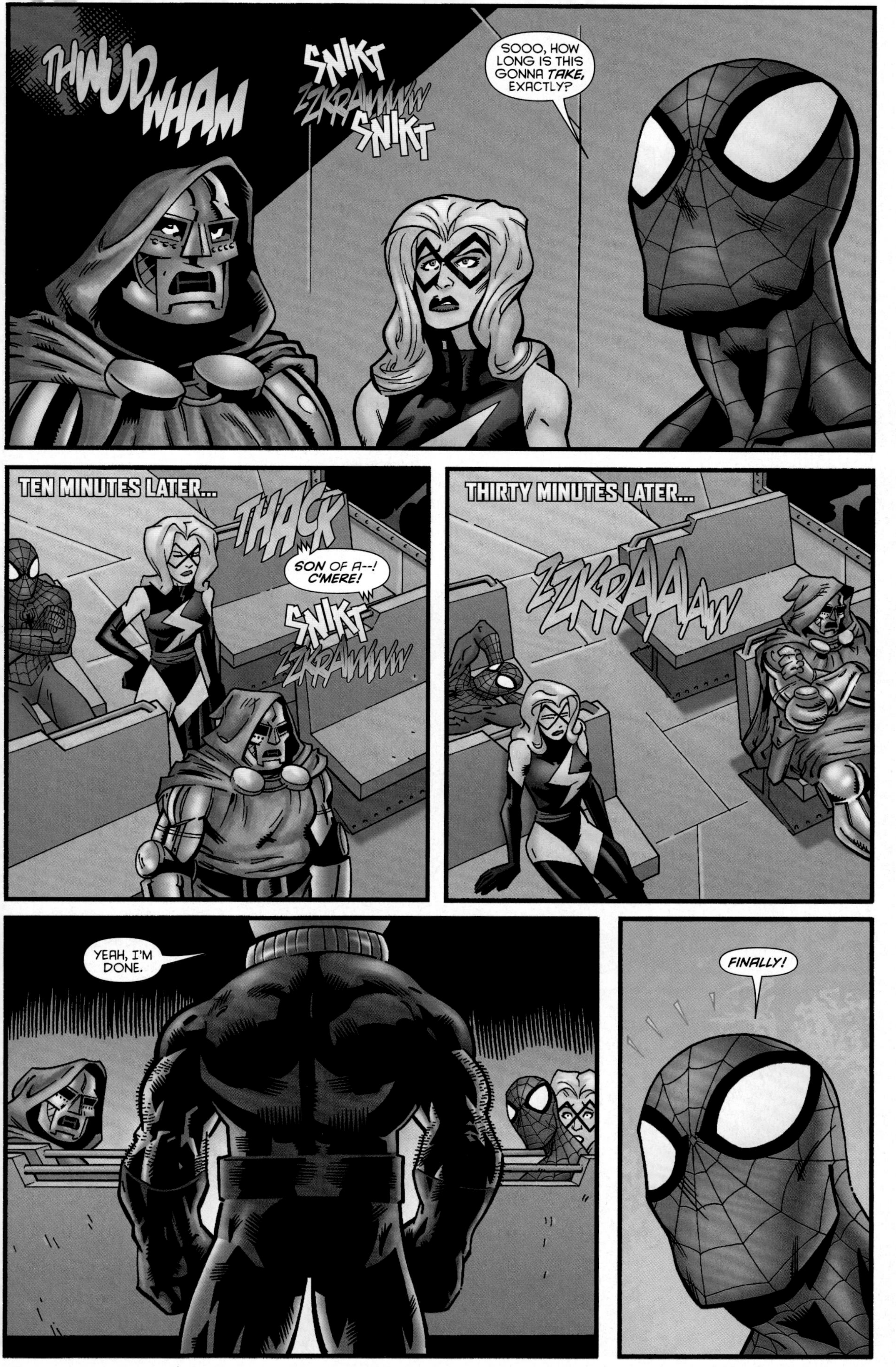
THWUD
WHAM
SNIKT
ZZKRAWWW
SNIKT
SOOO, HOW LONG IS THIS GONNA TAKE, EXACTLY?
TEN MINUTES LATER...
THACK
SON OF A--! C'MERE!
SNIKT
ZZKRAWWW
THIRTY MINUTES LATER...
ZZKRAAAAW
YEAH, I'M DONE.
FINALLY!

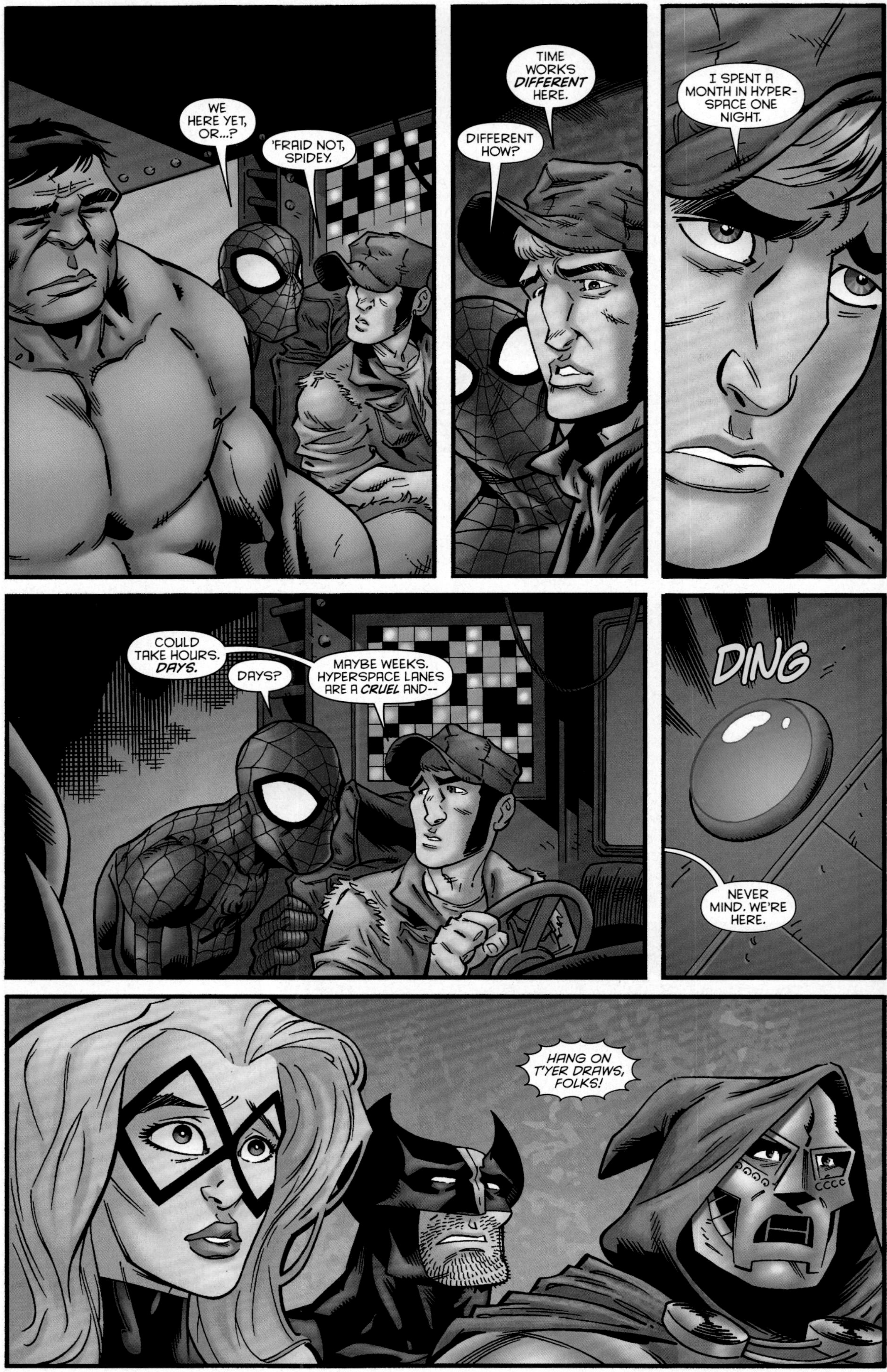
WE HERE YET, OR...?
'FRAID NOT, SPIDEY.
TIME WORKS DIFFERENT HERE.
DIFFERENT HOW?
I SPENT A MONTH IN HYPER-SPACE ONE NIGHT.
COULD TAKE HOURS. DAYS.
DAYS?
MAYBE WEEKS. HYPERSPACE LANES ARE A CRUEL AND--
DING
NEVER MIND. WE'RE HERE.
HANG ON T'YER DRAWS, FOLKS!

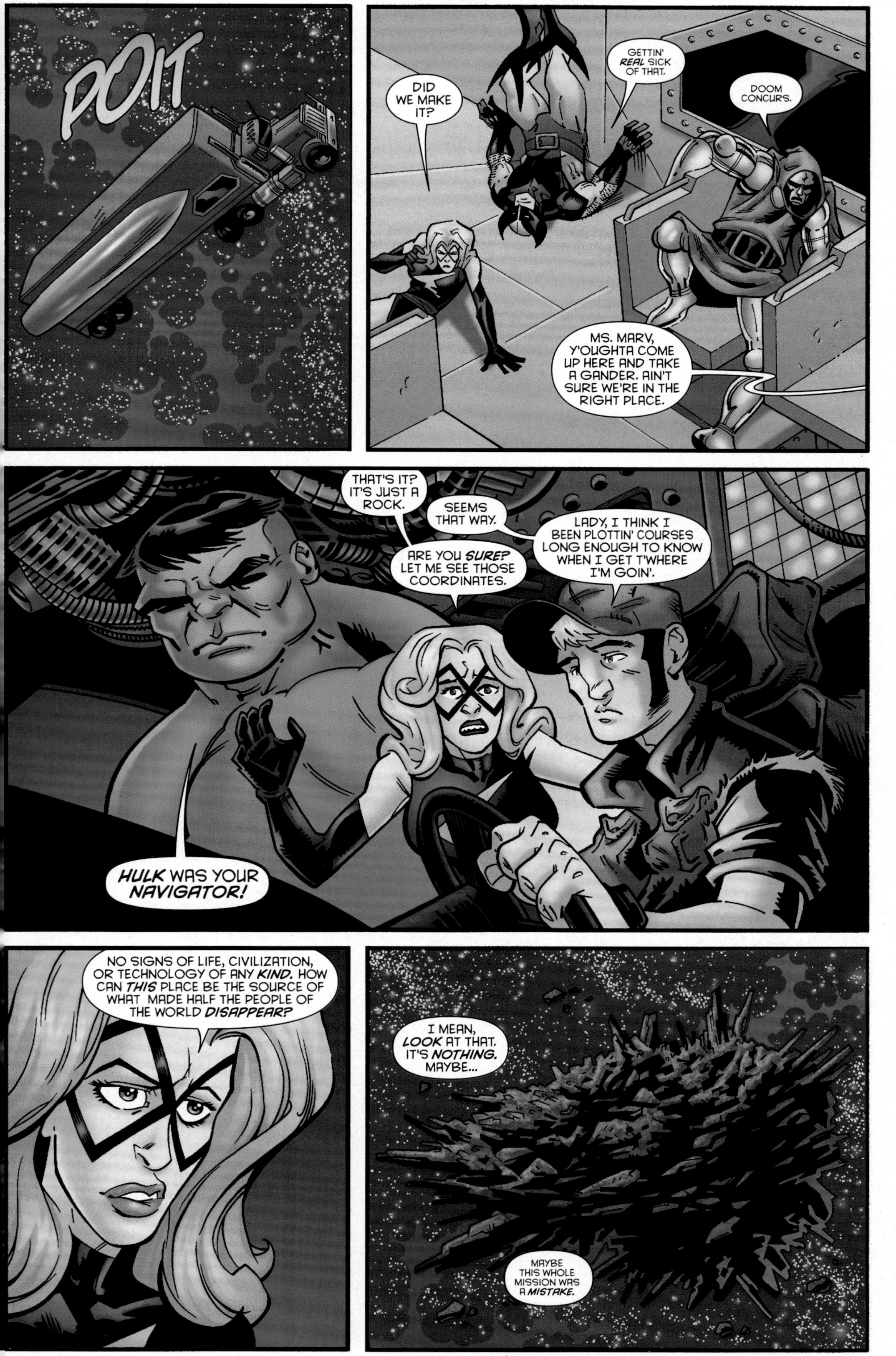
DOIT
DID WE MAKE IT?
GETTIN' REAL SICK OF THAT.
DOOM CONCURS.
MS. MARV, Y'OUGHTA COME UP HERE AND TAKE A GANDER. AIN'T SURE WE'RE IN THE RIGHT PLACE.
THAT'S IT? IT'S JUST A ROCK.
SEEMS THAT WAY.
LADY, I THINK I BEEN PLOTTIN' COURSES LONG ENOUGH TO KNOW WHEN I GET T'WHERE I'M GOIN'.
ARE YOU SURE? LET ME SEE THOSE COORDINATES.
HULK WAS YOUR NAVIGATOR!
NO SIGNS OF LIFE, CIVILIZATION, OR TECHNOLOGY OF ANY KIND. HOW CAN THIS PLACE BE THE SOURCE OF WHAT MADE HALF THE PEOPLE OF THE WORLD DISAPPEAR?
I MEAN, LOOK AT THAT. IT'S NOTHING. MAYBE...
MAYBE THIS WHOLE MISSION WAS A MISTAKE.

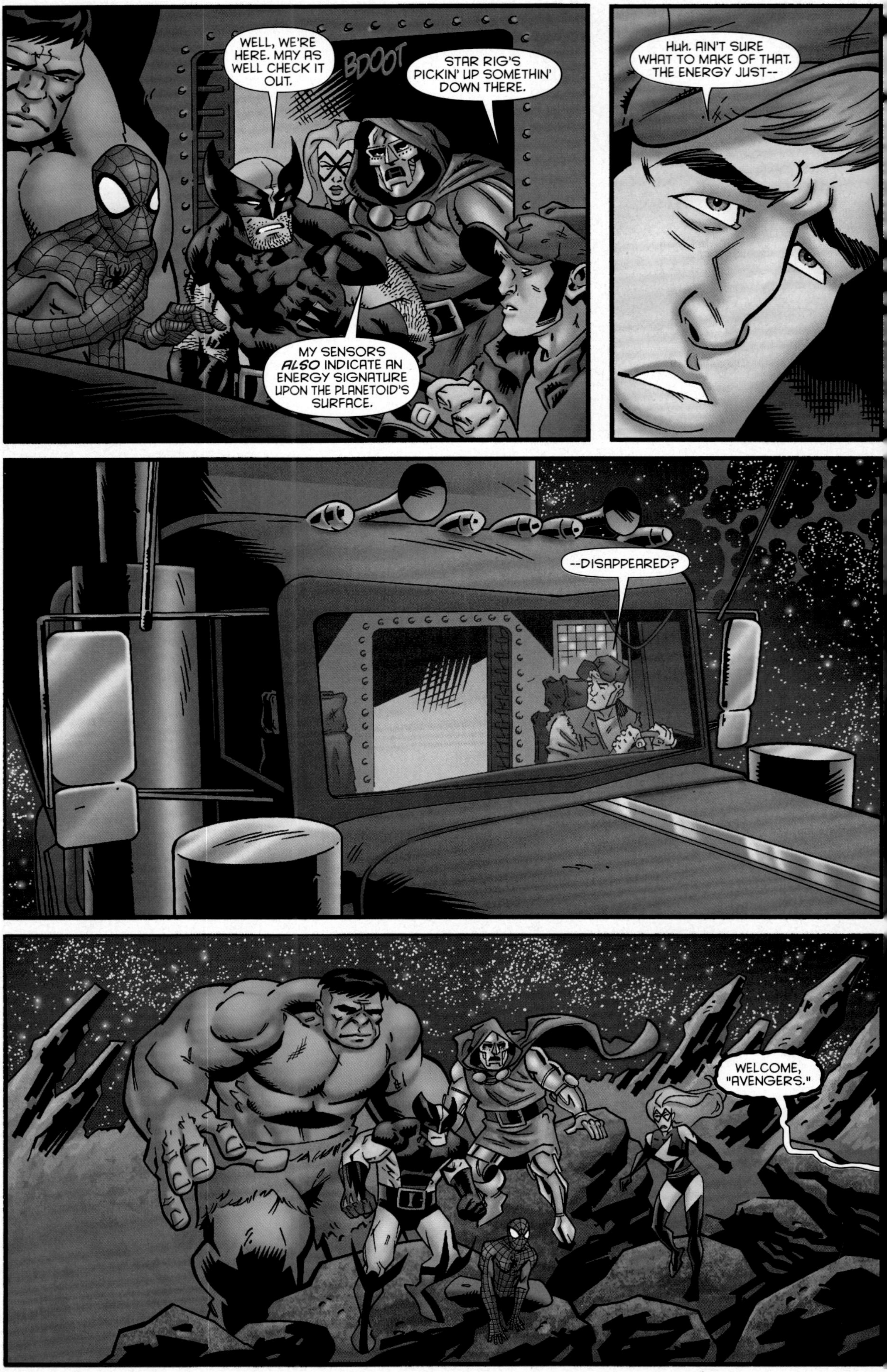
WELL, WE'RE HERE. MAY AS WELL CHECK IT OUT.
BDOOT
STAR RIG'S PICKIN' UP SOMETHIN' DOWN THERE.
MY SENSORS ALSO INDICATE AN ENERGY SIGNATURE UPON THE PLANETOID'S SURFACE.
Huh. AIN'T SURE WHAT TO MAKE OF THAT. THE ENERGY JUST--
--DISAPPEARED?
WELCOME, "AVENGERS."

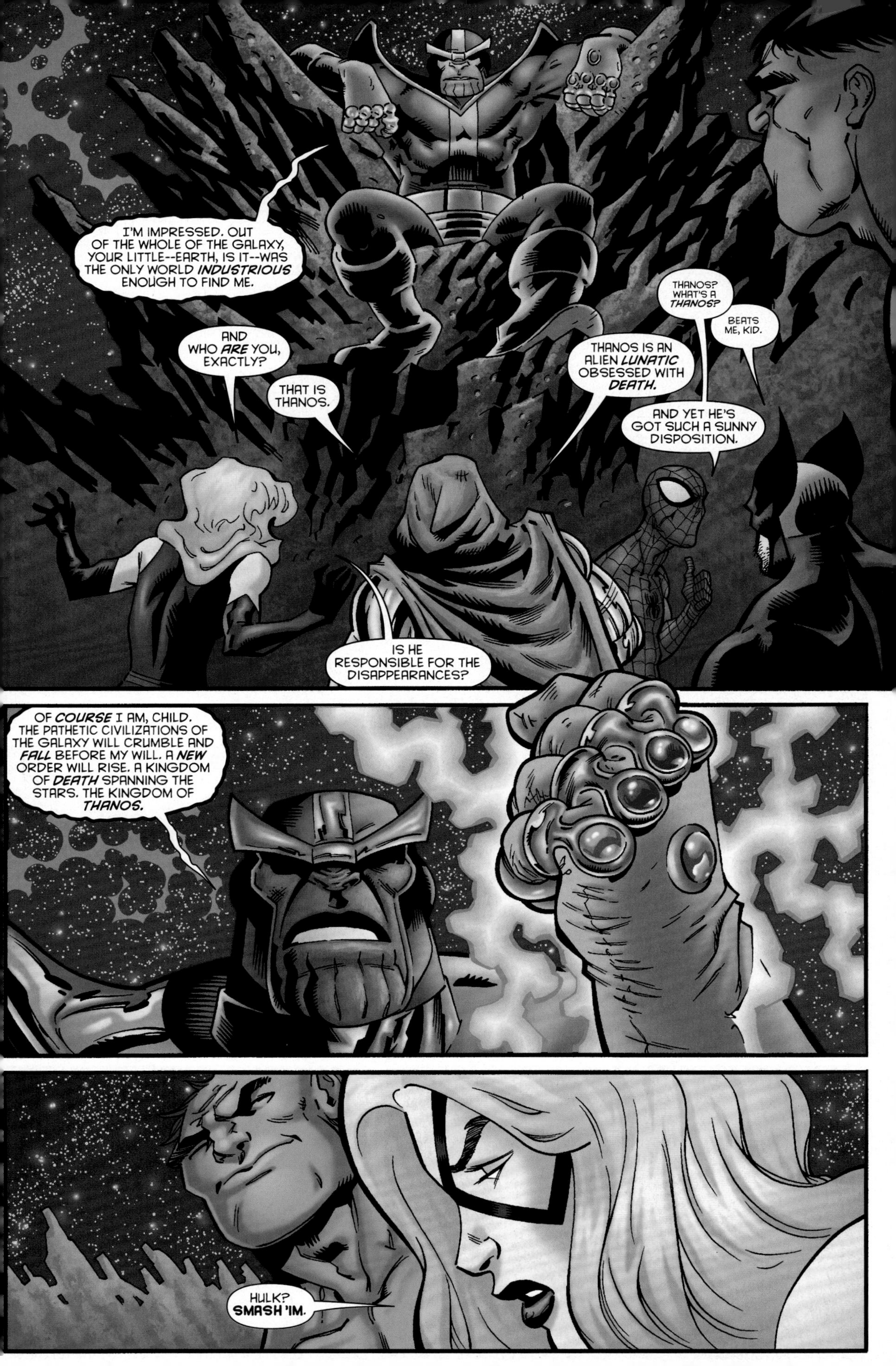
I'M IMPRESSED. OUT OF THE WHOLE OF THE GALAXY, YOUR LITTLE--EARTH, IS IT--WAS THE ONLY WORLD INDUSTRIOUS ENOUGH TO FIND ME.
AND WHO ARE YOU, EXACTLY?
THAT IS THANOS.
THANOS IS AN ALIEN LUNATIC OBSESSED WITH DEATH.
THANOS? WHAT'S A THANOS?
BEATS ME, KID.
AND YET HE'S GOT SUCH A SUNNY DISPOSITION.
IS HE RESPONSIBLE FOR THE DISAPPEARANCES?
OF COURSE I AM, CHILD. THE PATHETIC CIVILIZATIONS OF THE GALAXY WILL CRUMBLE AND FALL BEFORE MY WILL. A NEW ORDER WILL RISE. A KINGDOM OF DEATH SPANNING THE STARS. THE KINGDOM OF THANOS.
HULK? SMASH 'IM.

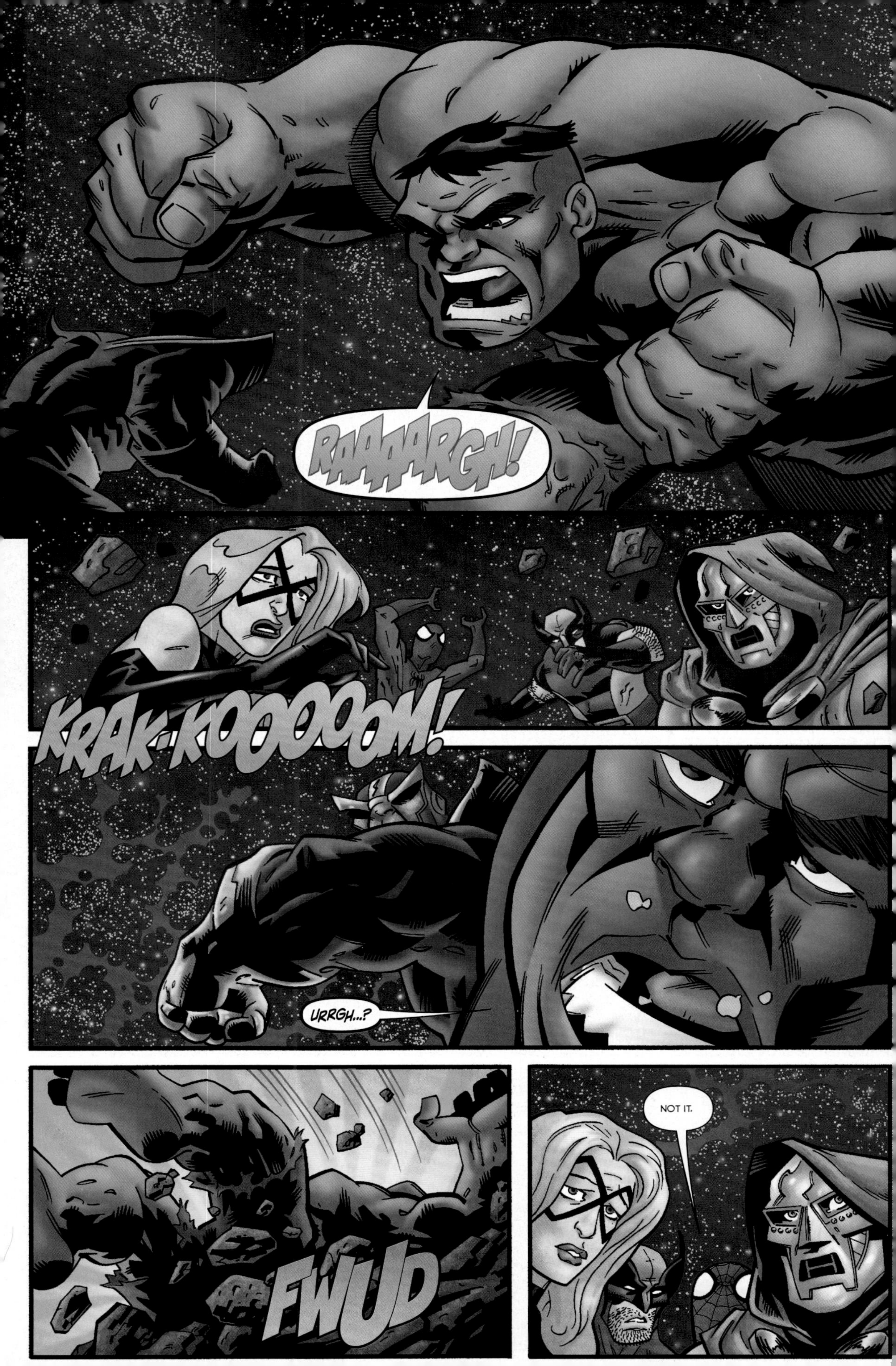
RAAAARGH!
KRAK-KOOOOOM!
URRGH...?
FWUD
NOT IT.

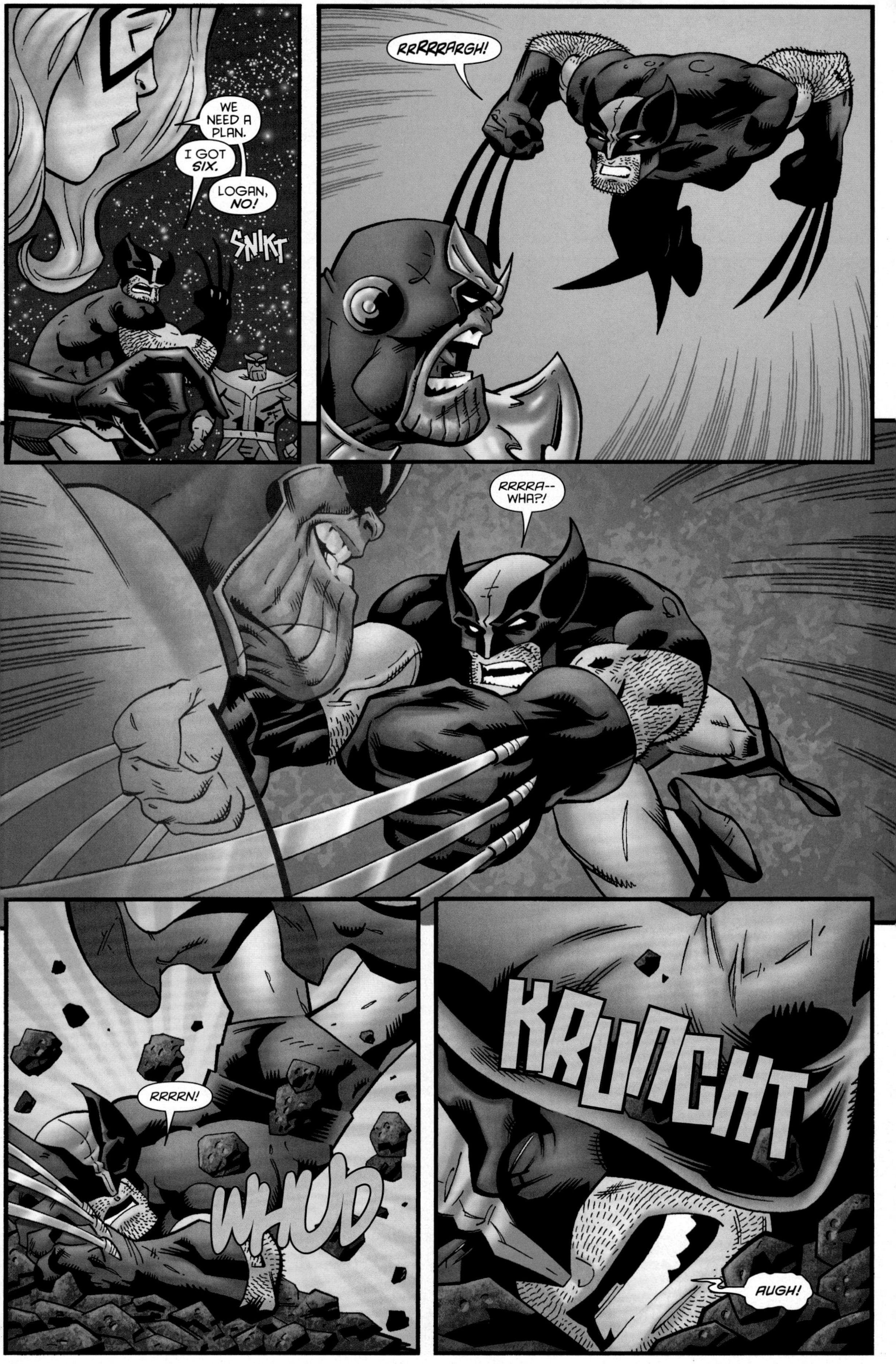
WE NEED A PLAN.
I GOT SIX.
LOGAN, NO!
SNIKT
RRRRRARGH!
RRRRA-- WHA?!
RRRRN!
WHUD
KRUNCHT
AUGH!

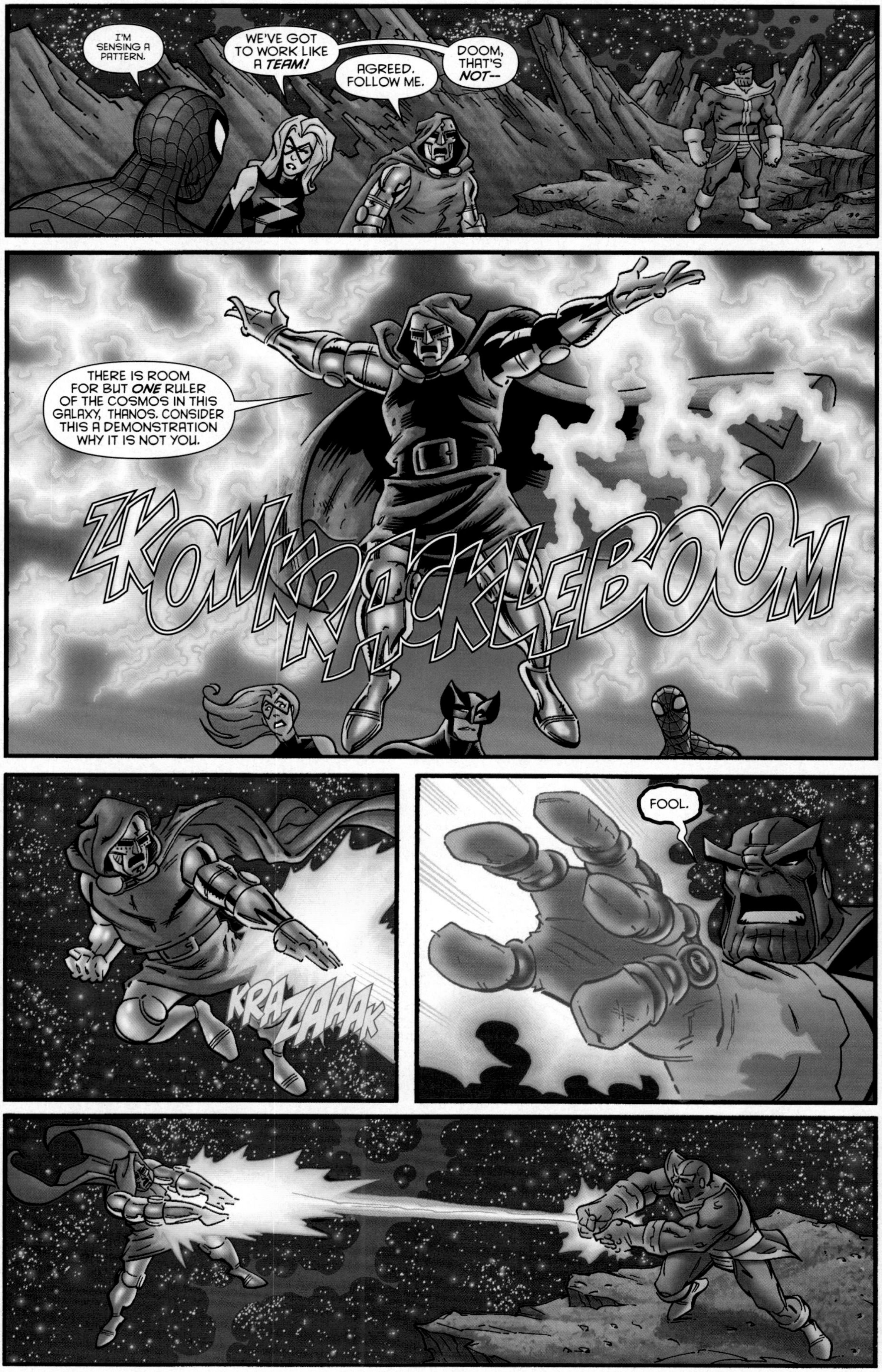
I'M SENSING A PATTERN.
WE'VE GOT TO WORK LIKE A TEAM!
AGREED. FOLLOW ME.
DOOM, THAT'S NOT--
THERE IS ROOM FOR BUT ONE RULER OF THE COSMOS IN THIS GALAXY, THANOS. CONSIDER THIS A DEMONSTRATION WHY IT IS NOT YOU.
KOWKRACKLEBOOM
KRAZAAAK
FOOL.

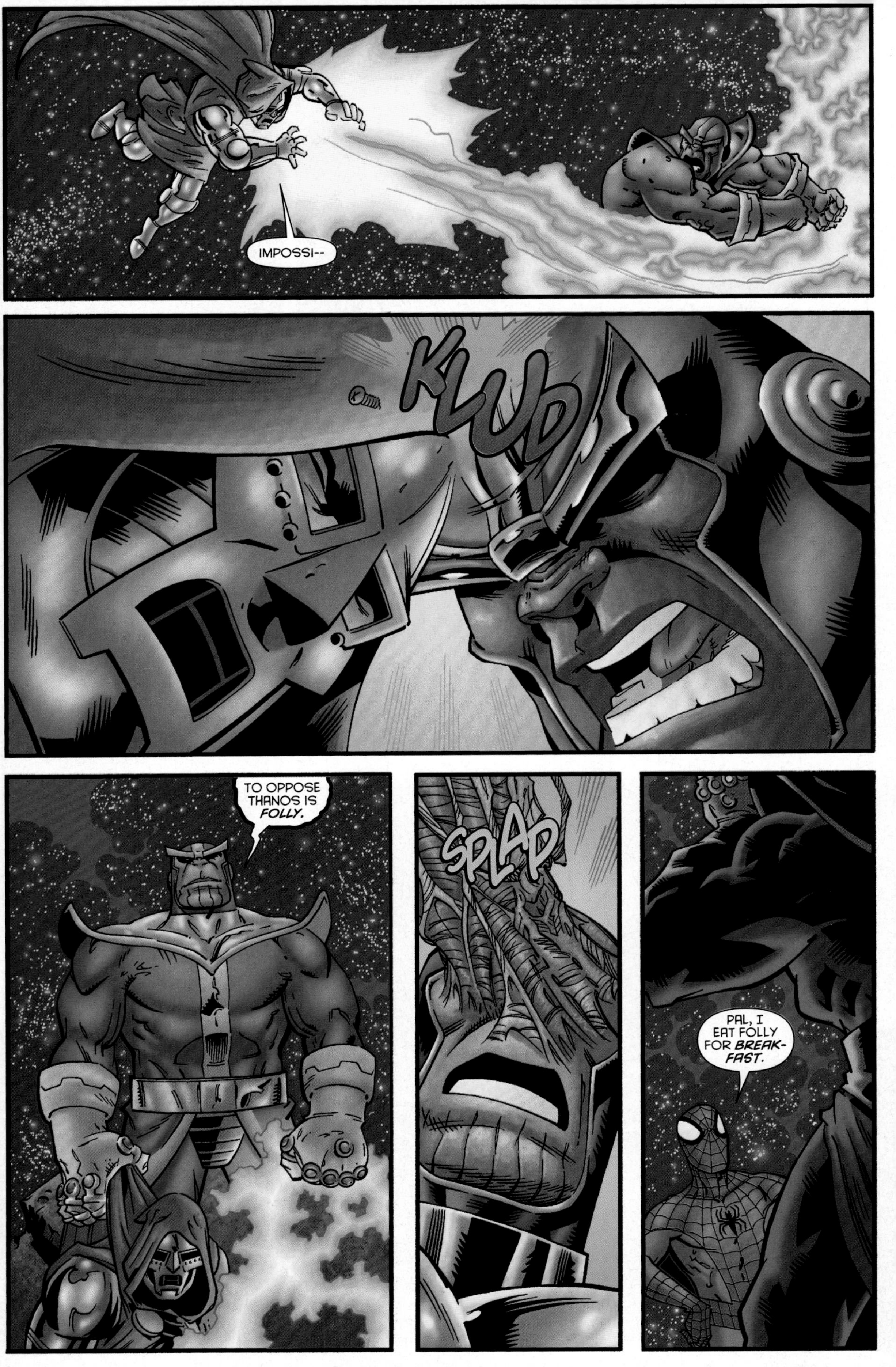
IMPOSSI--
KLUD
TO OPPOSE THANOS IS *FOLLY.*
SPLAP
PAL, I EAT FOLLY FOR *BREAK-FAST.*

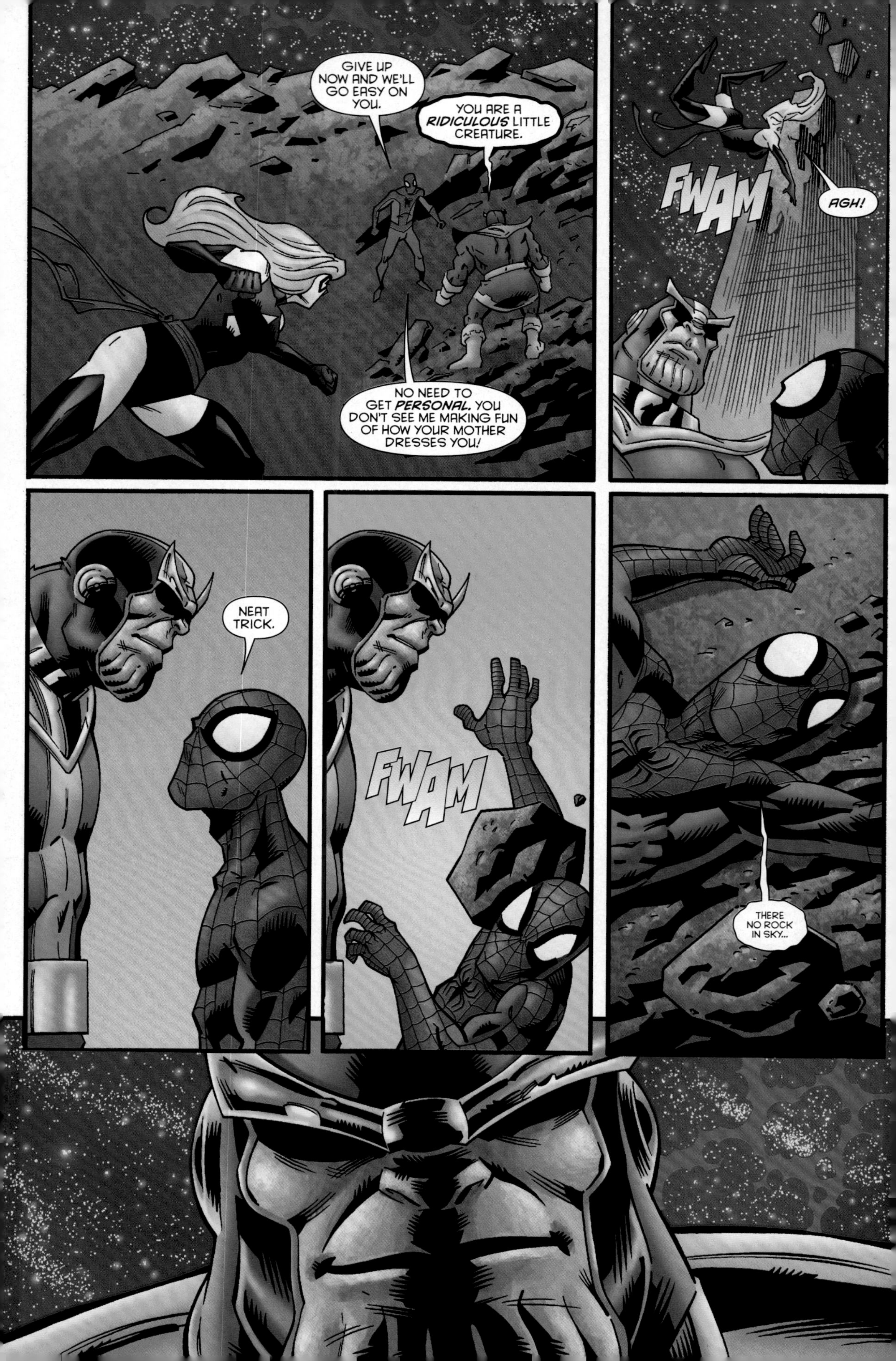
GIVE UP NOW AND WE'LL GO EASY ON YOU.
YOU ARE A RIDICULOUS LITTLE CREATURE.
NO NEED TO GET PERSONAL. YOU DON'T SEE ME MAKING FUN OF HOW YOUR MOTHER DRESSES YOU!
FWAM
AGH!
NEAT TRICK.
FWAM
THERE NO ROCK IN SKY...

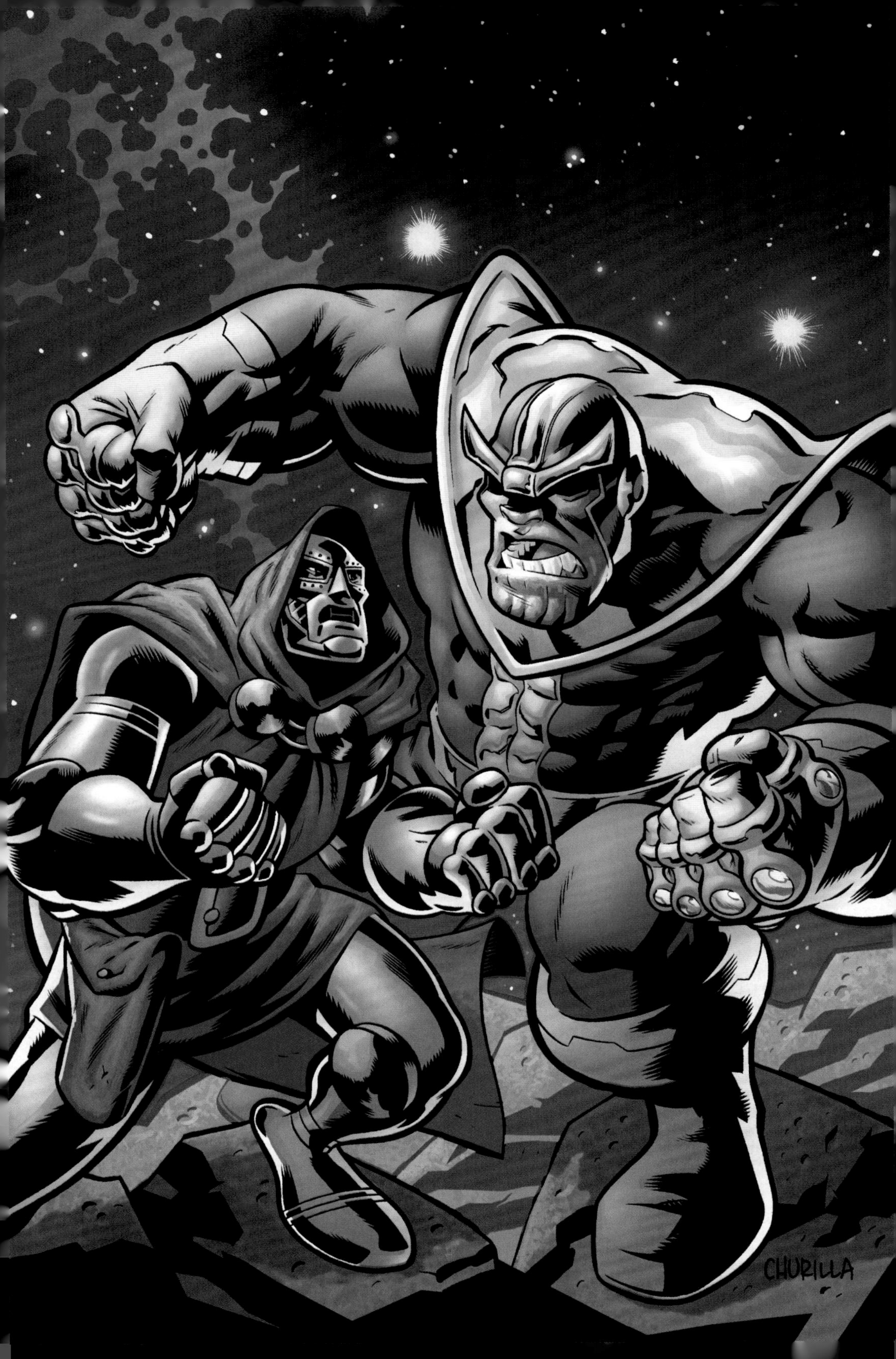
CHURILLA

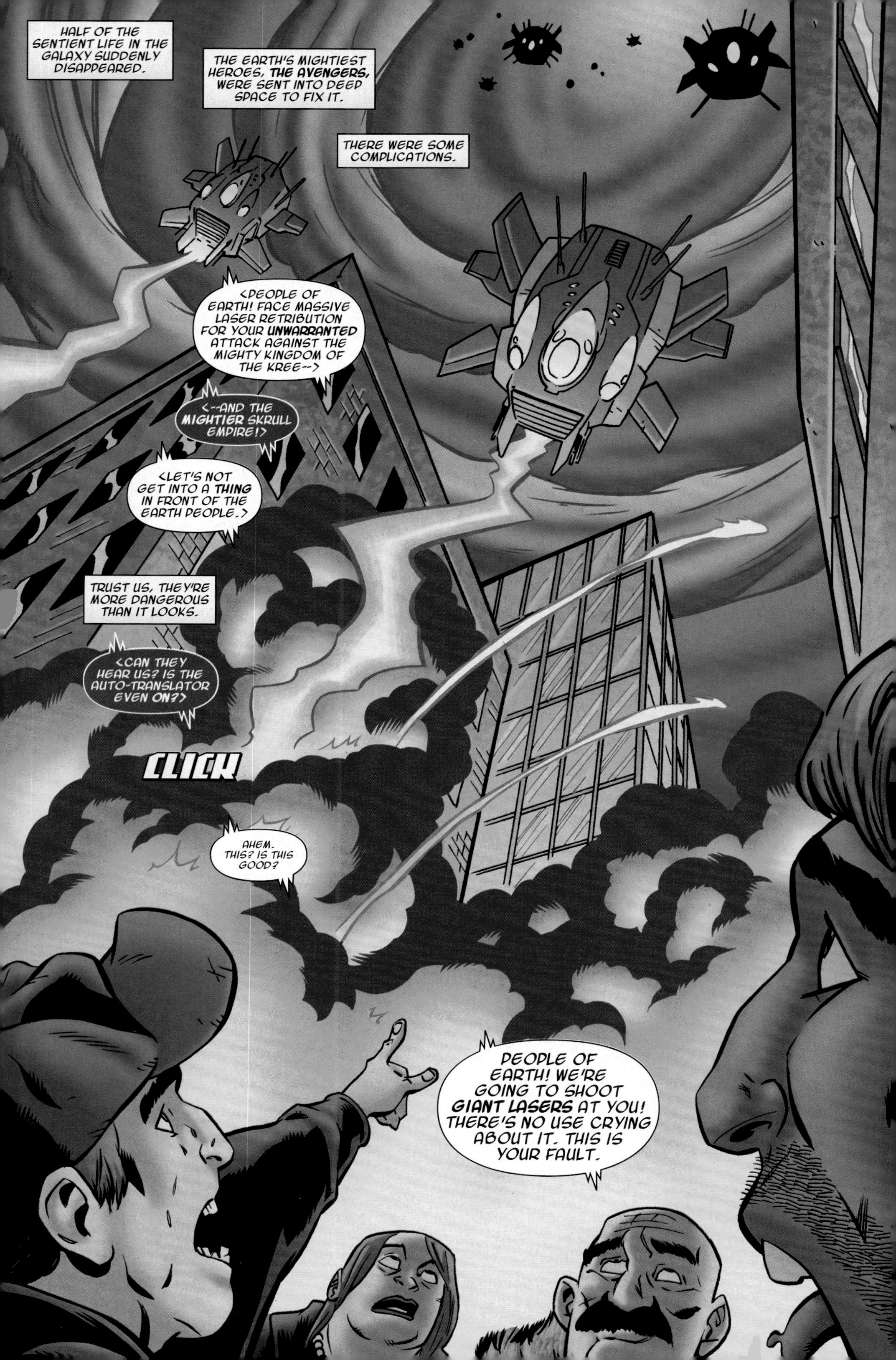
HALF OF THE SENTIENT LIFE IN THE GALAXY SUDDENLY DISAPPEARED.
THE EARTH'S MIGHTIEST HEROES, THE AVENGERS, WERE SENT INTO DEEP SPACE TO FIX IT.
THERE WERE SOME COMPLICATIONS.
<PEOPLE OF EARTH! FACE MASSIVE LASER RETRIBUTION FOR YOUR UNWARRANTED ATTACK AGAINST THE MIGHTY KINGDOM OF THE KREE-->
<--AND THE MIGHTIER SKRULL EMPIRE!>
<LET'S NOT GET INTO A THING IN FRONT OF THE EARTH PEOPLE.>
TRUST US, THEY'RE MORE DANGEROUS THAN IT LOOKS.
<CAN THEY HEAR US? IS THE AUTO-TRANSLATOR EVEN ON?>
CLICK
AHEM. THIS? IS THIS GOOD?
PEOPLE OF EARTH! WE'RE GOING TO SHOOT GIANT LASERS AT YOU! THERE'S NO USE CRYING ABOUT IT. THIS IS YOUR FAULT.

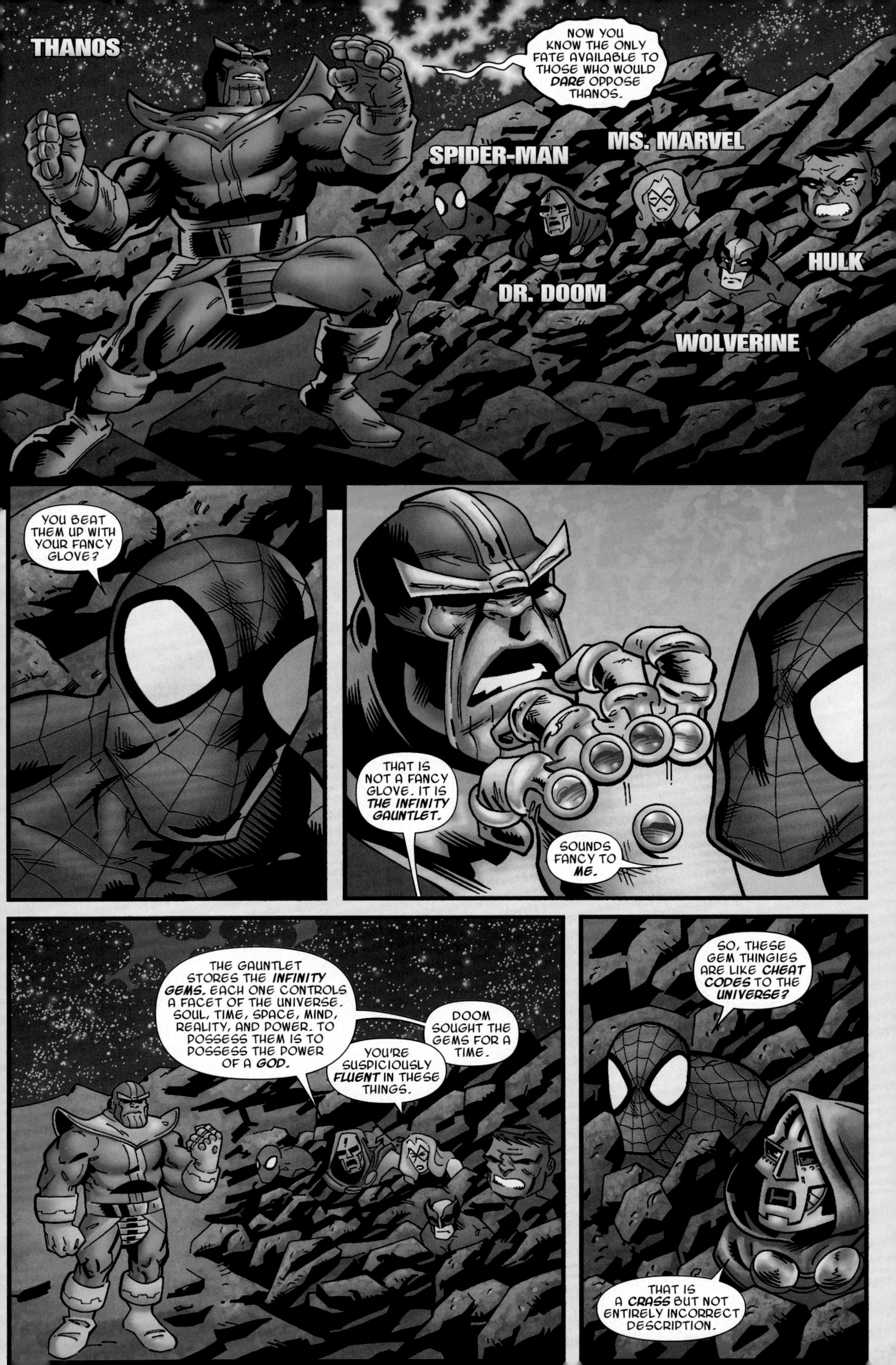
THANOS
NOW YOU KNOW THE ONLY FATE AVAILABLE TO THOSE WHO WOULD DARE OPPOSE THANOS.
SPIDER-MAN
MS. MARVEL
DR. DOOM
HULK
WOLVERINE
YOU BEAT THEM UP WITH YOUR FANCY GLOVE?
THAT IS NOT A FANCY GLOVE. IT IS THE INFINITY GAUNTLET.
SOUNDS FANCY TO ME.
THE GAUNTLET STORES THE INFINITY GEMS. EACH ONE CONTROLS A FACET OF THE UNIVERSE. SOUL, TIME, SPACE, MIND, REALITY, AND POWER. TO POSSESS THEM IS TO POSSESS THE POWER OF A GOD.
DOOM SOUGHT THE GEMS FOR A TIME.
YOU'RE SUSPICIOUSLY FLUENT IN THESE THINGS.
SO, THESE GEM THINGIES ARE LIKE CHEAT CODES TO THE UNIVERSE?
THAT IS A CRASS BUT NOT ENTIRELY INCORRECT DESCRIPTION.

DO NOT THINK OF THIS AS A DEFEAT. THINK OF IT AS AN *HONOR.*

HONOR?!

OF COURSE. KILLING HALF THE POPULATION OF THE MILKY WAY WAS ONLY THE BEGINNING. YOU WILL WITNESS FIRSTHAND AS THE GALAXY ITSELF IS REMADE IN MY IMAGE.

WHAT GIVES *YOU* THE RIGHT--!

I *WRESTED* THESE GEMS FROM THE ELDERS OF *CREATION.* CLAWED THEM FROM HYPOTHETICAL ENTITIES LOCKED IN *FORGOTTEN* CORNERS OF THE *NOTHINGVERSE.* STOLE THEM FROM THE ABYSSAL ENTRAILS OF STARWORMS GNAWING AT THE FRINGES OF *REALITY.*

WHAT GIVES *ME* THE RIGHT?

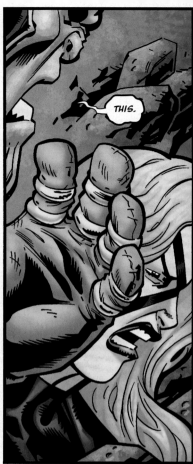

THIS.

AND *NOTHING* CAN STOP ME.

GIVE ME AND MY CLAWS *FIVE MINUTES* WITHOUT THAT *GAUNTLET* OF YOURS.

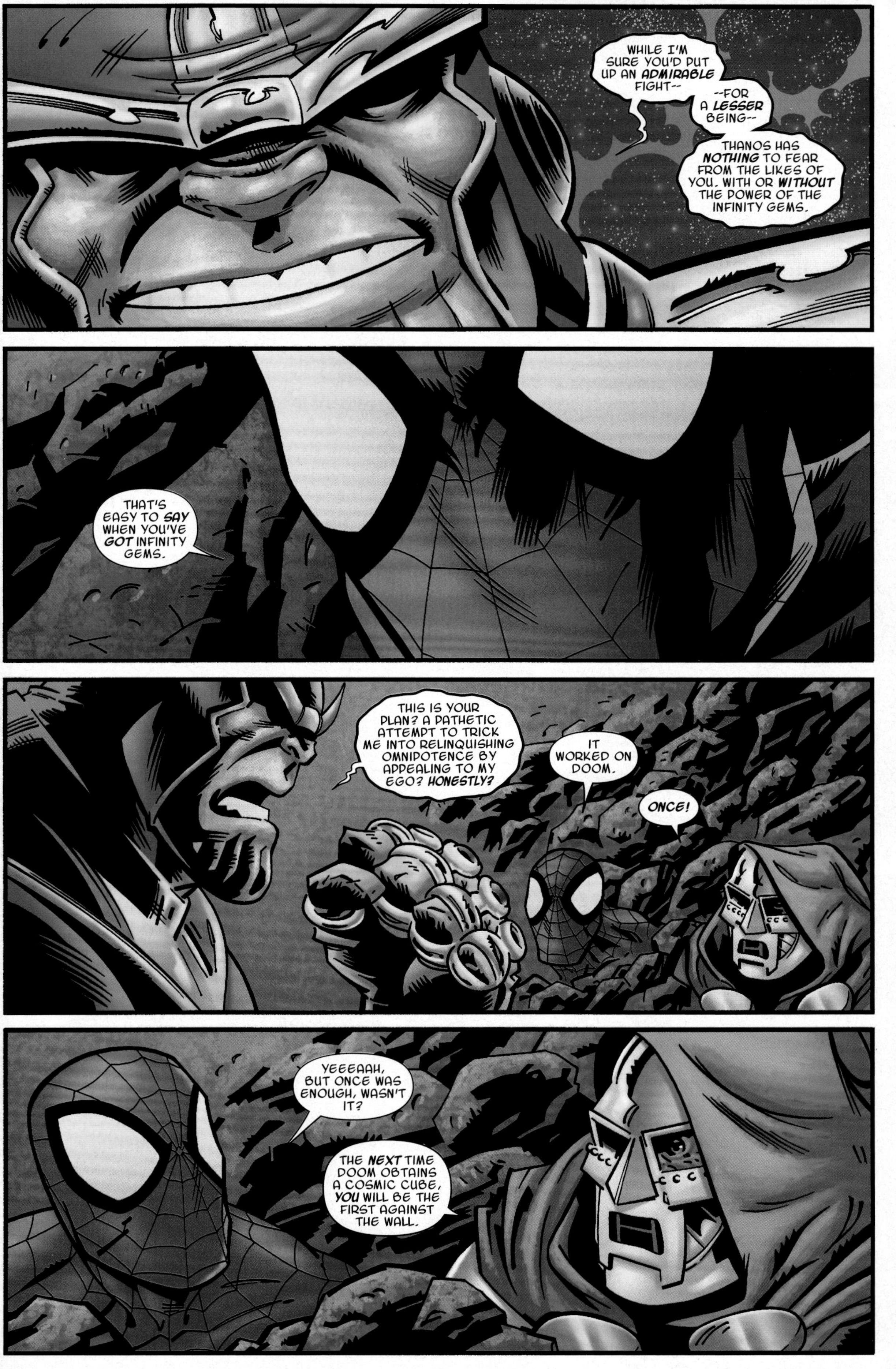
WHILE I'M SURE YOU'D PUT UP AN ADMIRABLE FIGHT--
--FOR A LESSER BEING--
THANOS HAS NOTHING TO FEAR FROM THE LIKES OF YOU. WITH OR WITHOUT THE POWER OF THE INFINITY GEMS.
THAT'S EASY TO SAY WHEN YOU'VE GOT INFINITY GEMS.
THIS IS YOUR PLAN? A PATHETIC ATTEMPT TO TRICK ME INTO RELINQUISHING OMNIPOTENCE BY APPEALING TO MY EGO? HONESTLY?
IT WORKED ON DOOM.
ONCE!
YEEEAAH, BUT ONCE WAS ENOUGH, WASN'T IT?
THE NEXT TIME DOOM OBTAINS A COSMIC CUBE, YOU WILL BE THE FIRST AGAINST THE WALL.

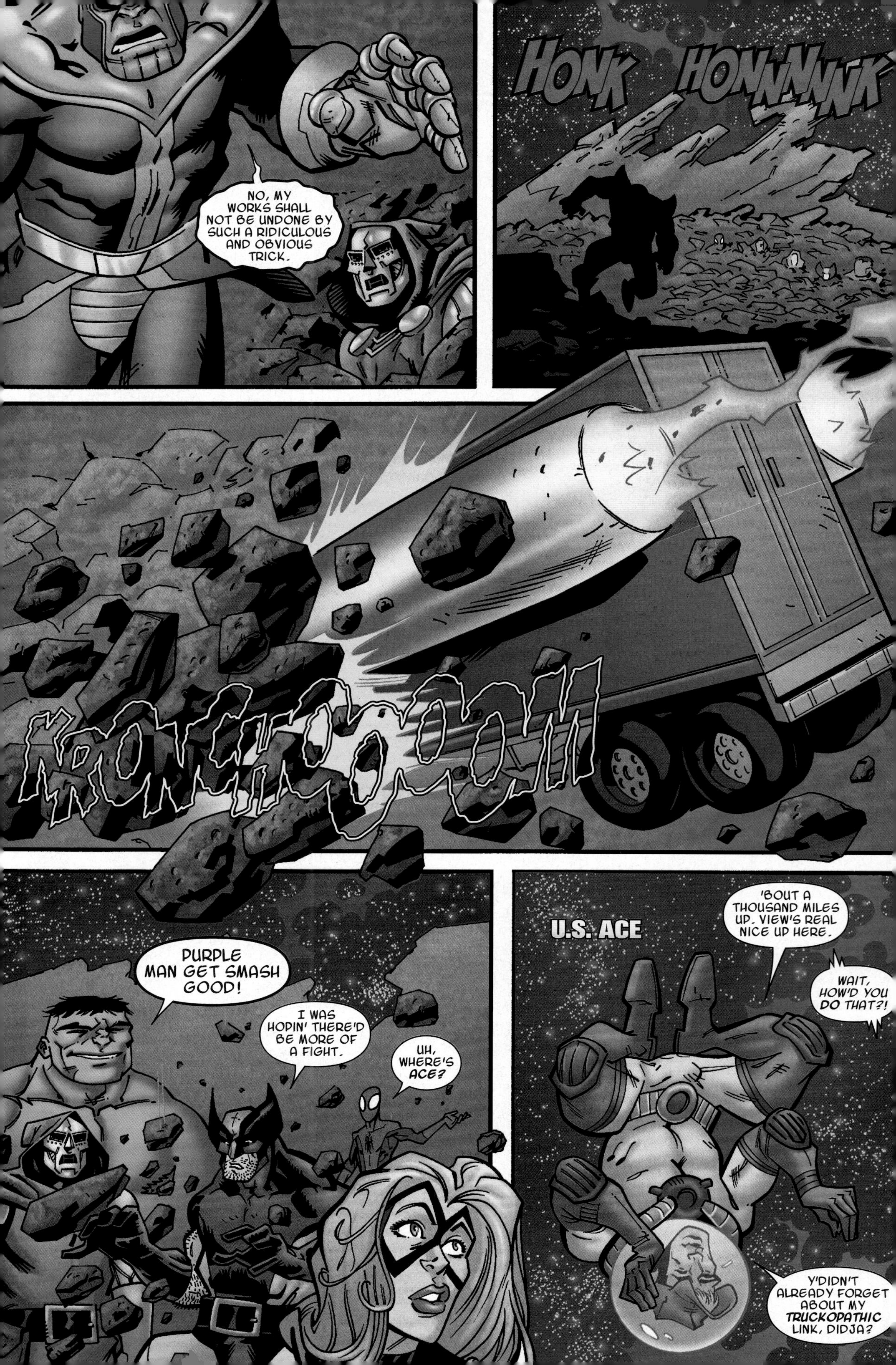

NO, MY WORKS SHALL NOT BE UNDONE BY SUCH A RIDICULOUS AND OBVIOUS TRICK.
HONK HONNNNNK
KRONCHOOOOOM
PURPLE MAN GET SMASH GOOD!
I WAS HOPIN' THERE'D BE MORE OF A FIGHT.
UH, WHERE'S ACE?
U.S. ACE
'BOUT A THOUSAND MILES UP. VIEW'S REAL NICE UP HERE.
WAIT, HOW'D YOU DO THAT?!
Y'DIDN'T ALREADY FORGET ABOUT MY TRUCKOPATHIC LINK, DIDJA?

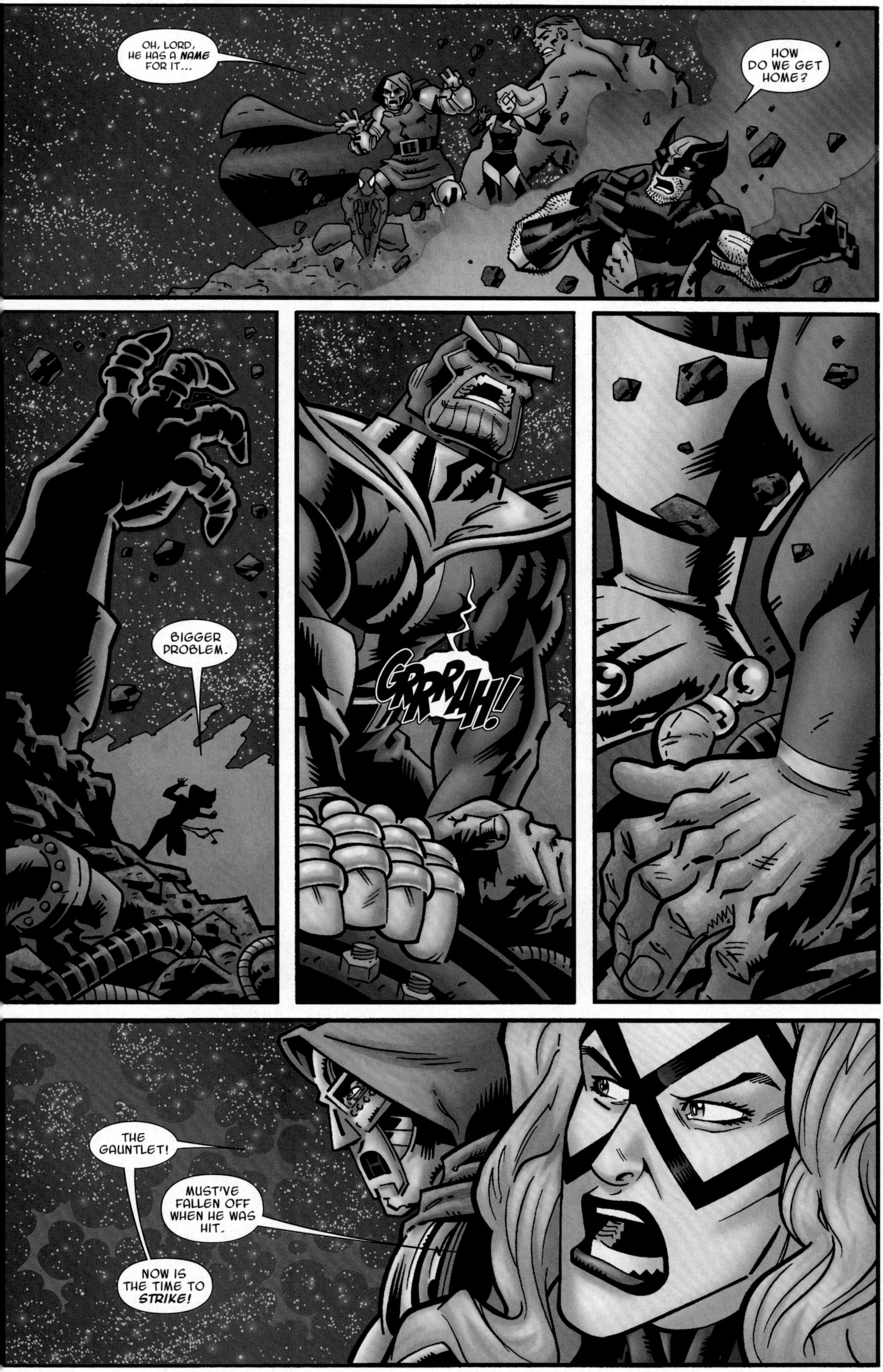
OH, LORD, HE HAS A NAME FOR IT...
HOW DO WE GET HOME?
BIGGER PROBLEM.
GRRRAH!
THE GAUNTLET!
MUST'VE FALLEN OFF WHEN HE WAS HIT.
NOW IS THE TIME TO STRIKE!

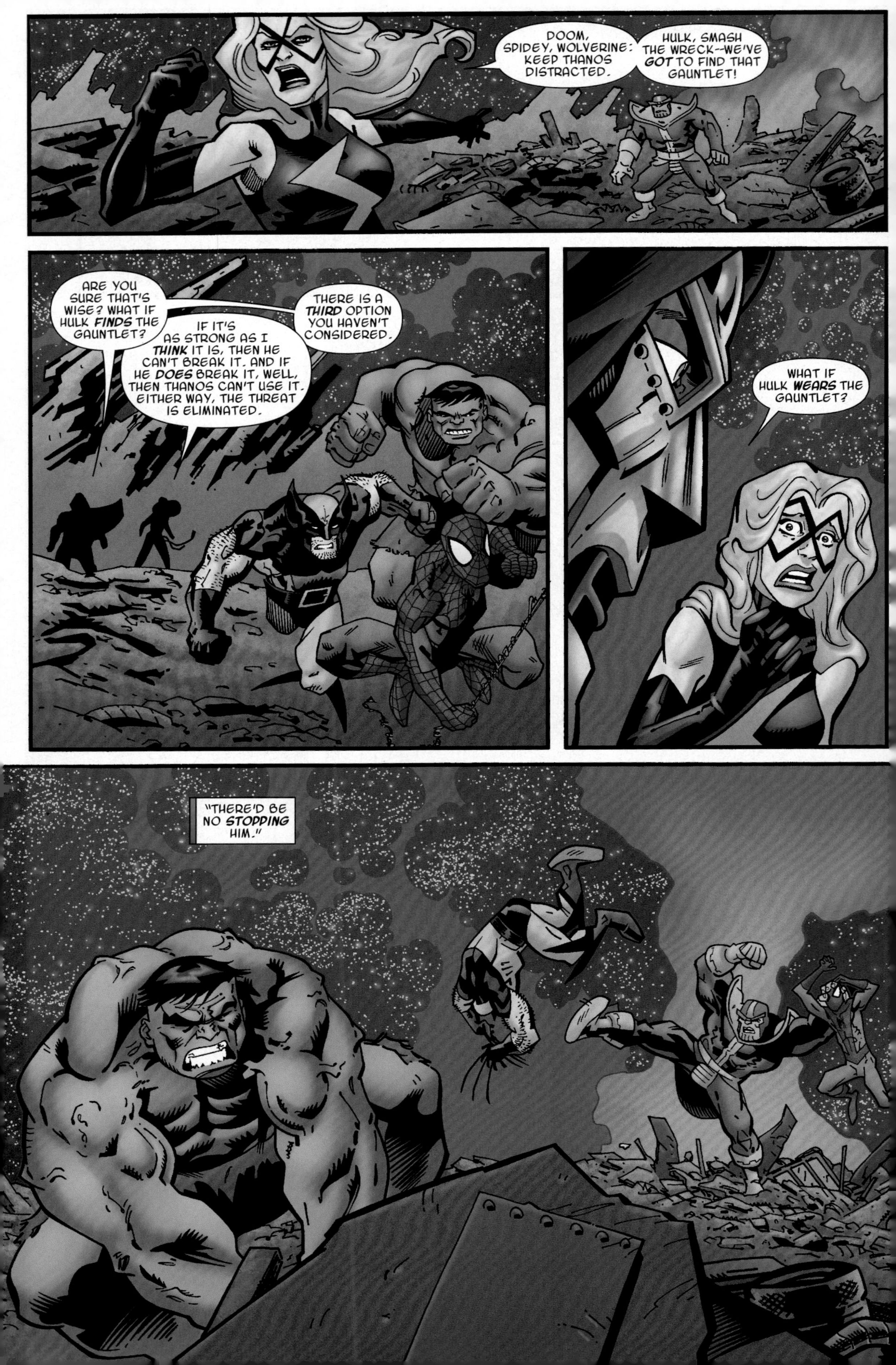
DOOM, SPIDEY, WOLVERINE: KEEP THANOS DISTRACTED.
HULK, SMASH THE WRECK--WE'VE GOT TO FIND THAT GAUNTLET!
ARE YOU SURE THAT'S WISE? WHAT IF HULK FINDS THE GAUNTLET?
IF IT'S AS STRONG AS I THINK IT IS, THEN HE CAN'T BREAK IT. AND IF HE DOES BREAK IT, WELL, THEN THANOS CAN'T USE IT. EITHER WAY, THE THREAT IS ELIMINATED.
THERE IS A THIRD OPTION YOU HAVEN'T CONSIDERED.
WHAT IF HULK WEARS THE GAUNTLET?
"THERE'D BE NO STOPPING HIM."

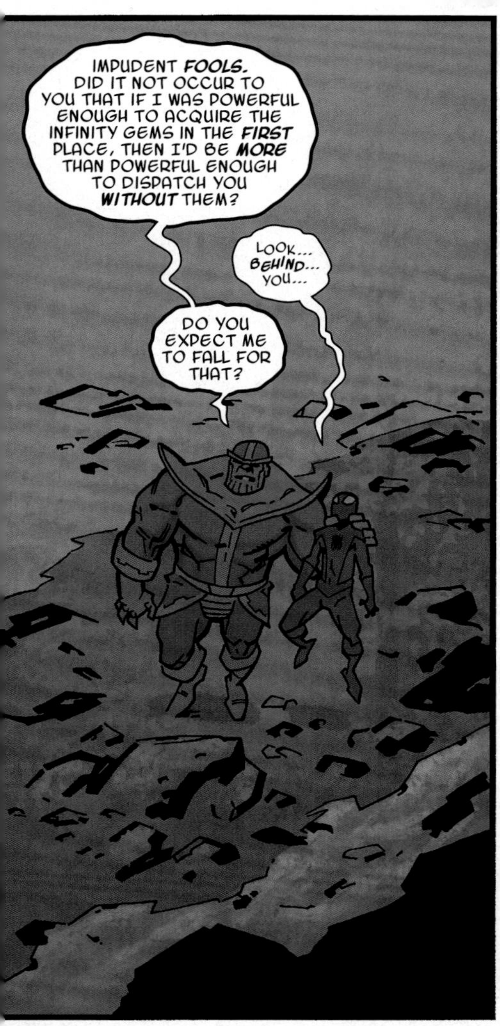
IMPUDENT FOOLS. DID IT NOT OCCUR TO YOU THAT IF I WAS POWERFUL ENOUGH TO ACQUIRE THE INFINITY GEMS IN THE FIRST PLACE, THEN I'D BE MORE THAN POWERFUL ENOUGH TO DISPATCH YOU WITHOUT THEM?
LOOK... BEHIND... YOU...
DO YOU EXPECT ME TO FALL FOR THAT?

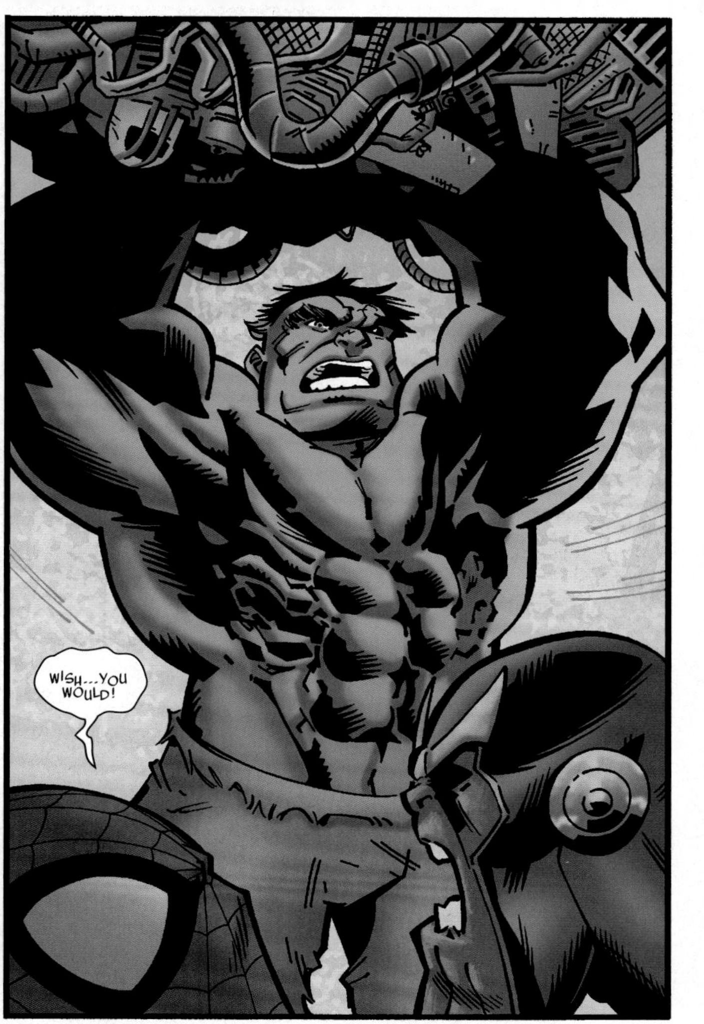
WISH...YOU WOULD!

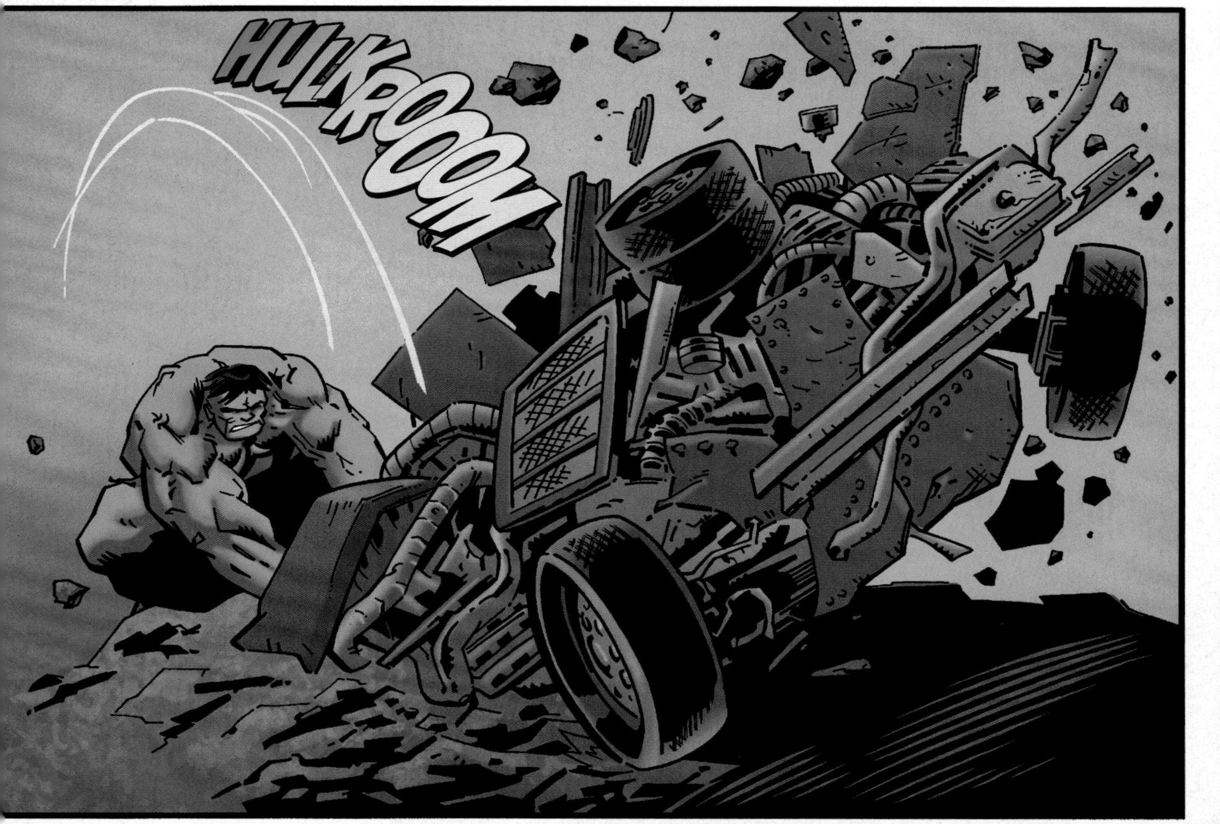
HULKROOOM

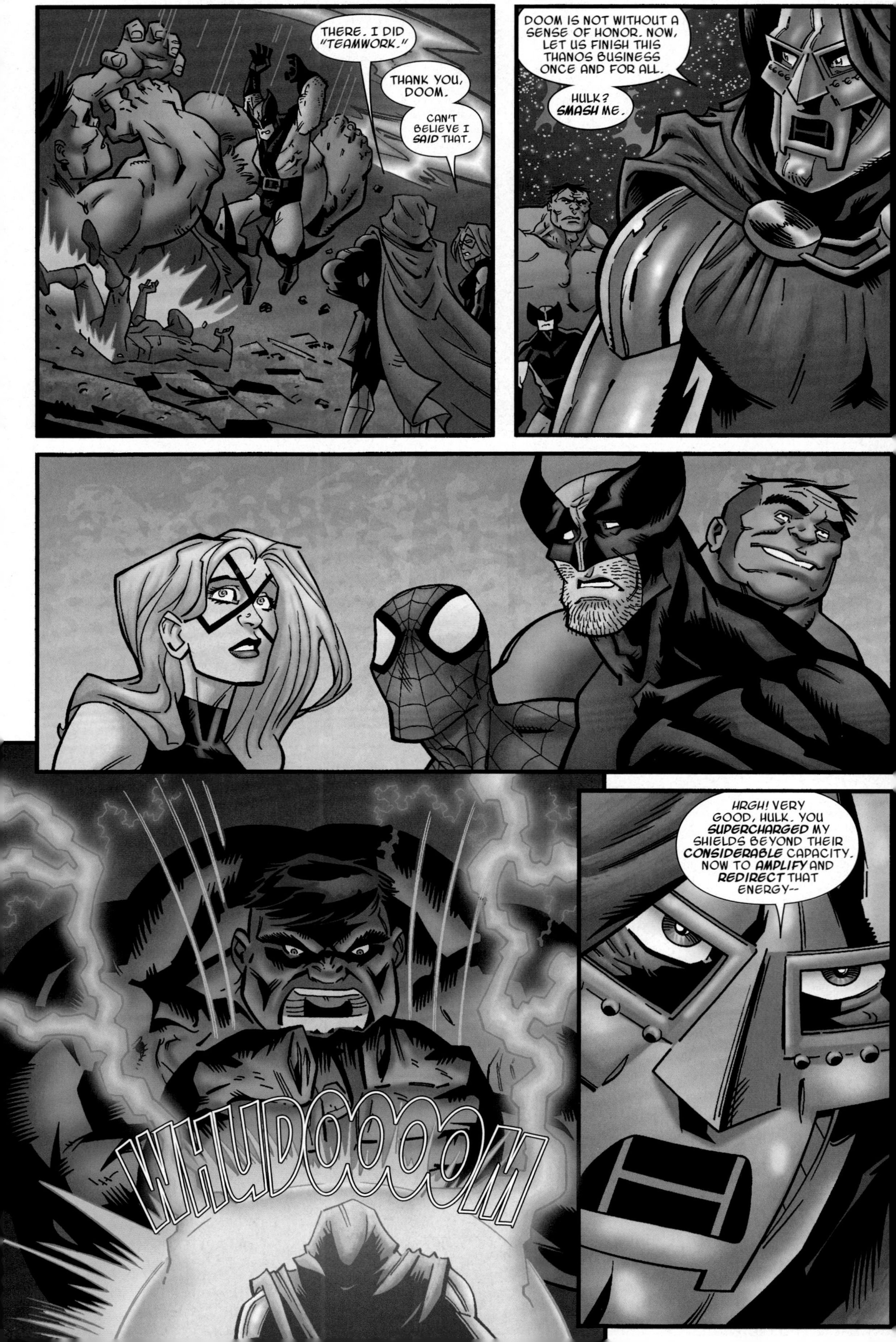
THERE. I DID "TEAMWORK."
THANK YOU, DOOM.
CAN'T BELIEVE I SAID THAT.
DOOM IS NOT WITHOUT A SENSE OF HONOR. NOW, LET US FINISH THIS THANOS BUSINESS ONCE AND FOR ALL.
HULK? SMASH ME.
WHUDOOOOM
HRGH! VERY GOOD, HULK. YOU SUPERCHARGED MY SHIELDS BEYOND THEIR CONSIDERABLE CAPACITY. NOW TO AMPLIFY AND REDIRECT THAT ENERGY--

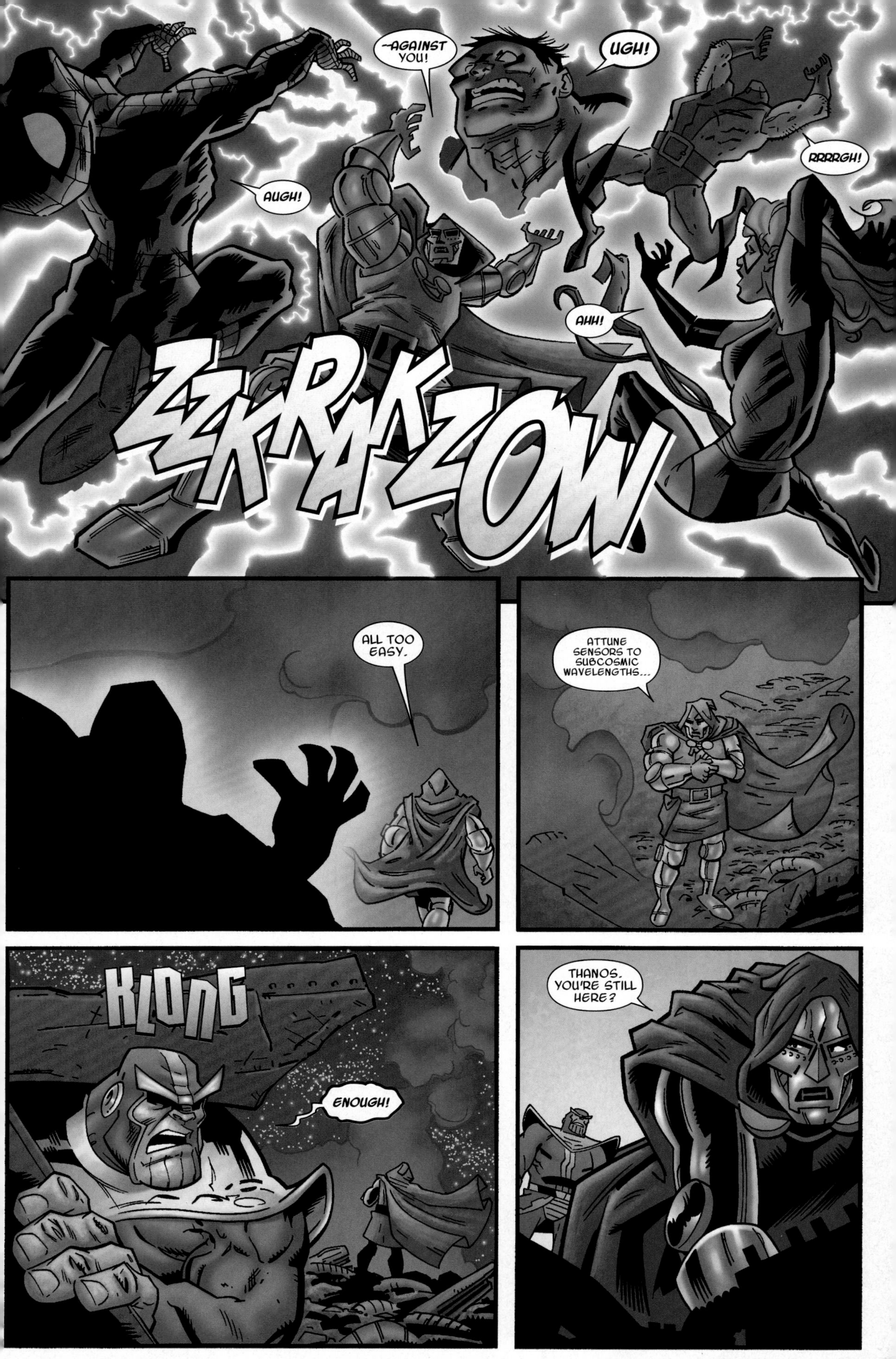
—AGAINST YOU!
UGH!
RRRRGH!
AUGH!
AHH!
ZZKRAKKAZOW
ALL TOO EASY.
ATTUNE SENSORS TO SUBCOSMIC WAVELENGTHS...
KLONG
ENOUGH!
THANOS. YOU'RE STILL HERE?

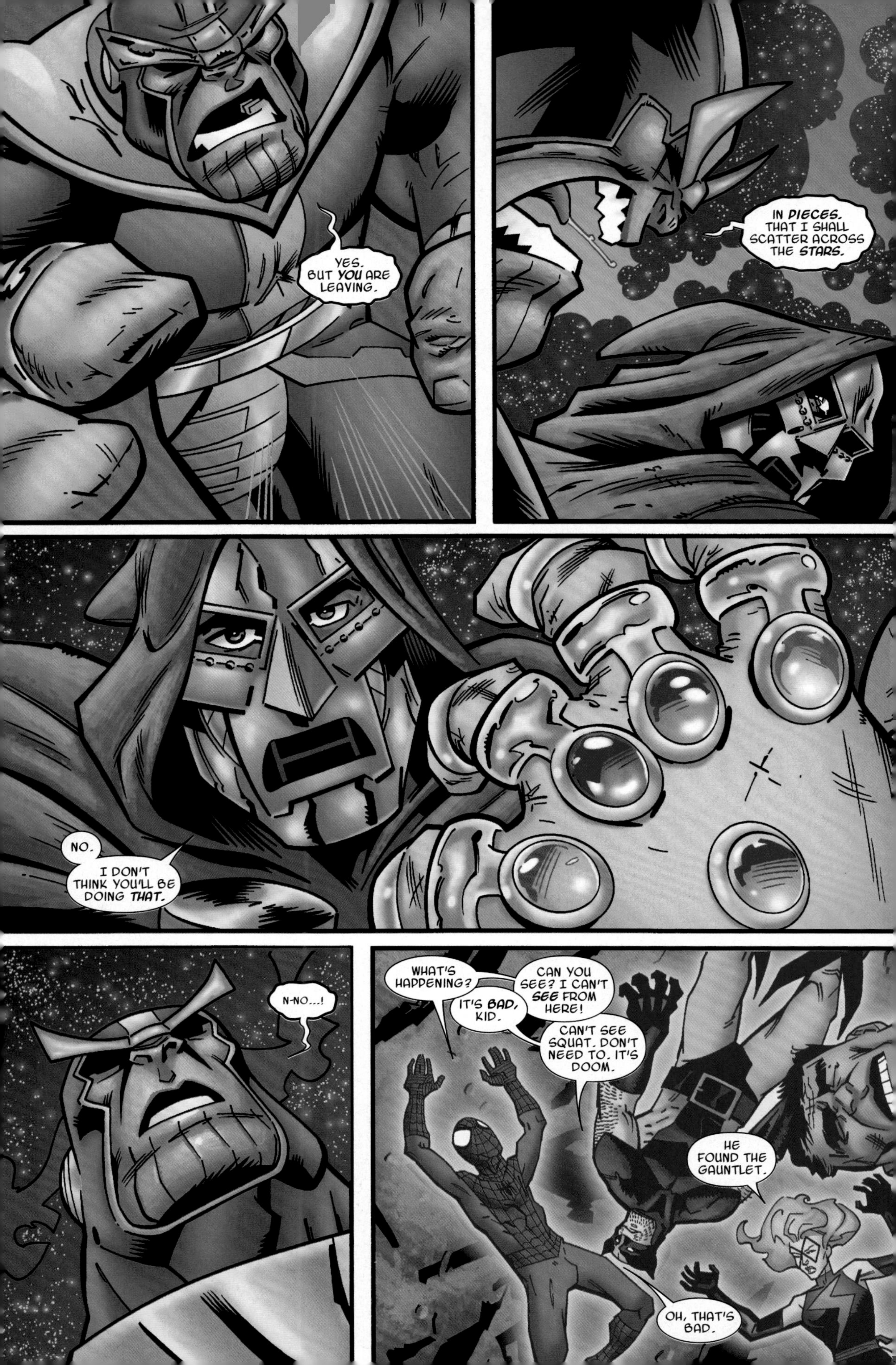
YES. BUT YOU ARE LEAVING.
IN PIECES. THAT I SHALL SCATTER ACROSS THE STARS.
NO. I DON'T THINK YOU'LL BE DOING THAT.
N-NO...!
WHAT'S HAPPENING?
CAN YOU SEE? I CAN'T SEE FROM HERE!
IT'S BAD, KID.
CAN'T SEE SQUAT. DON'T NEED TO. IT'S DOOM.
HE FOUND THE GAUNTLET.
OH, THAT'S BAD.

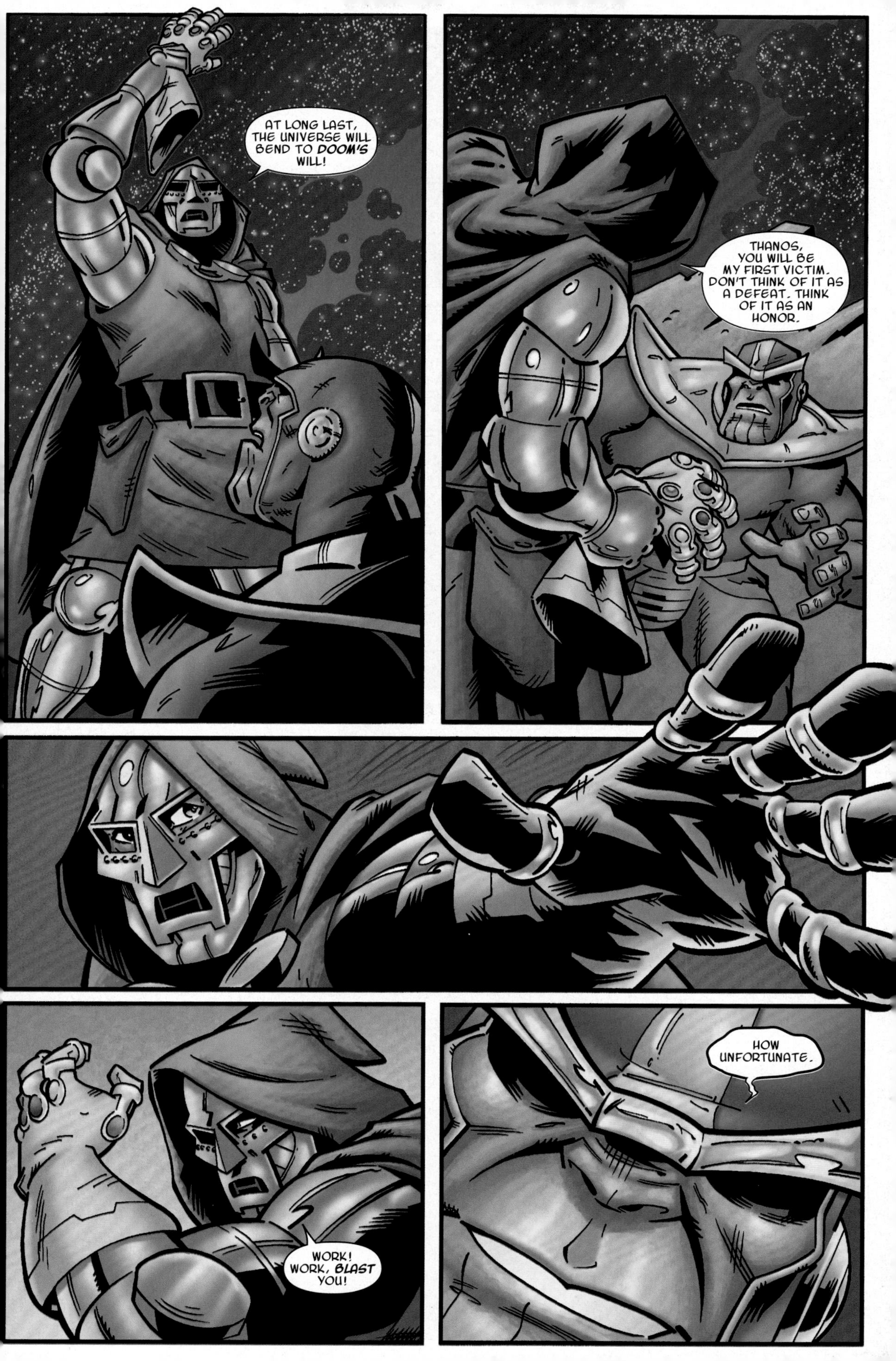
AT LONG LAST, THE UNIVERSE WILL BEND TO DOOM'S WILL!
THANOS, YOU WILL BE MY FIRST VICTIM. DON'T THINK OF IT AS A DEFEAT. THINK OF IT AS AN HONOR.
WORK! WORK, BLAST YOU!
HOW UNFORTUNATE.

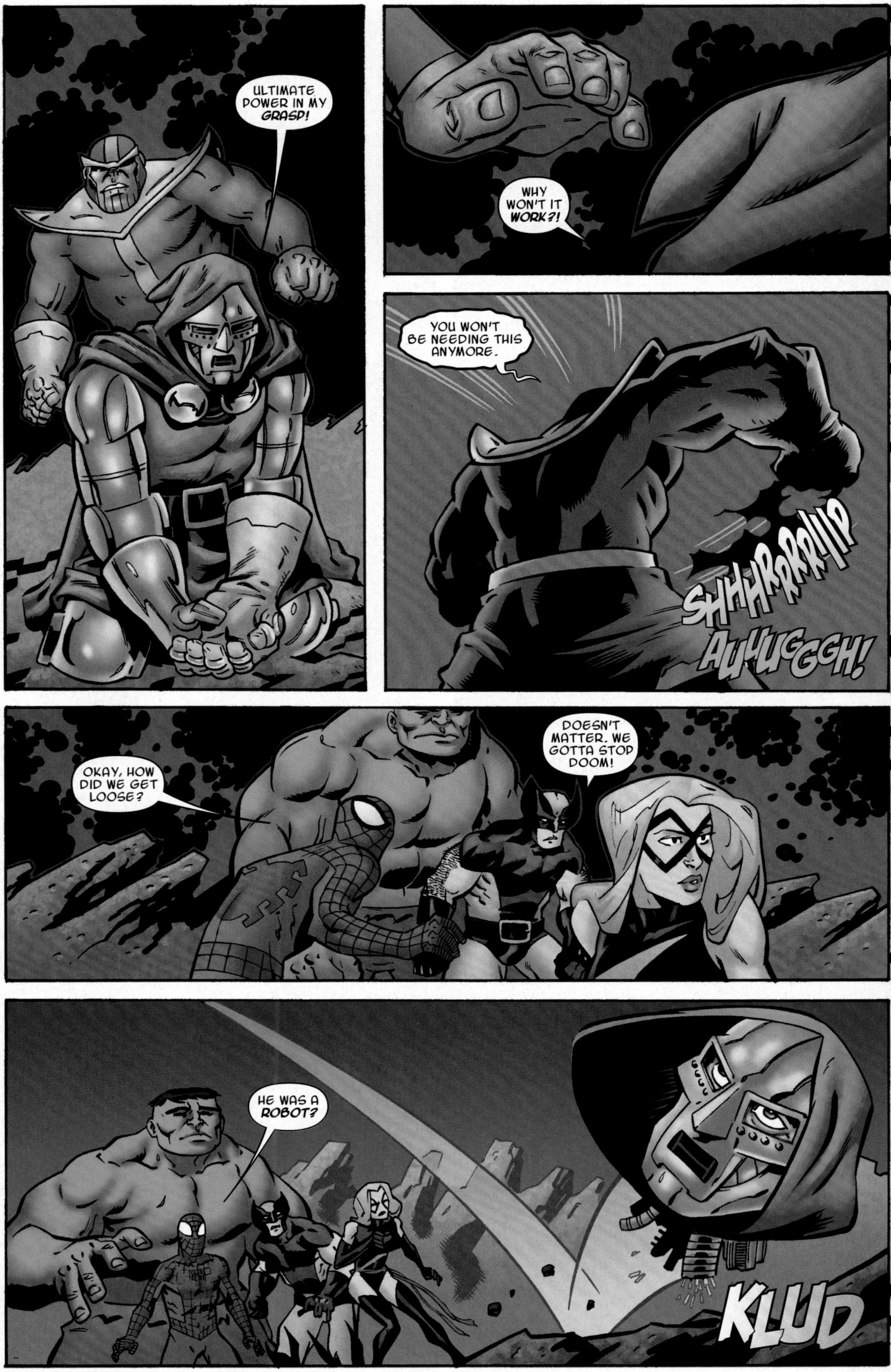
ULTIMATE POWER IN MY GRASP!
WHY WON'T IT WORK?!
YOU WON'T BE NEEDING THIS ANYMORE.
SHHHRRRRRIIP
AUUUGGGH!
OKAY, HOW DID WE GET LOOSE?
DOESN'T MATTER. WE GOTTA STOP DOOM!
HE WAS A ROBOT?
KLUD

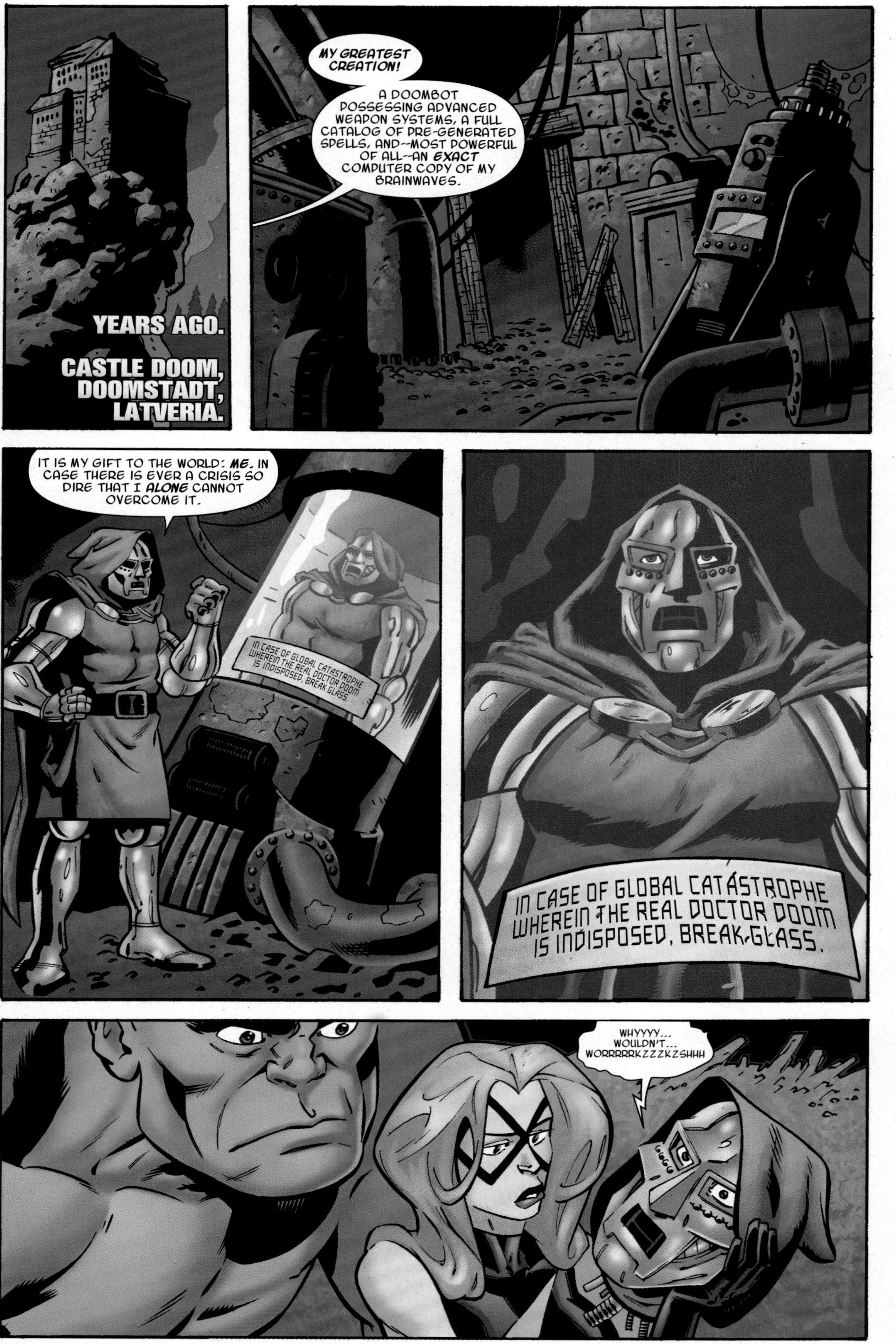
YEARS AGO.
CASTLE DOOM, DOOMSTADT, LATVERIA.
MY GREATEST CREATION!
A DOOMBOT POSSESSING ADVANCED WEAPON SYSTEMS, A FULL CATALOG OF PRE-GENERATED SPELLS, AND--MOST POWERFUL OF ALL--AN EXACT COMPUTER COPY OF MY BRAINWAVES.
IT IS MY GIFT TO THE WORLD: ME. IN CASE THERE IS EVER A CRISIS SO DIRE THAT I ALONE CANNOT OVERCOME IT.
IN CASE OF GLOBAL CATASTROPHE WHEREIN THE REAL DOCTOR DOOM IS INDISPOSED, BREAK GLASS.
IN CASE OF GLOBAL CATÁSTROPHE WHEREIN THE REAL DOCTOR DOOM IS INDISPOSED, BREAK GLASS.
WHYYYY... WOULDN'T... WORRRRRRKZZZKZSHHH

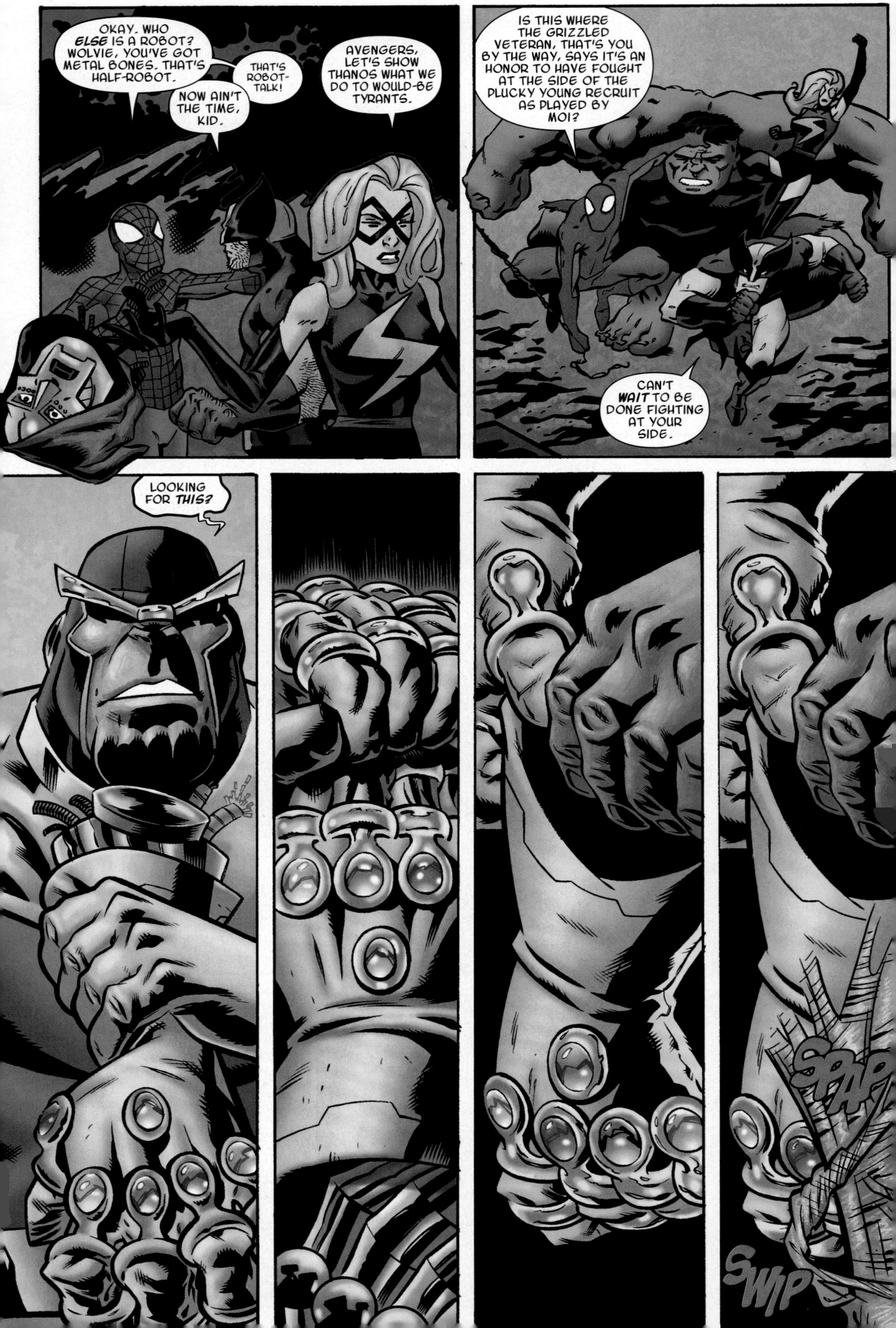

OKAY. WHO *ELSE* IS A ROBOT? WOLVIE, YOU'VE GOT METAL BONES. THAT'S HALF-ROBOT.
THAT'S ROBOT-TALK!
NOW AIN'T THE TIME, KID.
AVENGERS, LET'S SHOW THANOS WHAT WE DO TO WOULD-BE TYRANTS.
IS THIS WHERE THE GRIZZLED VETERAN, THAT'S YOU BY THE WAY, SAYS IT'S AN HONOR TO HAVE FOUGHT AT THE SIDE OF THE PLUCKY YOUNG RECRUIT AS PLAYED BY MOI?
CAN'T *WAIT* TO BE DONE FIGHTING AT YOUR SIDE.
LOOKING FOR *THIS?*
SPAP
SWIP

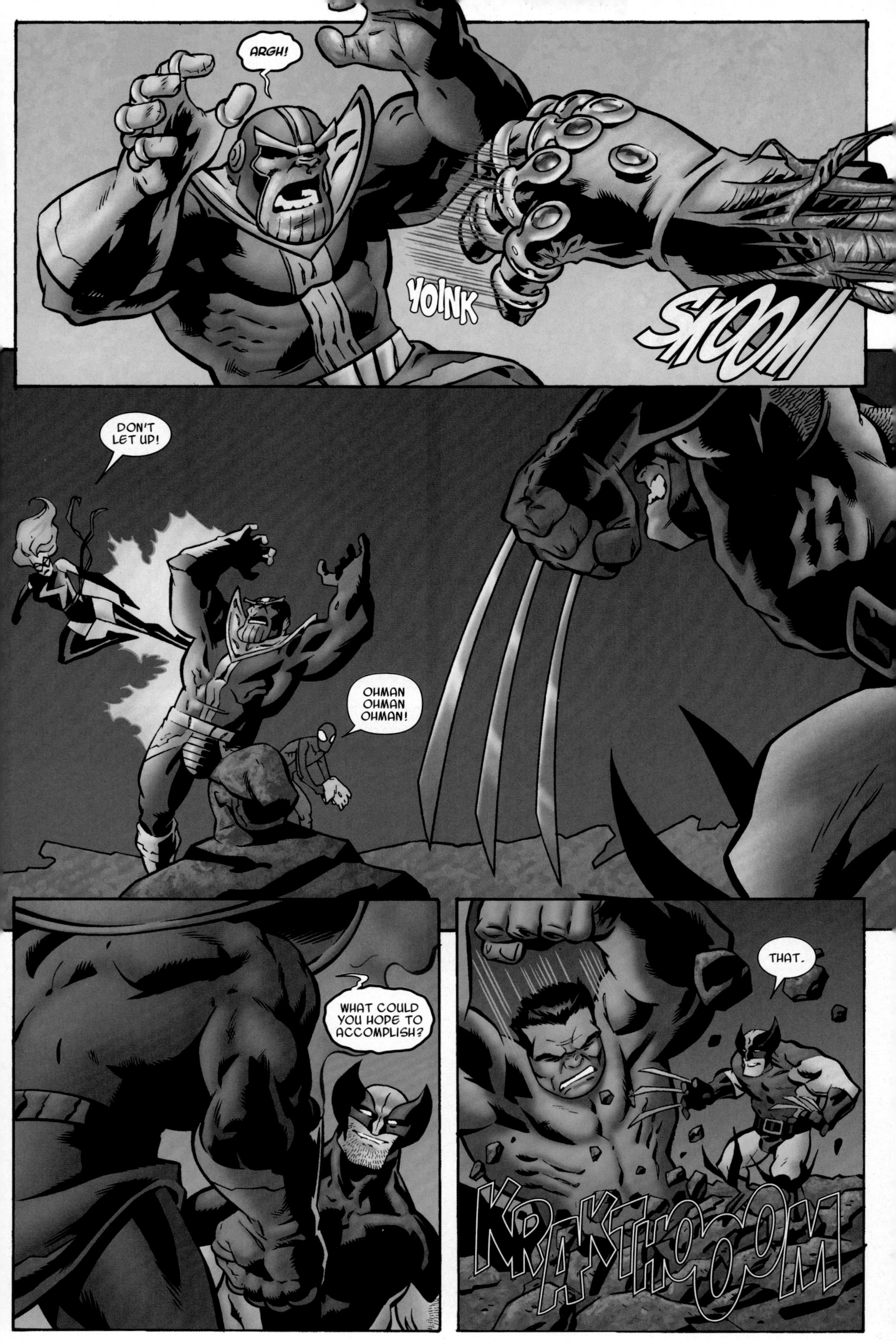
ARGH!
YOINK
SKOOM
DON'T LET UP!
OHMAN OHMAN OHMAN!
WHAT COULD YOU HOPE TO ACCOMPLISH?
THAT.
KRAKTHOOOOM

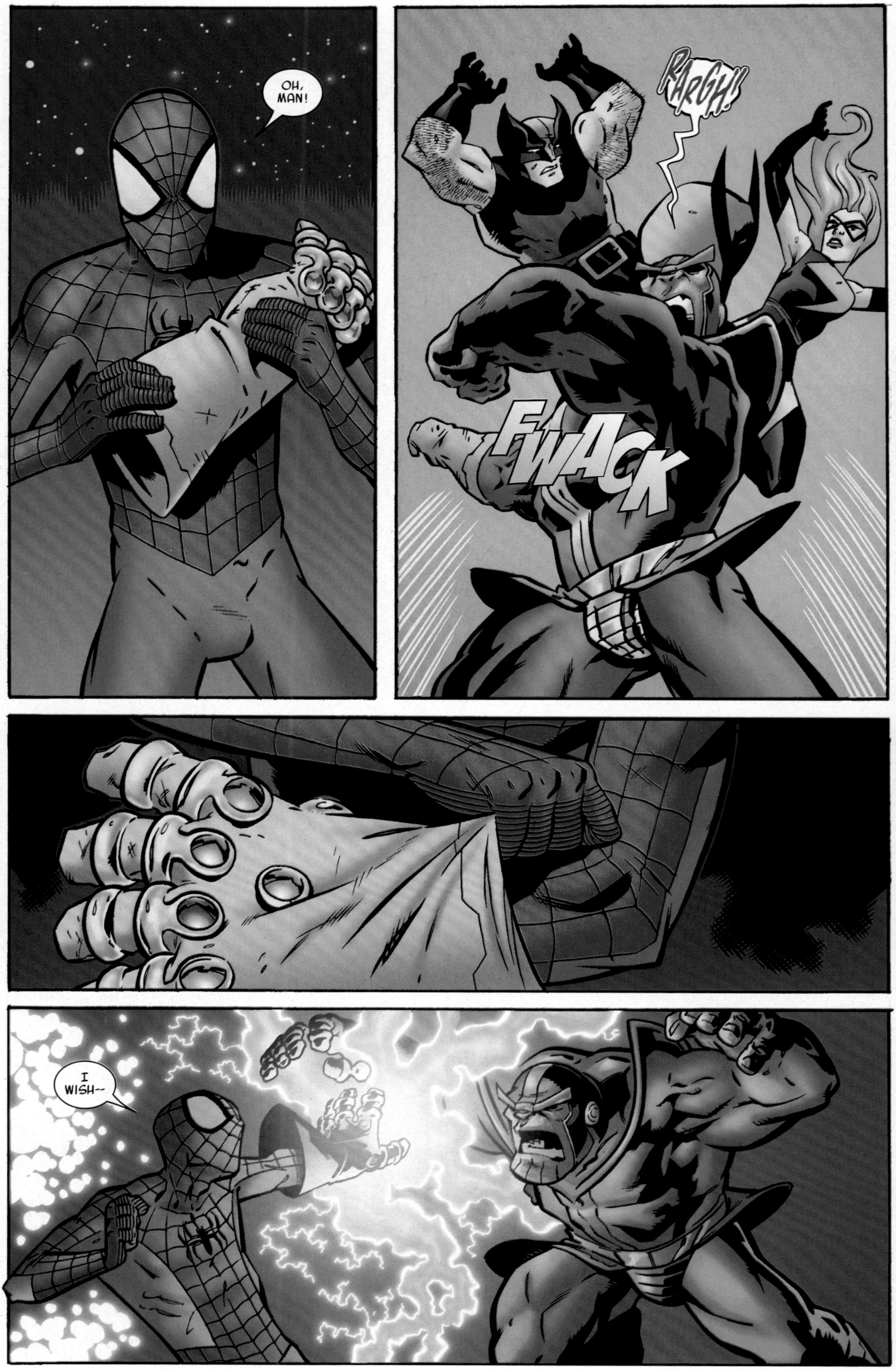
OH, MAN!
RARGH!!
FWACK
I WISH--

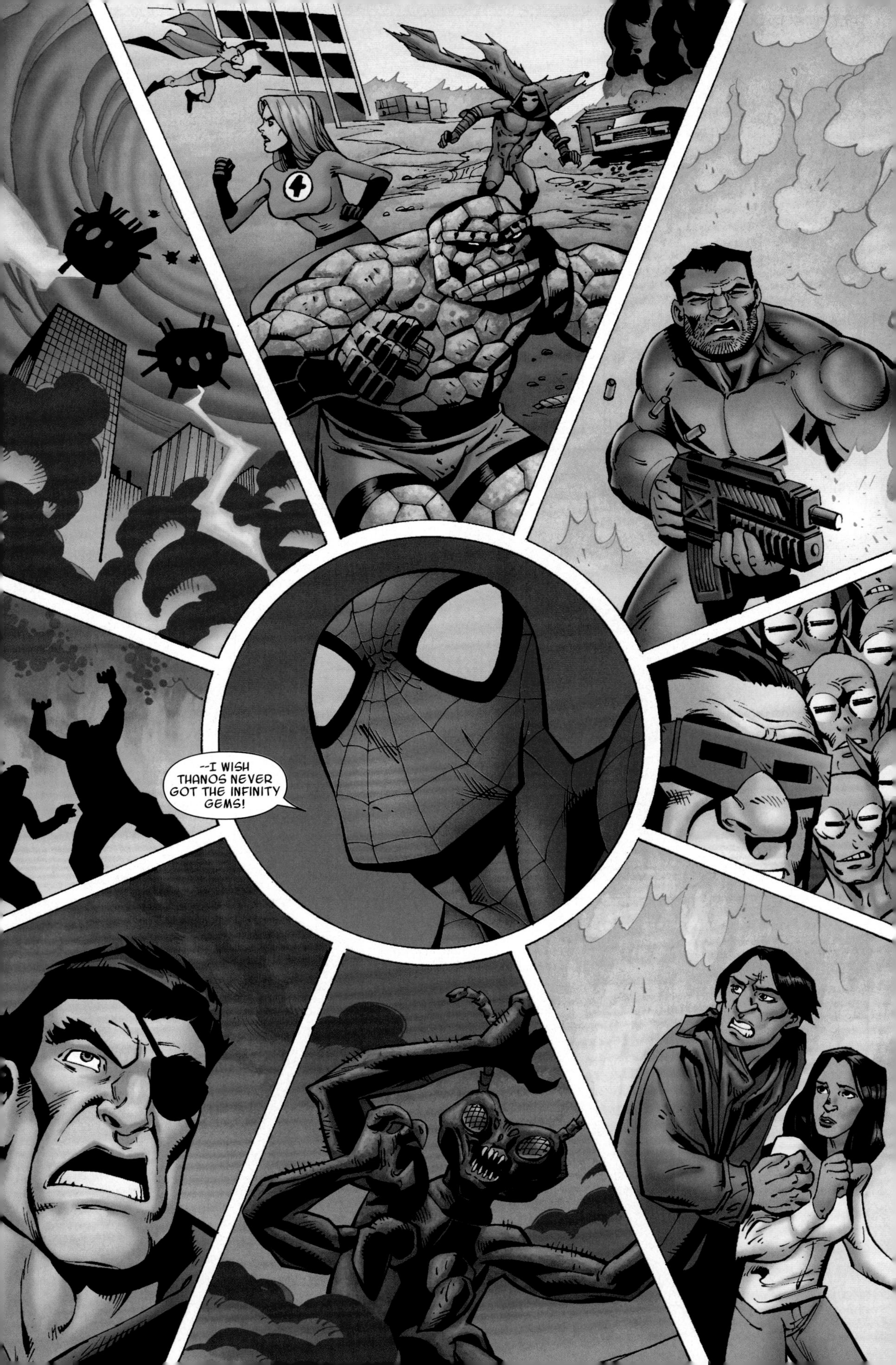
--I WISH THANOS NEVER GOT THE INFINITY GEMS!

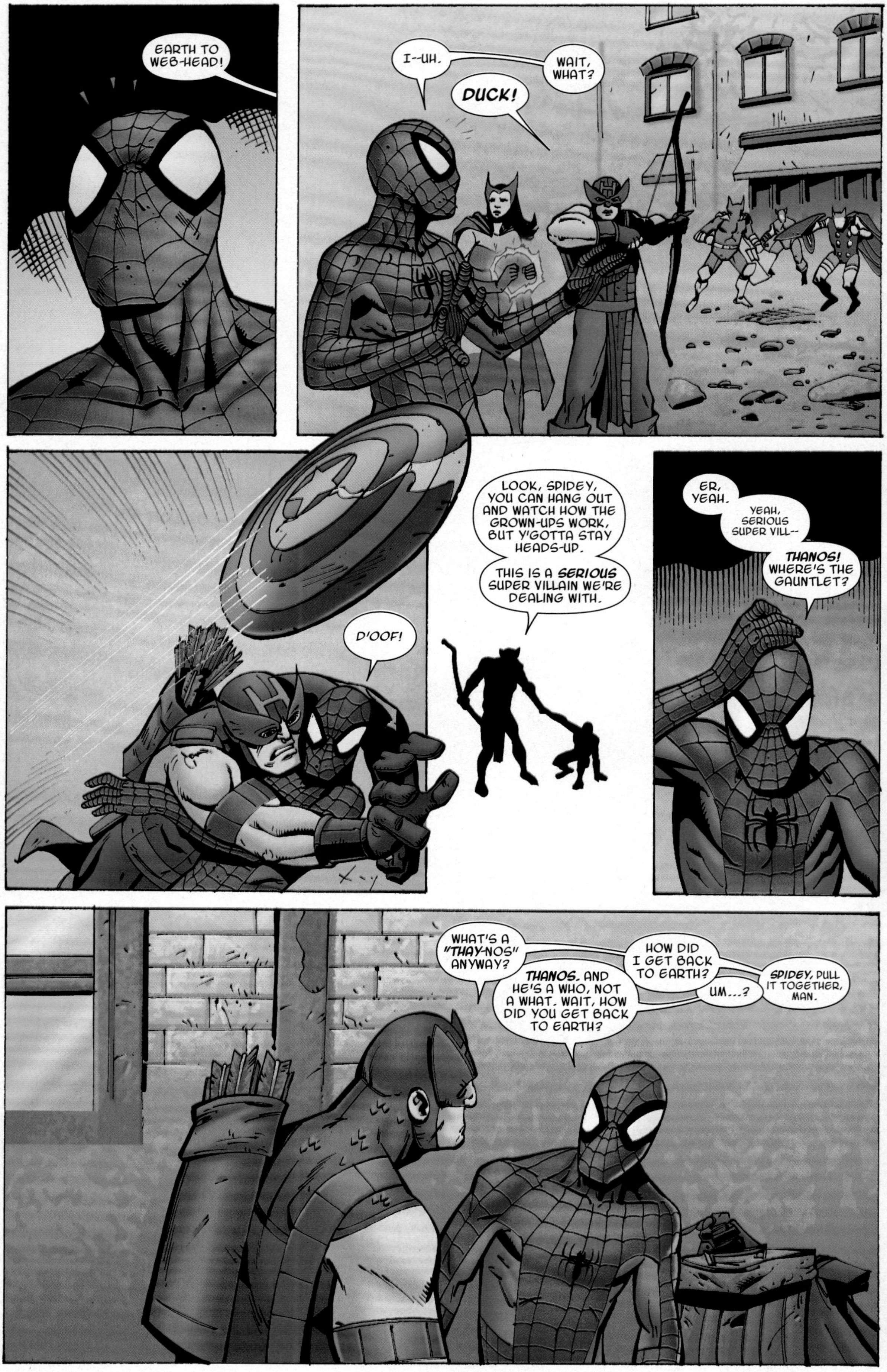
EARTH TO WEB-HEAD!
I--UH.
WAIT, WHAT?
DUCK!
D'OOF!
LOOK, SPIDEY, YOU CAN HANG OUT AND WATCH HOW THE GROWN-UPS WORK, BUT Y'GOTTA STAY HEADS-UP.
THIS IS A SERIOUS SUPER VILLAIN WE'RE DEALING WITH.
ER, YEAH.
YEAH, SERIOUS SUPER VILL--
THANOS! WHERE'S THE GAUNTLET?
WHAT'S A "THAY-NOS" ANYWAY?
THANOS. AND HE'S A WHO, NOT A WHAT. WAIT, HOW DID YOU GET BACK TO EARTH?
HOW DID I GET BACK TO EARTH?
UM...?
SPIDEY, PULL IT TOGETHER, MAN.

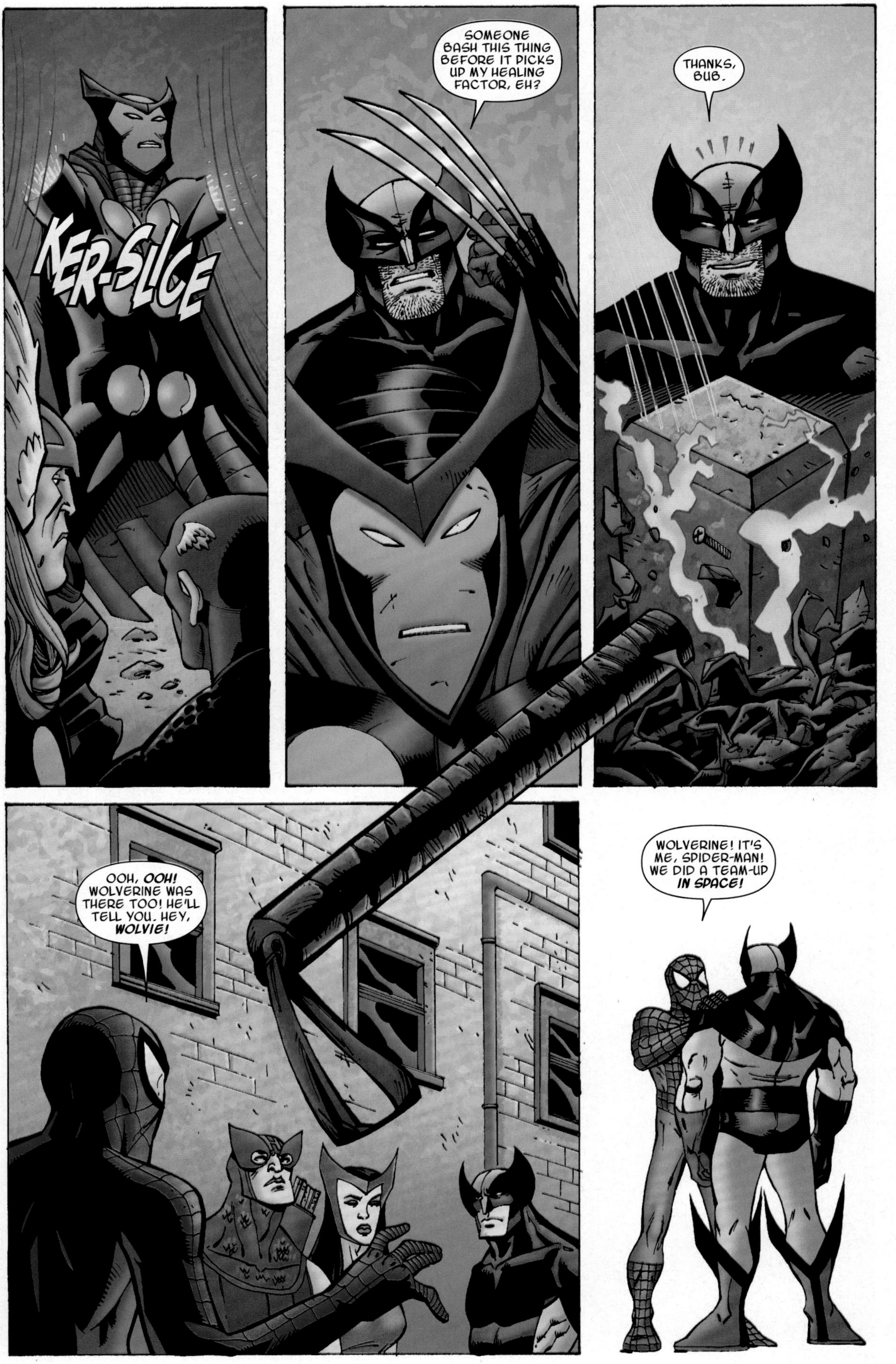
KER-SLICE
SOMEONE BASH THIS THING BEFORE IT PICKS UP MY HEALING FACTOR, EH?
THANKS, BUB.
OOH, OOH! WOLVERINE WAS THERE TOO! HE'LL TELL YOU. HEY, WOLVIE!
WOLVERINE! IT'S ME, SPIDER-MAN! WE DID A TEAM-UP IN SPACE!

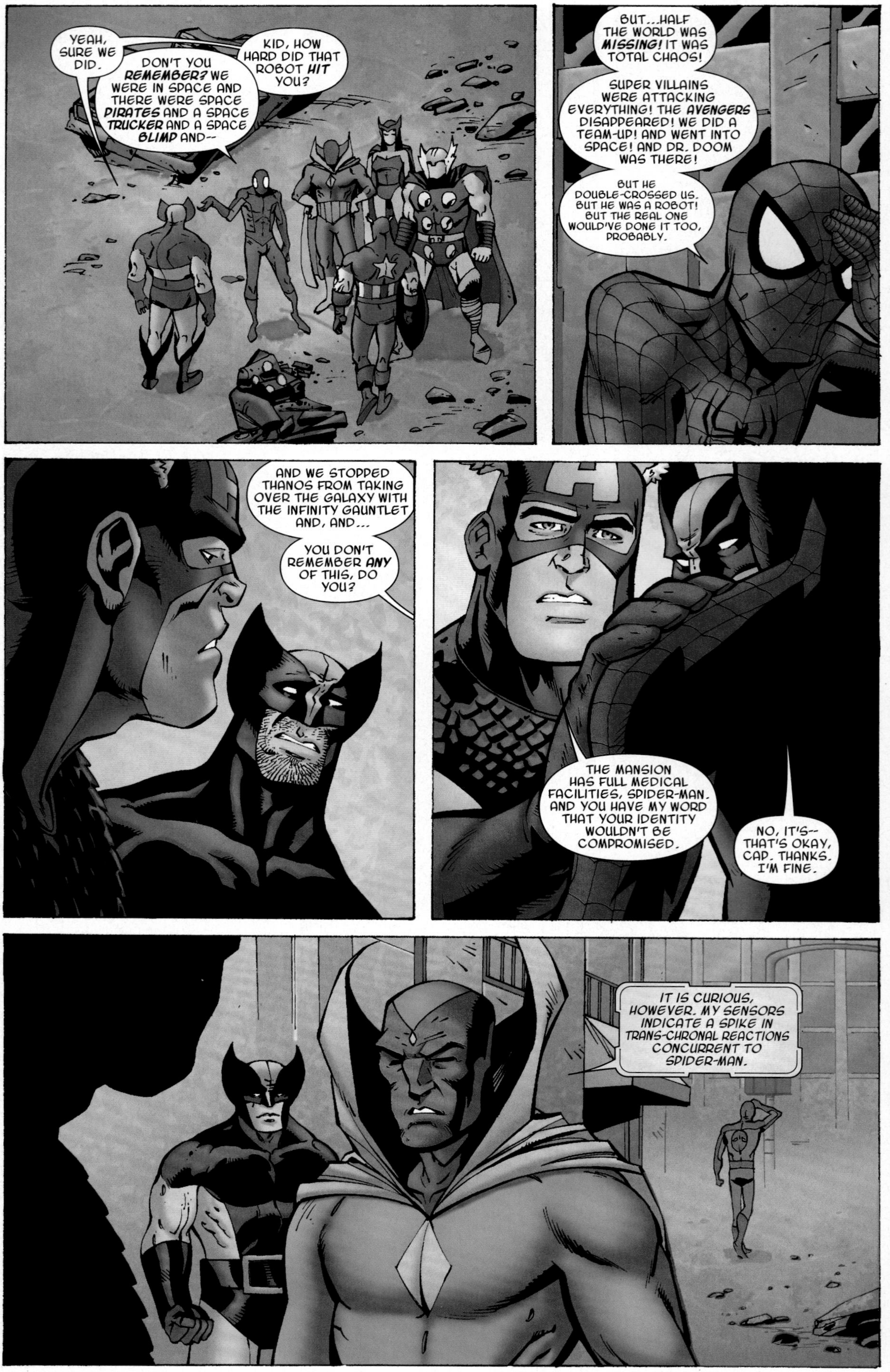
YEAH, SURE WE DID.
DON'T YOU REMEMBER? WE WERE IN SPACE AND THERE WERE SPACE PIRATES AND A SPACE TRUCKER AND A SPACE BLIMP AND--
KID, HOW HARD DID THAT ROBOT HIT YOU?
BUT...HALF THE WORLD WAS MISSING! IT WAS TOTAL CHAOS!
SUPER VILLAINS WERE ATTACKING EVERYTHING! THE AVENGERS DISAPPEARED! WE DID A TEAM-UP! AND WENT INTO SPACE! AND DR. DOOM WAS THERE!
BUT HE DOUBLE-CROSSED US. BUT HE WAS A ROBOT! BUT THE REAL ONE WOULD'VE DONE IT TOO, PROBABLY.
AND WE STOPPED THANOS FROM TAKING OVER THE GALAXY WITH THE INFINITY GAUNTLET AND, AND...
YOU DON'T REMEMBER ANY OF THIS, DO YOU?
THE MANSION HAS FULL MEDICAL FACILITIES, SPIDER-MAN. AND YOU HAVE MY WORD THAT YOUR IDENTITY WOULDN'T BE COMPROMISED.
NO, IT'S-- THAT'S OKAY, CAP. THANKS. I'M FINE.
IT IS CURIOUS, HOWEVER. MY SENSORS INDICATE A SPIKE IN TRANS-CHRONAL REACTIONS CONCURRENT TO SPIDER-MAN.

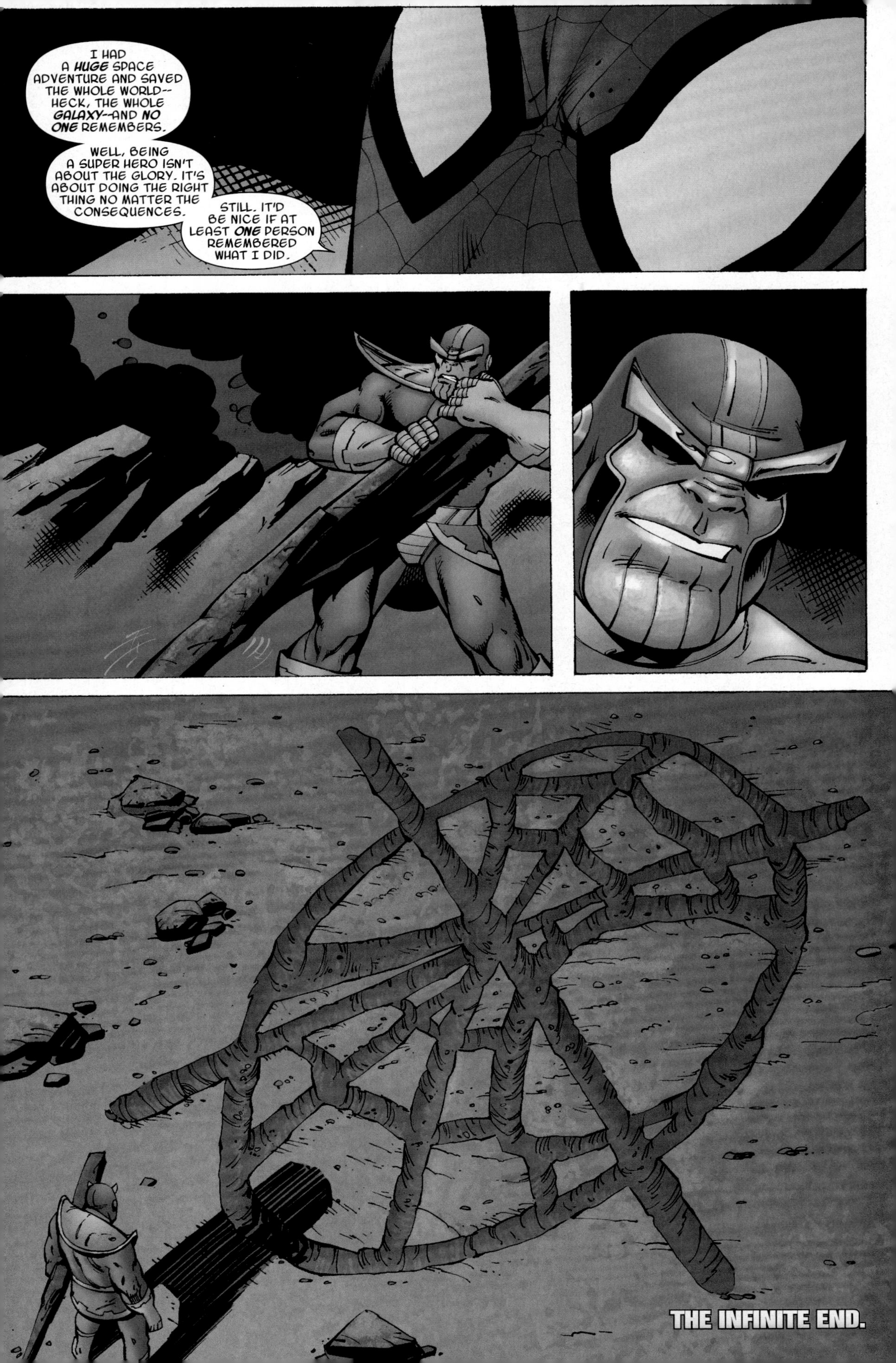
I HAD A **HUGE** SPACE ADVENTURE AND SAVED THE WHOLE WORLD-- HECK, THE WHOLE **GALAXY**--AND **NO ONE** REMEMBERS.
WELL, BEING A SUPER HERO ISN'T ABOUT THE GLORY. IT'S ABOUT DOING THE RIGHT THING NO MATTER THE CONSEQUENCES.
STILL. IT'D BE NICE IF AT LEAST **ONE** PERSON REMEMBERED WHAT I DID.
THE INFINITE END.

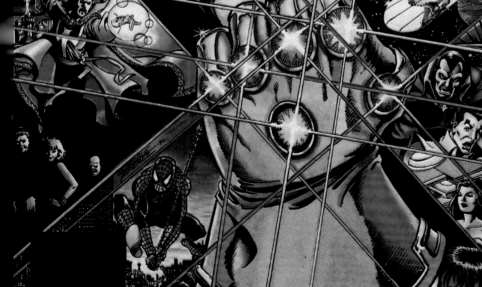

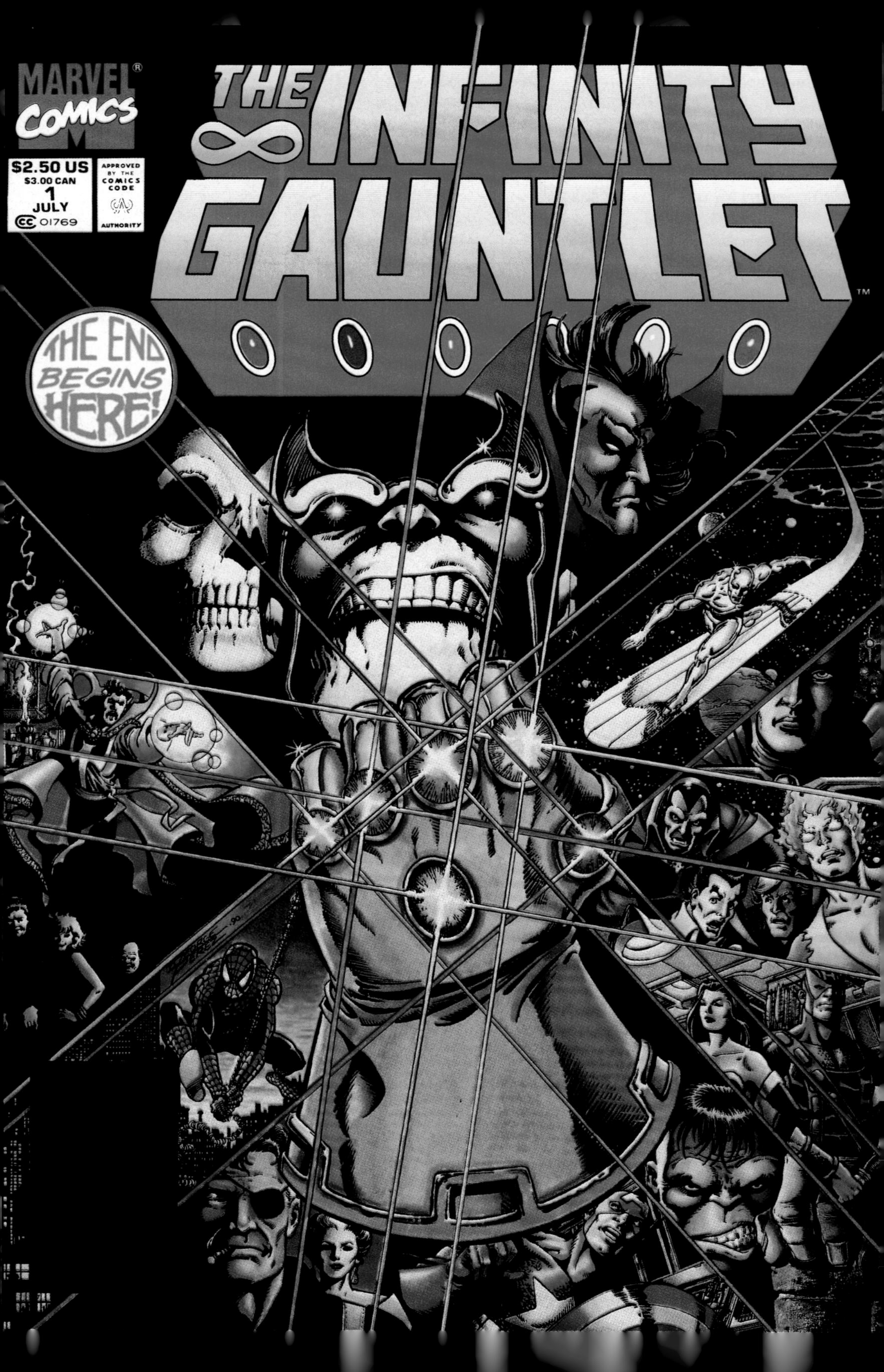

MARVEL COMICS ®

$2.50 US
$3.00 CAN
1 JULY

APPROVED BY THE COMICS CODE AUTHORITY

01769

THE ∞ INFINITY GAUNTLET ™

THE END BEGINS HERE!

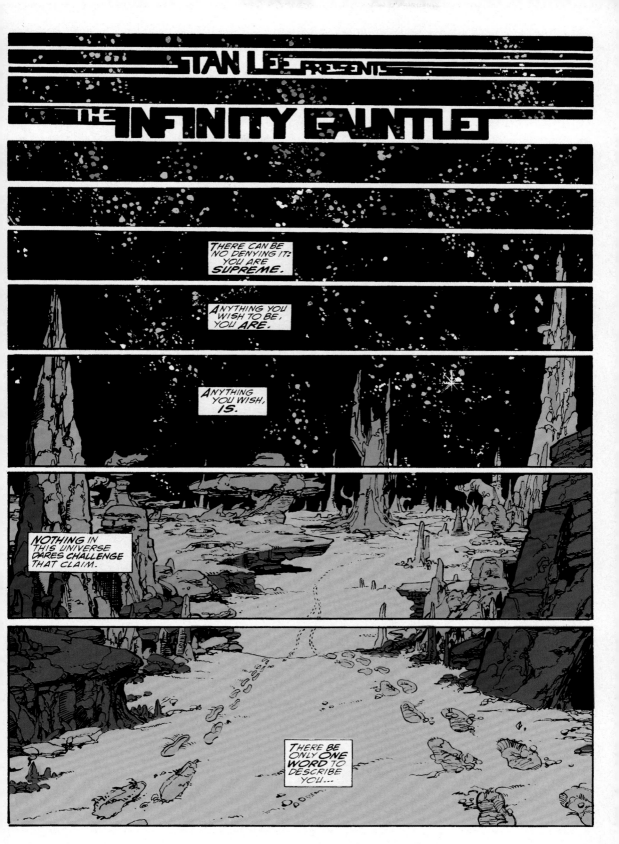

STAN LEE PRESENTS

THE INFINITY GAUNTLET

THERE CAN BE NO DENYING IT: YOU ARE **SUPREME.**

ANYTHING YOU WISH TO BE, YOU **ARE.**

ANYTHING YOU WISH, **IS.**

NOTHING IN THIS UNIVERSE DARES CHALLENGE THAT CLAIM.

THERE BE ONLY **ONE WORD** TO DESCRIBE YOU...

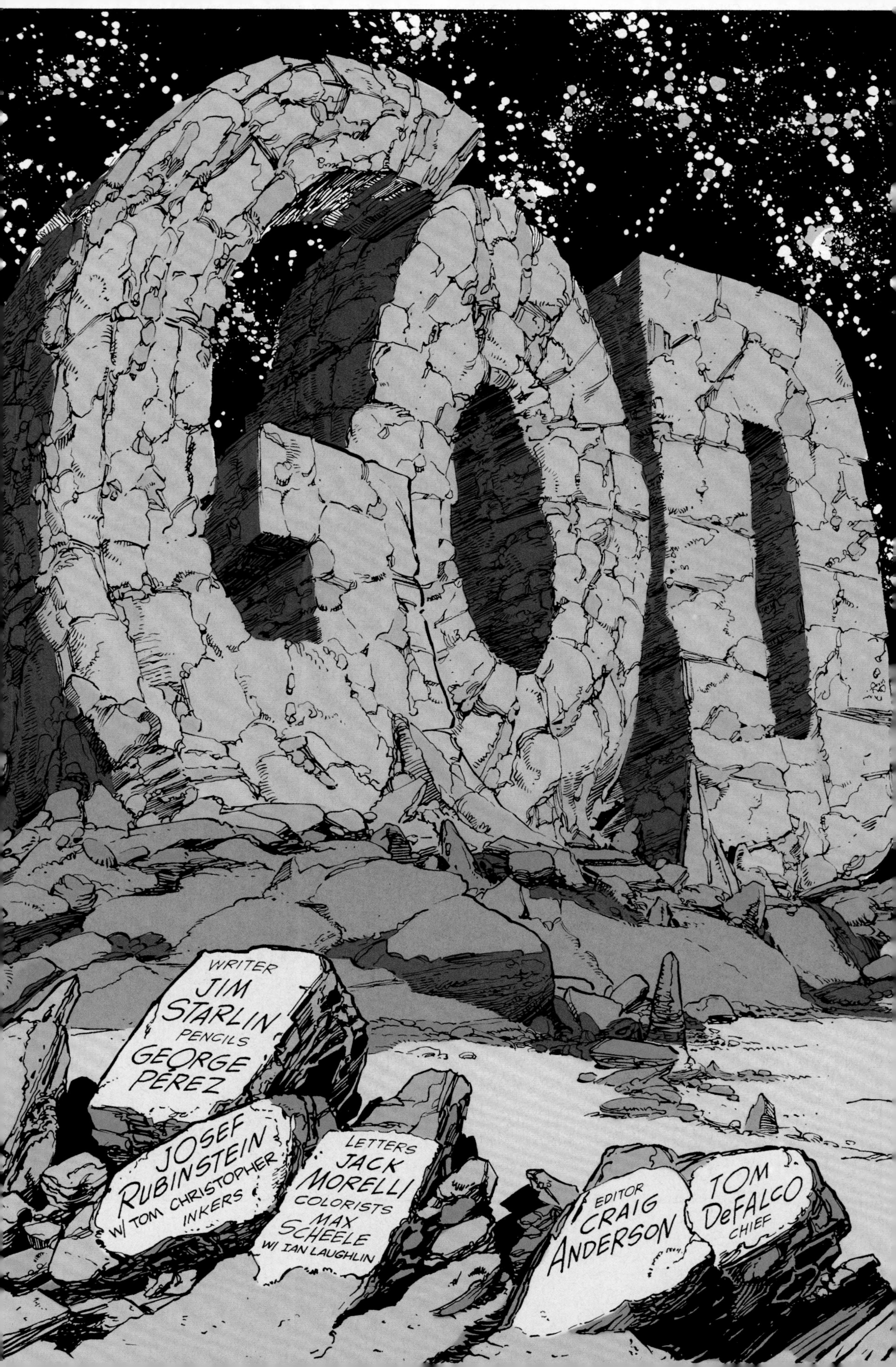
GOD
WRITER
JIM STARLIN
PENCILS
GEORGE PEREZ
JOSEF RUBINSTEIN
W/ TOM CHRISTOPHER
INKERS
LETTERS
JACK MORELLI
COLORISTS
MAX SCHEELE
W/ IAN LAUGHLIN
EDITOR
CRAIG ANDERSON
TOM DeFALCO
CHIEF

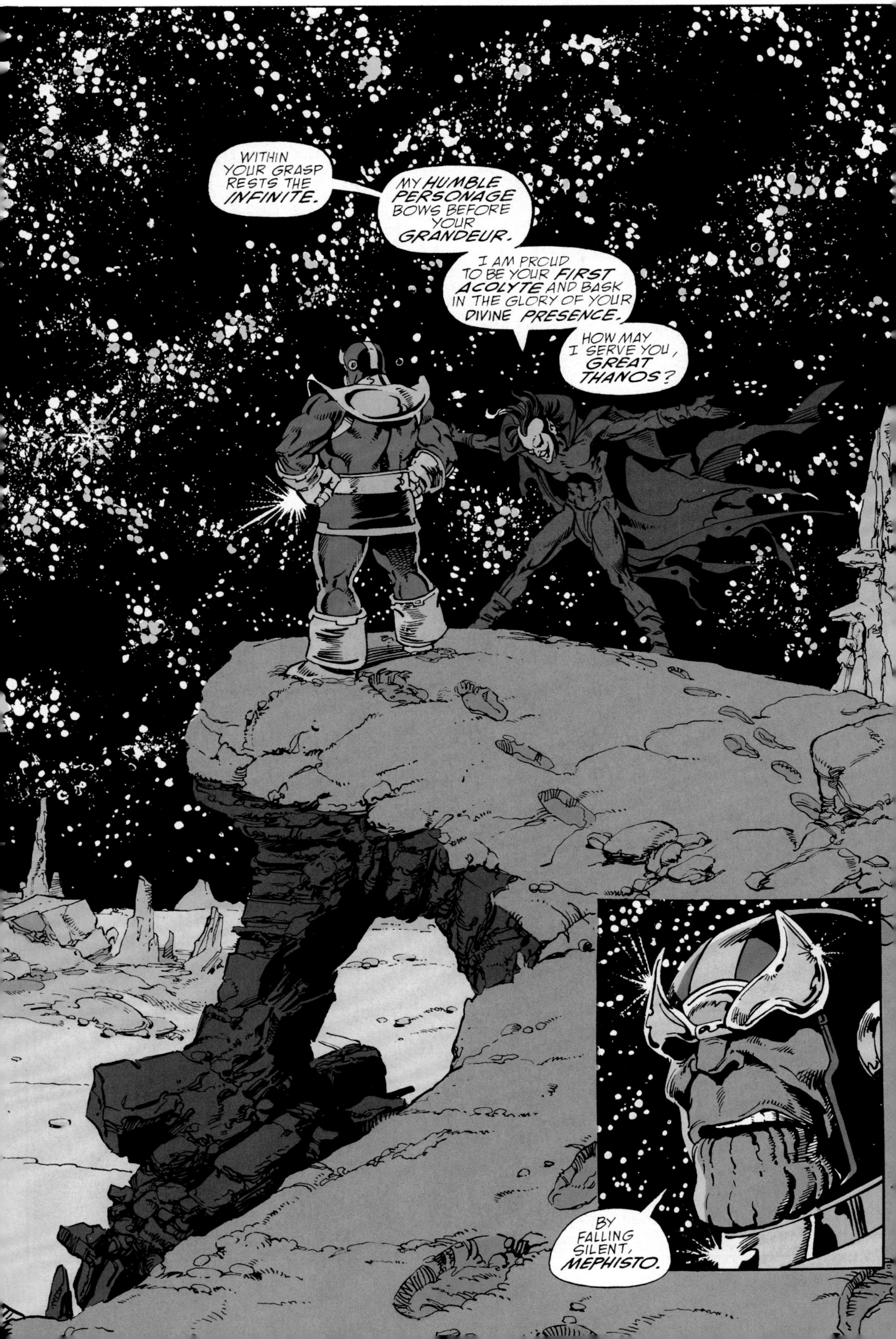
WITHIN YOUR GRASP RESTS THE INFINITE.
MY HUMBLE PERSONAGE BOWS BEFORE YOUR GRANDEUR.
I AM PROUD TO BE YOUR FIRST ACOLYTE AND BASK IN THE GLORY OF YOUR DIVINE PRESENCE.
HOW MAY I SERVE YOU, GREAT THANOS?
BY FALLING SILENT, MEPHISTO.

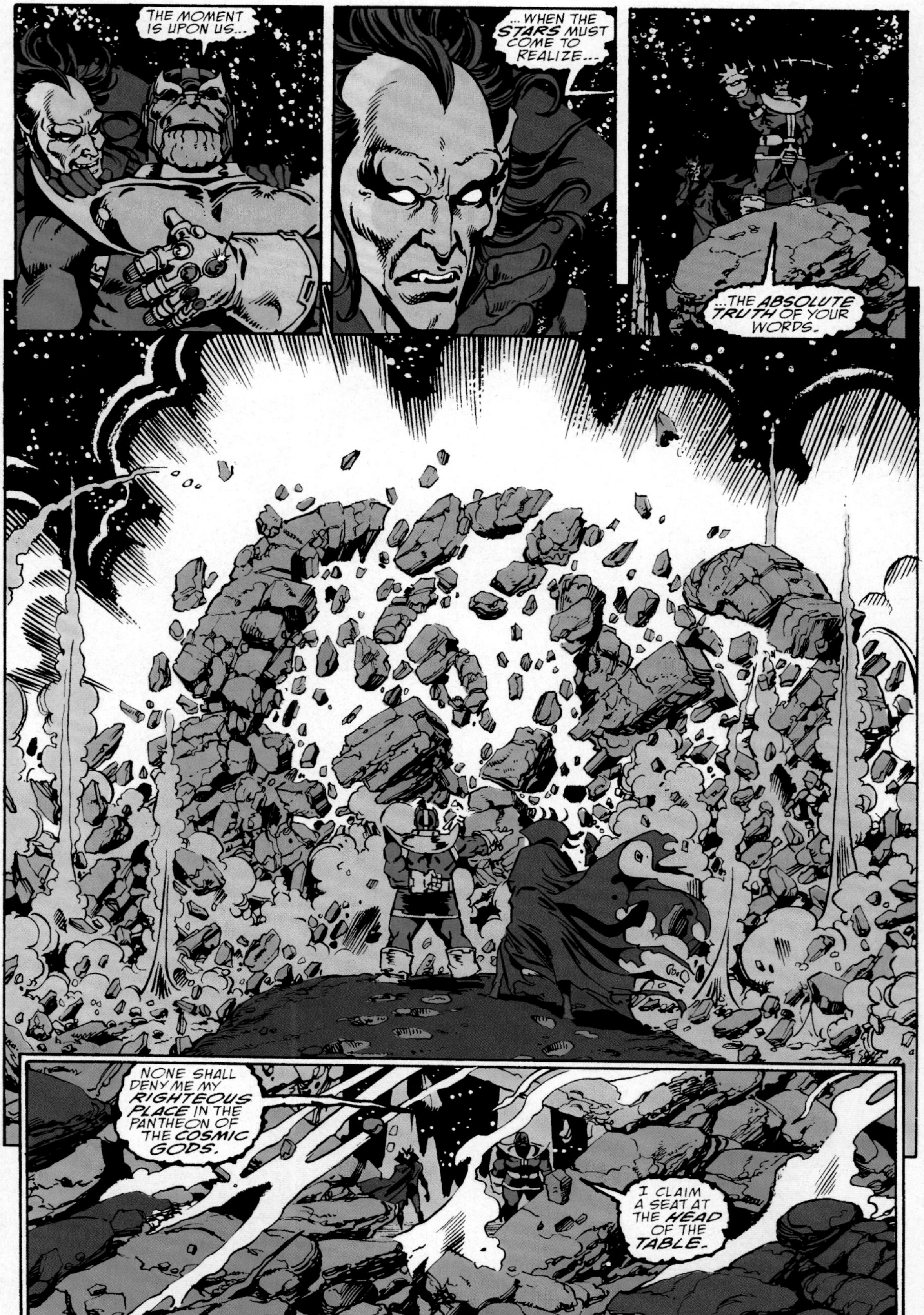
THE MOMENT IS UPON US...
...WHEN THE STARS MUST COME TO REALIZE...
...THE ABSOLUTE TRUTH OF YOUR WORDS.
NONE SHALL DENY ME MY RIGHTEOUS PLACE IN THE PANTHEON OF THE COSMIC GODS.
I CLAIM A SEAT AT THE HEAD OF THE TABLE.

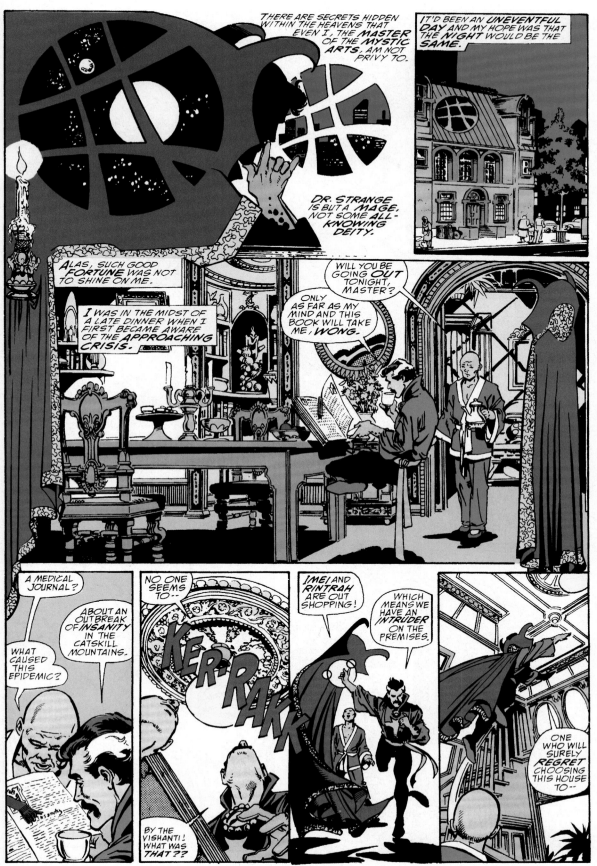

THERE ARE SECRETS HIDDEN WITHIN THE HEAVENS THAT EVEN I, THE *MASTER* OF THE *MYSTIC ARTS*, AM NOT PRIVY TO.

IT'D BEEN AN *UNEVENTFUL DAY* AND MY HOPE WAS THAT THE *NIGHT* WOULD BE THE *SAME.*

DR. STRANGE IS BUT A *MAGE,* NOT SOME *ALL-KNOWING DEITY.*

ALAS, SUCH GOOD *FORTUNE* WAS NOT TO SHINE ON ME.

I WAS IN THE MIDST OF A LATE DINNER WHEN I FIRST BECAME AWARE OF THE *APPROACHING CRISIS.*

WILL YOU BE GOING *OUT* TONIGHT, *MASTER?*

ONLY AS FAR AS MY *MIND* AND THIS *BOOK* WILL TAKE ME, *WONG.*

A *MEDICAL JOURNAL?*

ABOUT AN *OUTBREAK* OF *INSANITY* IN THE *CATSKILL* MOUNTAINS.

WHAT CAUSED THIS *EPIDEMIC?*

NO ONE SEEMS TO--

KER-RAKK

BY THE *VISHANTI!* WHAT WAS *THAT??*

MEI AND *RINTRAH* ARE OUT *SHOPPING!*

WHICH MEANS WE HAVE AN *INTRUDER* ON THE PREMISES.

ONE WHO WILL SURELY *REGRET* CHOOSING THIS HOUSE TO--

99

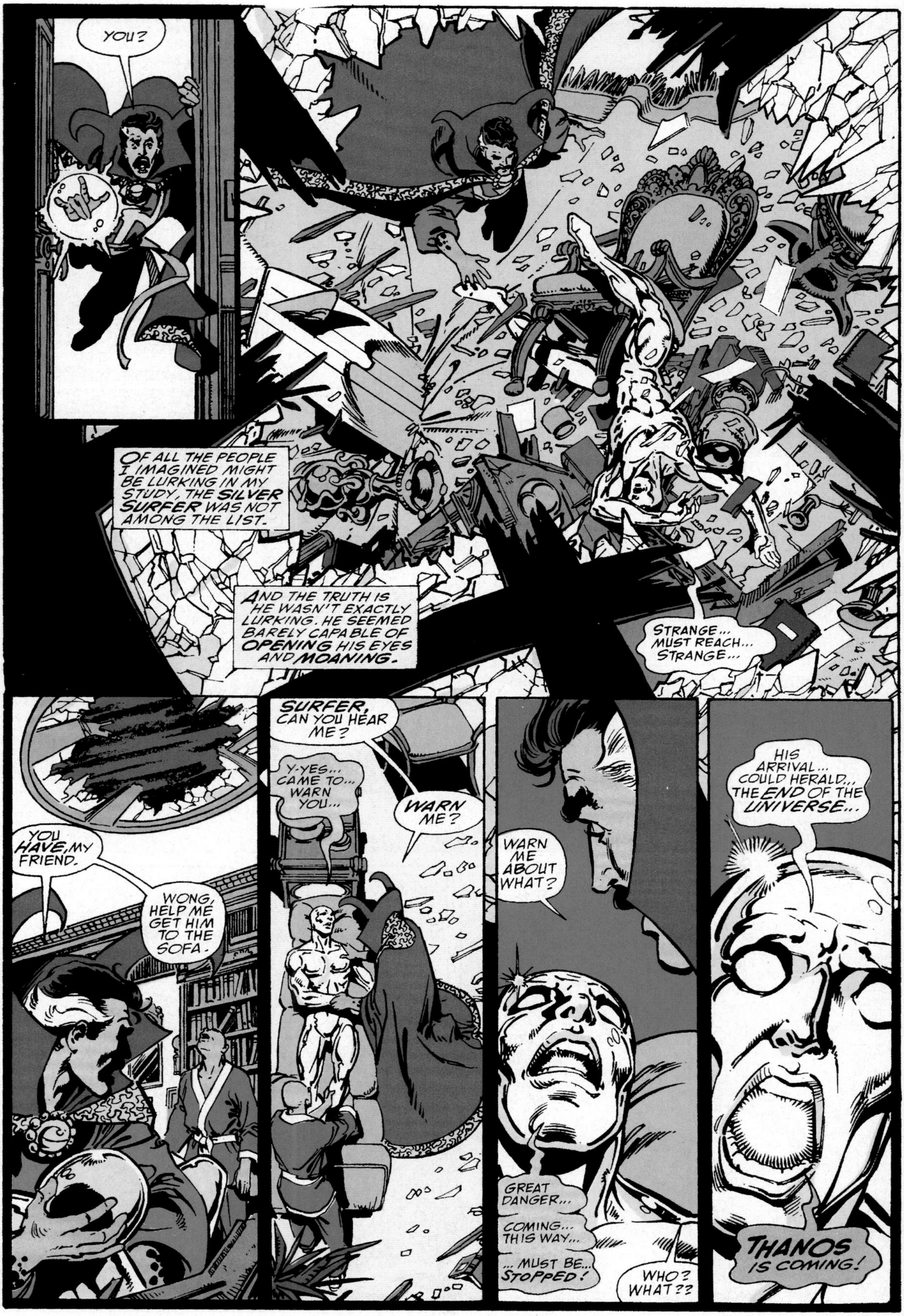
YOU?
OF ALL THE PEOPLE I IMAGINED MIGHT BE LURKING IN MY STUDY, THE SILVER SURFER WAS NOT AMONG THE LIST.
AND THE TRUTH IS HE WASN'T EXACTLY LURKING. HE SEEMED BARELY CAPABLE OF OPENING HIS EYES AND MOANING.
STRANGE... MUST REACH... STRANGE...
YOU HAVE, MY FRIEND.
WONG, HELP ME GET HIM TO THE SOFA.
SURFER, CAN YOU HEAR ME?
Y-YES... CAME TO... WARN YOU...
WARN ME?
WARN ME ABOUT WHAT?
GREAT DANGER...
COMING... THIS WAY...
... MUST BE... STOPPED!
WHO? WHAT??
HIS ARRIVAL... COULD HERALD... THE END OF THE UNIVERSE...
THANOS IS COMING!

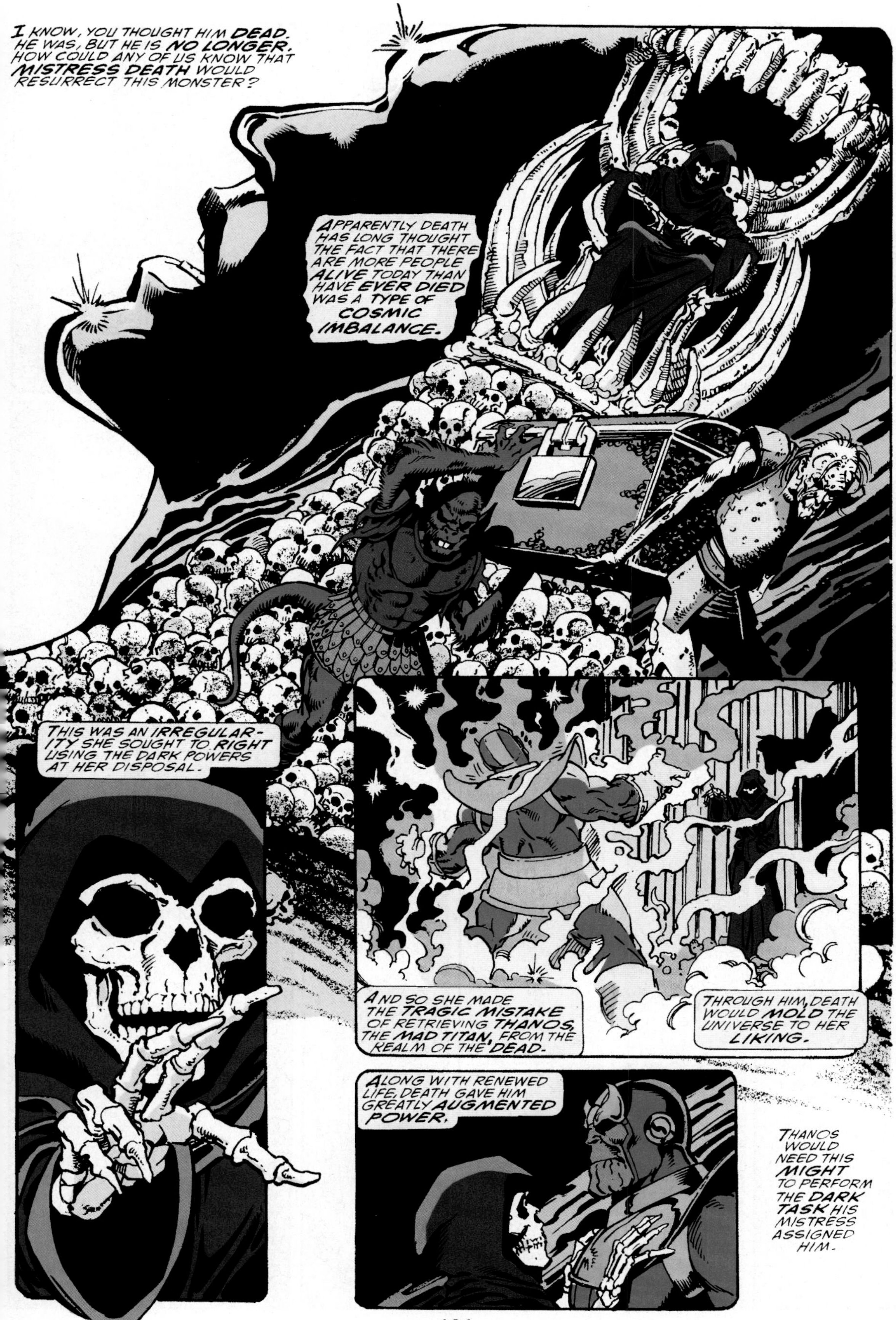
I KNOW, YOU THOUGHT HIM DEAD. HE WAS, BUT HE IS NO LONGER. HOW COULD ANY OF US KNOW THAT MISTRESS DEATH WOULD RESURRECT THIS MONSTER?
APPARENTLY DEATH HAS LONG THOUGHT THE FACT THAT THERE ARE MORE PEOPLE ALIVE TODAY THAN HAVE EVER DIED WAS A TYPE OF COSMIC IMBALANCE.
THIS WAS AN IRREGULARITY SHE SOUGHT TO RIGHT USING THE DARK POWERS AT HER DISPOSAL.
AND SO SHE MADE THE TRAGIC MISTAKE OF RETRIEVING THANOS, THE MAD TITAN, FROM THE REALM OF THE DEAD.
THROUGH HIM, DEATH WOULD MOLD THE UNIVERSE TO HER LIKING.
ALONG WITH RENEWED LIFE, DEATH GAVE HIM GREATLY AUGMENTED POWER.
THANOS WOULD NEED THIS MIGHT TO PERFORM THE DARK TASK HIS MISTRESS ASSIGNED HIM.

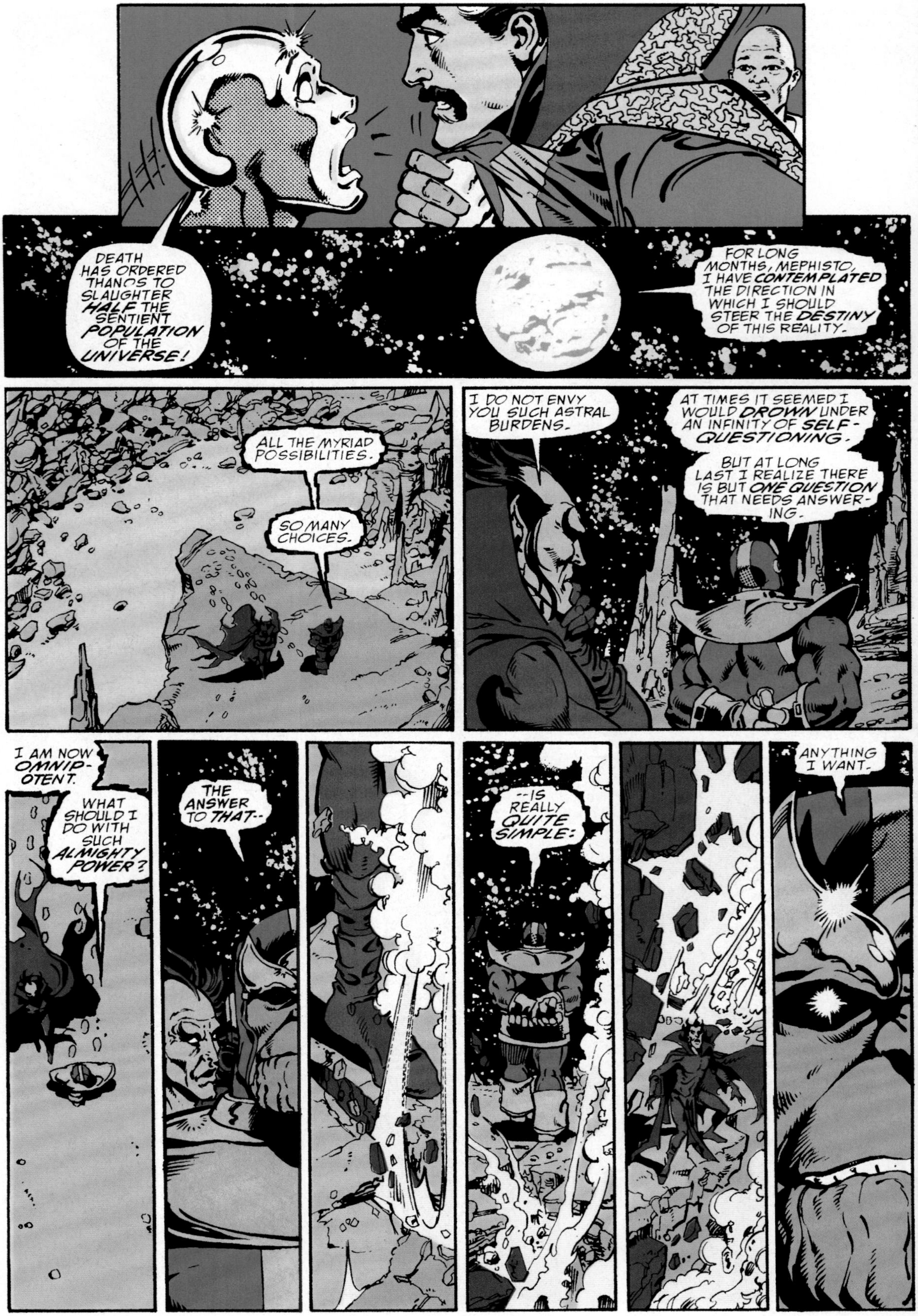
DEATH HAS ORDERED THANOS TO SLAUGHTER HALF THE SENTIENT POPULATION OF THE UNIVERSE!
FOR LONG MONTHS, MEPHISTO, I HAVE CONTEMPLATED THE DIRECTION IN WHICH I SHOULD STEER THE DESTINY OF THIS REALITY.
ALL THE MYRIAD POSSIBILITIES.
SO MANY CHOICES.
I DO NOT ENVY YOU SUCH ASTRAL BURDENS.
AT TIMES IT SEEMED I WOULD DROWN UNDER AN INFINITY OF SELF-QUESTIONING.
BUT AT LONG LAST I REALIZE THERE IS BUT ONE QUESTION THAT NEEDS ANSWERING.
I AM NOW OMNIPOTENT.
WHAT SHOULD I DO WITH SUCH ALMIGHTY POWER?
THE ANSWER TO THAT--
--IS REALLY QUITE SIMPLE:
ANYTHING I WANT.

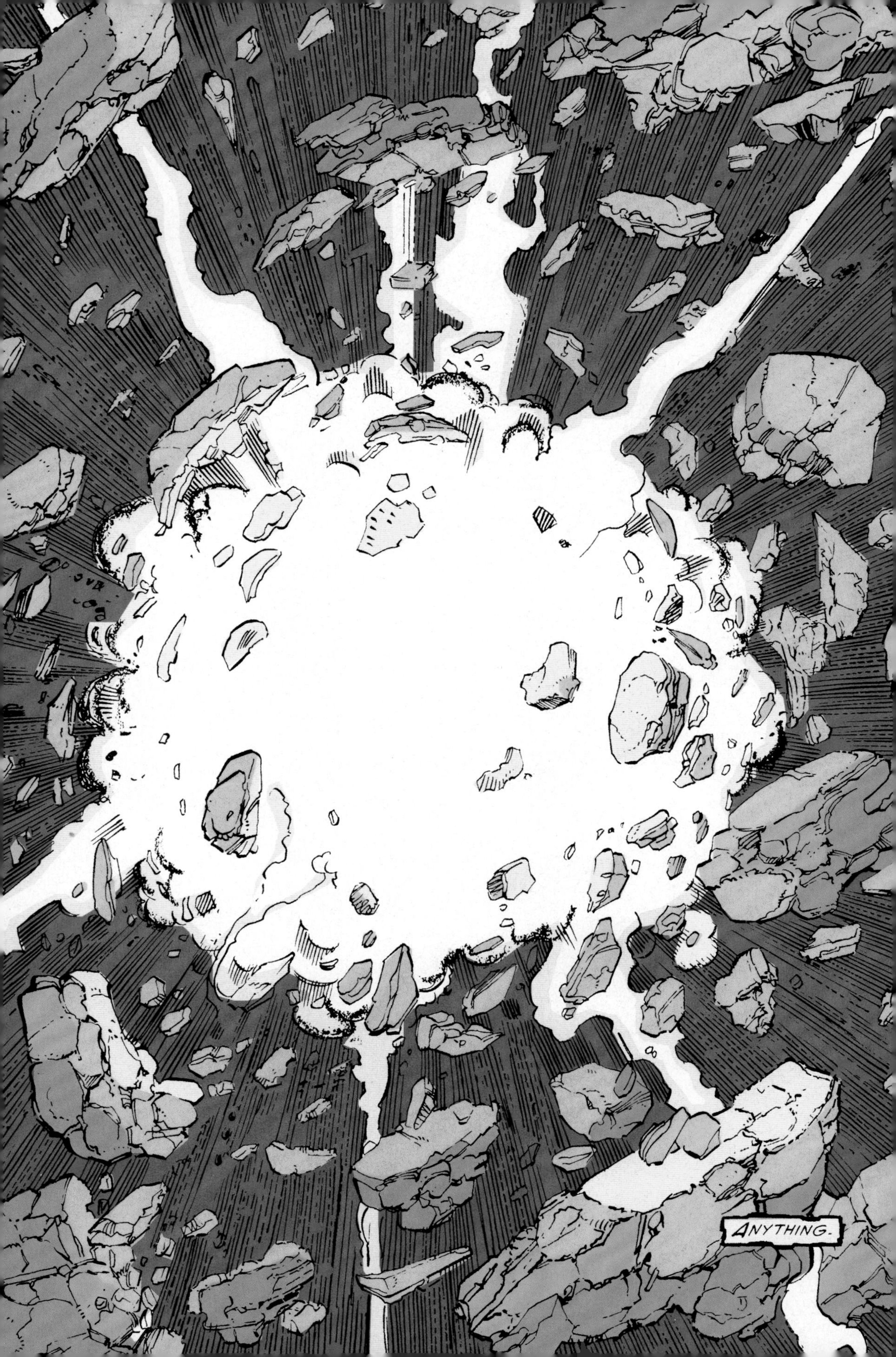
ANYTHING.

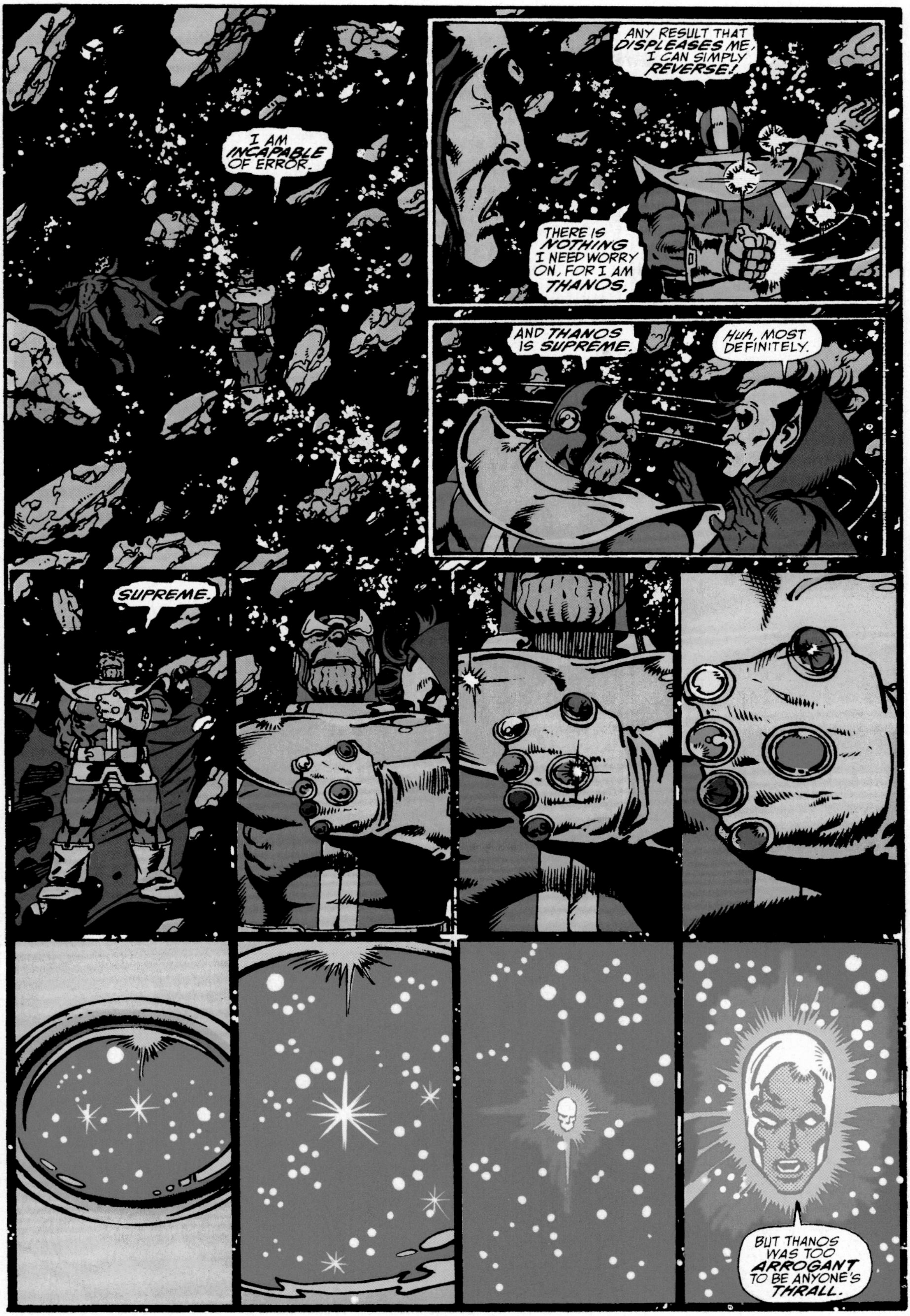
I AM INCAPABLE OF ERROR.
ANY RESULT THAT DISPLEASES ME, I CAN SIMPLY REVERSE!
THERE IS NOTHING I NEED WORRY ON, FOR I AM THANOS.
AND THANOS IS SUPREME.
Huh, MOST DEFINITELY.
SUPREME.
BUT THANOS WAS TOO ARROGANT TO BE ANYONE'S THRALL.

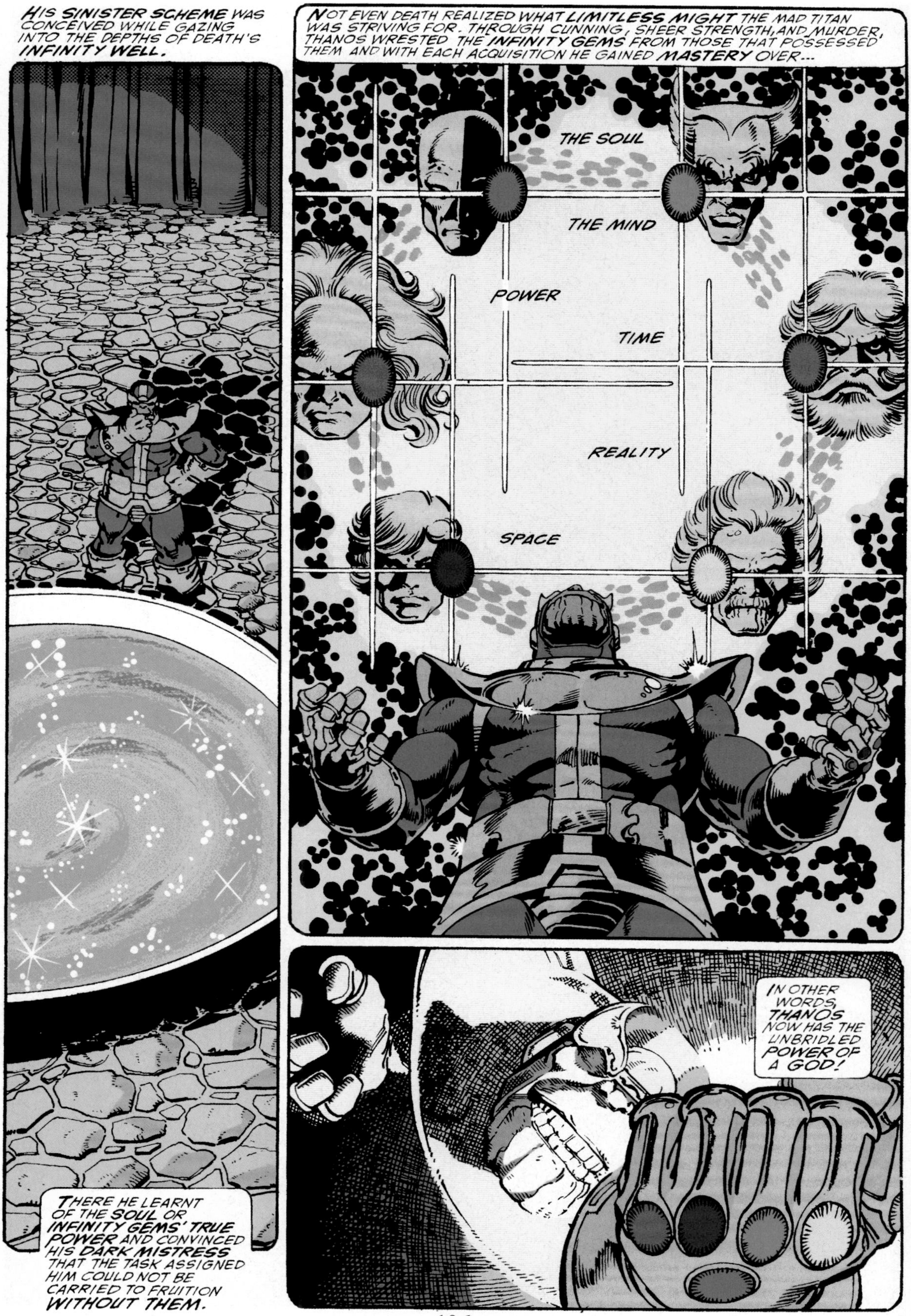
HIS SINISTER SCHEME WAS CONCEIVED WHILE GAZING INTO THE DEPTHS OF DEATH'S INFINITY WELL.
THERE HE LEARNT OF THE SOUL OR INFINITY GEMS' TRUE POWER AND CONVINCED HIS DARK MISTRESS THAT THE TASK ASSIGNED HIM COULD NOT BE CARRIED TO FRUITION WITHOUT THEM.
NOT EVEN DEATH REALIZED WHAT LIMITLESS MIGHT THE MAD TITAN WAS STRIVING FOR. THROUGH CUNNING, SHEER STRENGTH, AND MURDER, THANOS WRESTED THE INFINITY GEMS FROM THOSE THAT POSSESSED THEM AND WITH EACH ACQUISITION HE GAINED MASTERY OVER...
THE SOUL
THE MIND
POWER
TIME
REALITY
SPACE
IN OTHER WORDS, THANOS NOW HAS THE UNBRIDLED POWER OF A GOD!

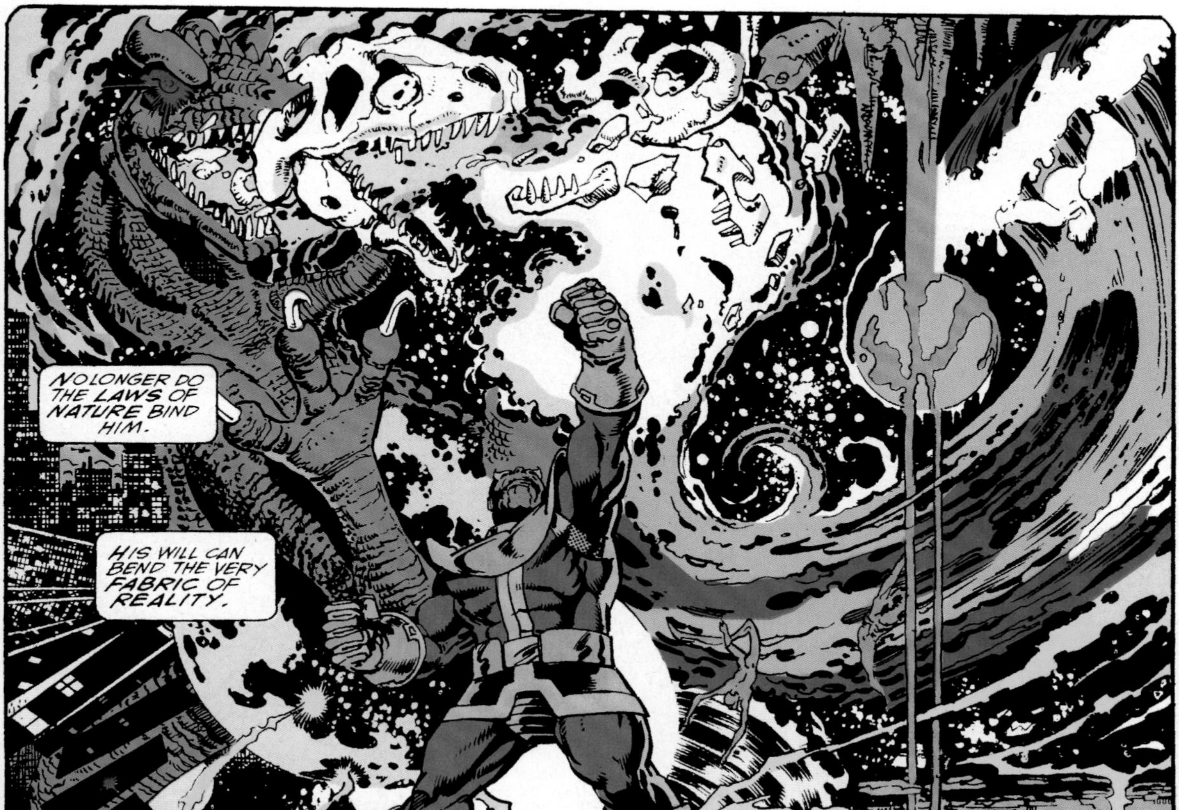
NO LONGER DO THE LAWS OF NATURE BIND HIM.
HIS WILL CAN BEND THE VERY FABRIC OF REALITY.
HE IS ALL AND ALL THERE IS IS NOW HIS TO COMMAND.
THANOS IS NOW MIGHTIER THAN DEATH HERSELF.
MORE POWERFUL THAN ANY FORCE IN THE UNIVERSE.

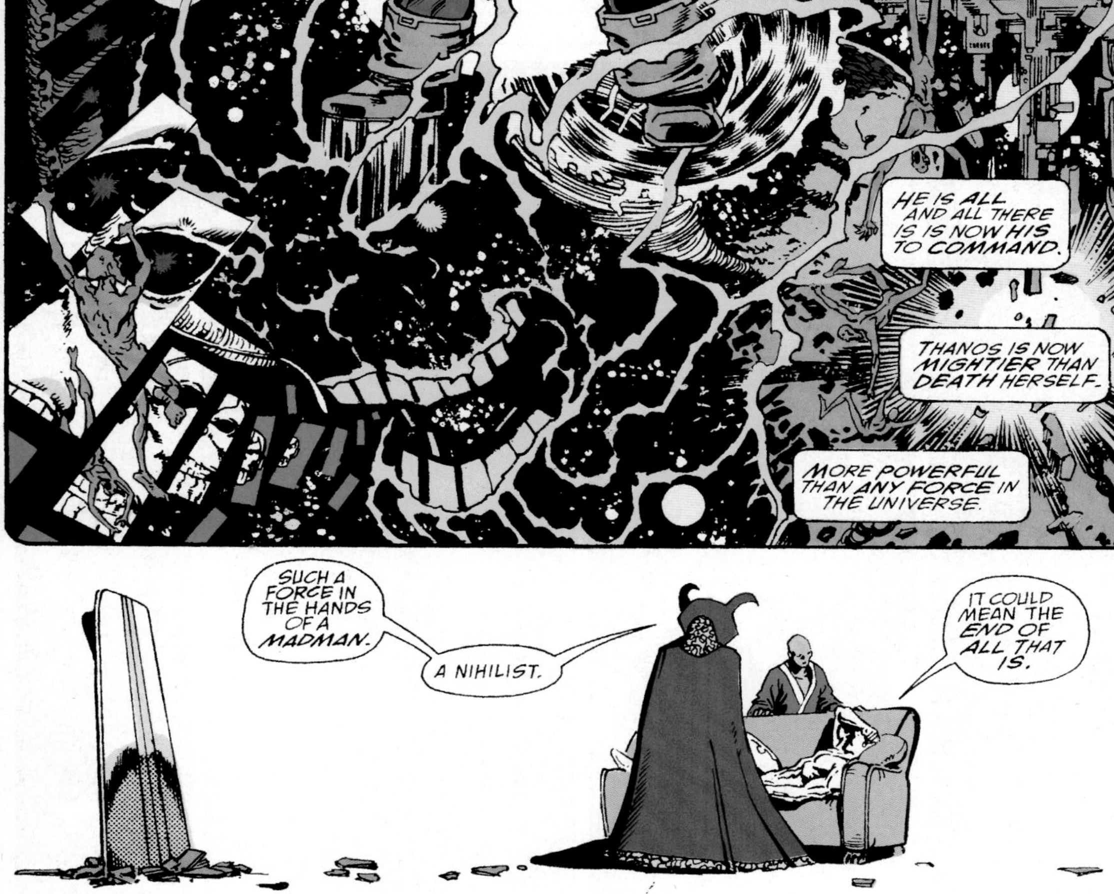
SUCH A FORCE IN THE HANDS OF A MADMAN.
A NIHILIST.
IT COULD MEAN THE END OF ALL THAT IS.

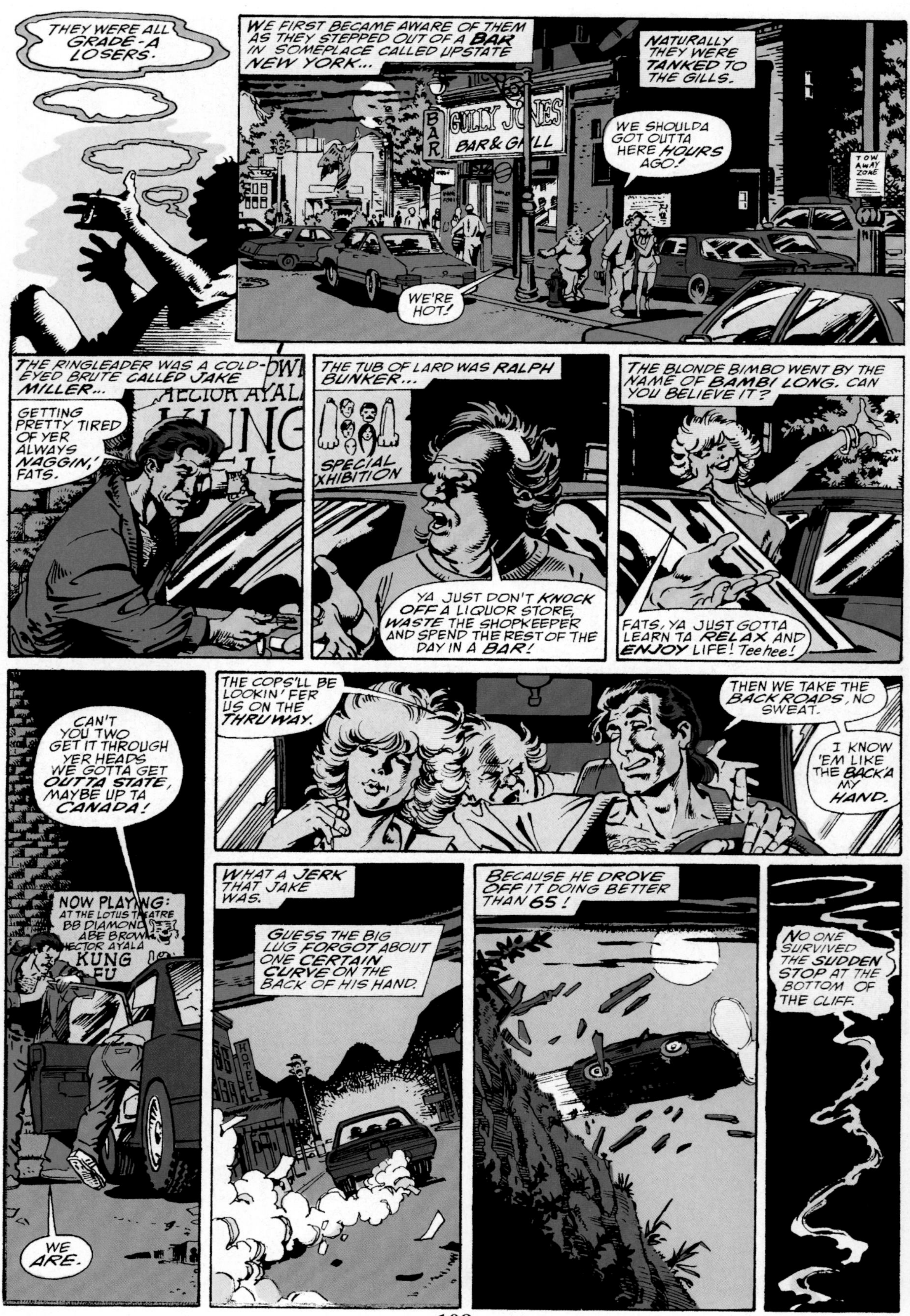

THEY WERE ALL GRADE-A LOSERS.
WE FIRST BECAME AWARE OF THEM AS THEY STEPPED OUT OF A BAR IN SOMEPLACE CALLED UPSTATE NEW YORK...
NATURALLY THEY WERE TANKED TO THE GILLS.
GULLY JONES BAR & GRILL
BAR
WE SHOULDA GOT OUTTA HERE HOURS AGO!
TOW AWAY ZONE
WE'RE HOT!
THE RINGLEADER WAS A COLD-EYED BRUTE CALLED JAKE MILLER...
GETTING PRETTY TIRED OF YER ALWAYS NAGGIN,' FATS.
THE TUB OF LARD WAS RALPH BUNKER...
SPECIAL XHIBITION
YA JUST DON'T KNOCK OFF A LIQUOR STORE, WASTE THE SHOPKEEPER AND SPEND THE REST OF THE DAY IN A BAR!
THE BLONDE BIMBO WENT BY THE NAME OF BAMBI LONG. CAN YOU BELIEVE IT?
FATS, YA JUST GOTTA LEARN TA RELAX AND ENJOY LIFE! Teehee!
CAN'T YOU TWO GET IT THROUGH YER HEADS WE GOTTA GET OUTTA STATE, MAYBE UP TA CANADA!
NOW PLAYING: AT THE LOTUS THEATRE BB DIAMOND ABE BROWN HECTOR AYALA KUNG FU
WE ARE.
THE COPS'LL BE LOOKIN' FER US ON THE THRUWAY.
THEN WE TAKE THE BACK ROADS, NO SWEAT.
I KNOW 'EM LIKE THE BACK'A MY HAND.
WHAT A JERK THAT JAKE WAS.
GUESS THE BIG LUG FORGOT ABOUT ONE CERTAIN CURVE ON THE BACK OF HIS HAND.
HOTEL
BECAUSE HE DROVE OFF IT DOING BETTER THAN 65!
NO ONE SURVIVED THE SUDDEN STOP AT THE BOTTOM OF THE CLIFF.

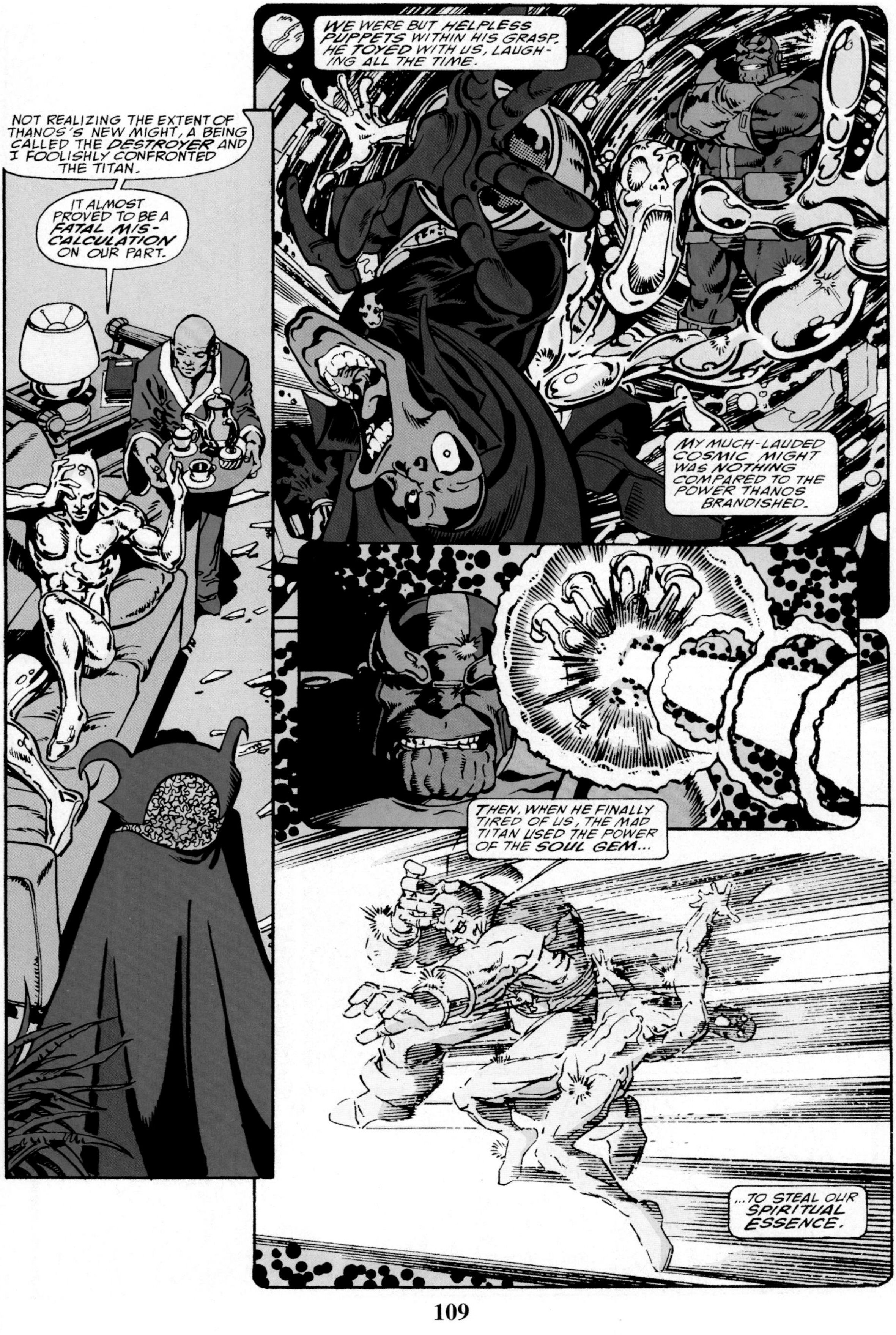
NOT REALIZING THE EXTENT OF THANOS'S NEW MIGHT, A BEING CALLED THE DESTROYER AND I FOOLISHLY CONFRONTED THE TITAN.
IT ALMOST PROVED TO BE A FATAL MIS-CALCULATION ON OUR PART.
WE WERE BUT HELPLESS PUPPETS WITHIN HIS GRASP. HE TOYED WITH US, LAUGHING ALL THE TIME.
MY MUCH-LAUDED COSMIC MIGHT WAS NOTHING COMPARED TO THE POWER THANOS BRANDISHED.
THEN, WHEN HE FINALLY TIRED OF US, THE MAD TITAN USED THE POWER OF THE SOUL GEM...
...TO STEAL OUR SPIRITUAL ESSENCE.

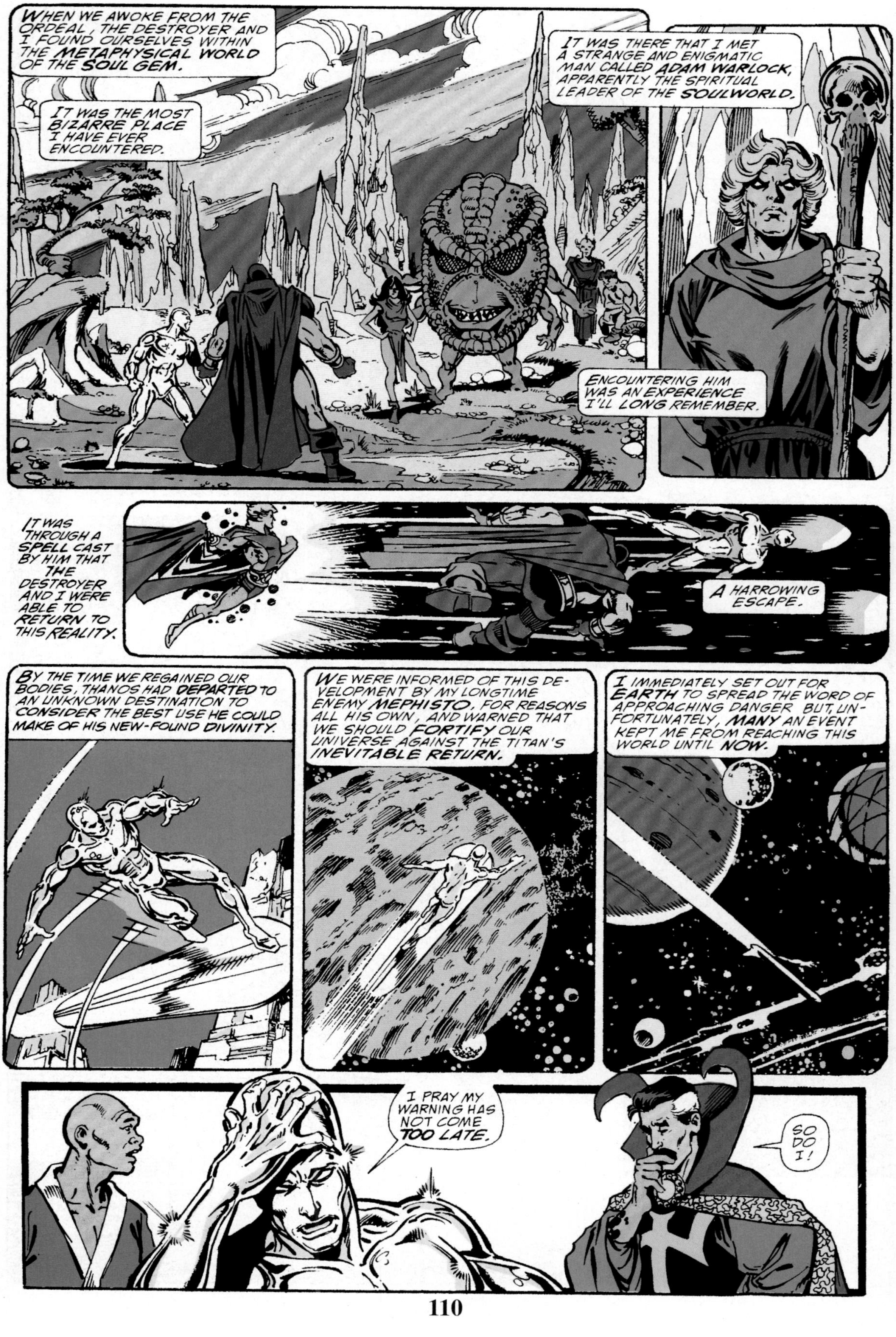
WHEN WE AWOKE FROM THE ORDEAL, THE DESTROYER AND I FOUND OURSELVES WITHIN THE METAPHYSICAL WORLD OF THE SOUL GEM.
IT WAS THE MOST BIZARRE PLACE I HAVE EVER ENCOUNTERED.
IT WAS THERE THAT I MET A STRANGE AND ENIGMATIC MAN CALLED ADAM WARLOCK, APPARENTLY THE SPIRITUAL LEADER OF THE SOULWORLD.
ENCOUNTERING HIM WAS AN EXPERIENCE I'LL LONG REMEMBER.
IT WAS THROUGH A SPELL CAST BY HIM THAT THE DESTROYER AND I WERE ABLE TO RETURN TO THIS REALITY.
A HARROWING ESCAPE.
BY THE TIME WE REGAINED OUR BODIES, THANOS HAD DEPARTED TO AN UNKNOWN DESTINATION TO CONSIDER THE BEST USE HE COULD MAKE OF HIS NEW-FOUND DIVINITY.
WE WERE INFORMED OF THIS DEVELOPMENT BY MY LONGTIME ENEMY MEPHISTO, FOR REASONS ALL HIS OWN, AND WARNED THAT WE SHOULD FORTIFY OUR UNIVERSE AGAINST THE TITAN'S INEVITABLE RETURN.
I IMMEDIATELY SET OUT FOR EARTH TO SPREAD THE WORD OF APPROACHING DANGER BUT, UNFORTUNATELY, MANY AN EVENT KEPT ME FROM REACHING THIS WORLD UNTIL NOW.
I PRAY MY WARNING HAS NOT COME TOO LATE.
SO DO I!

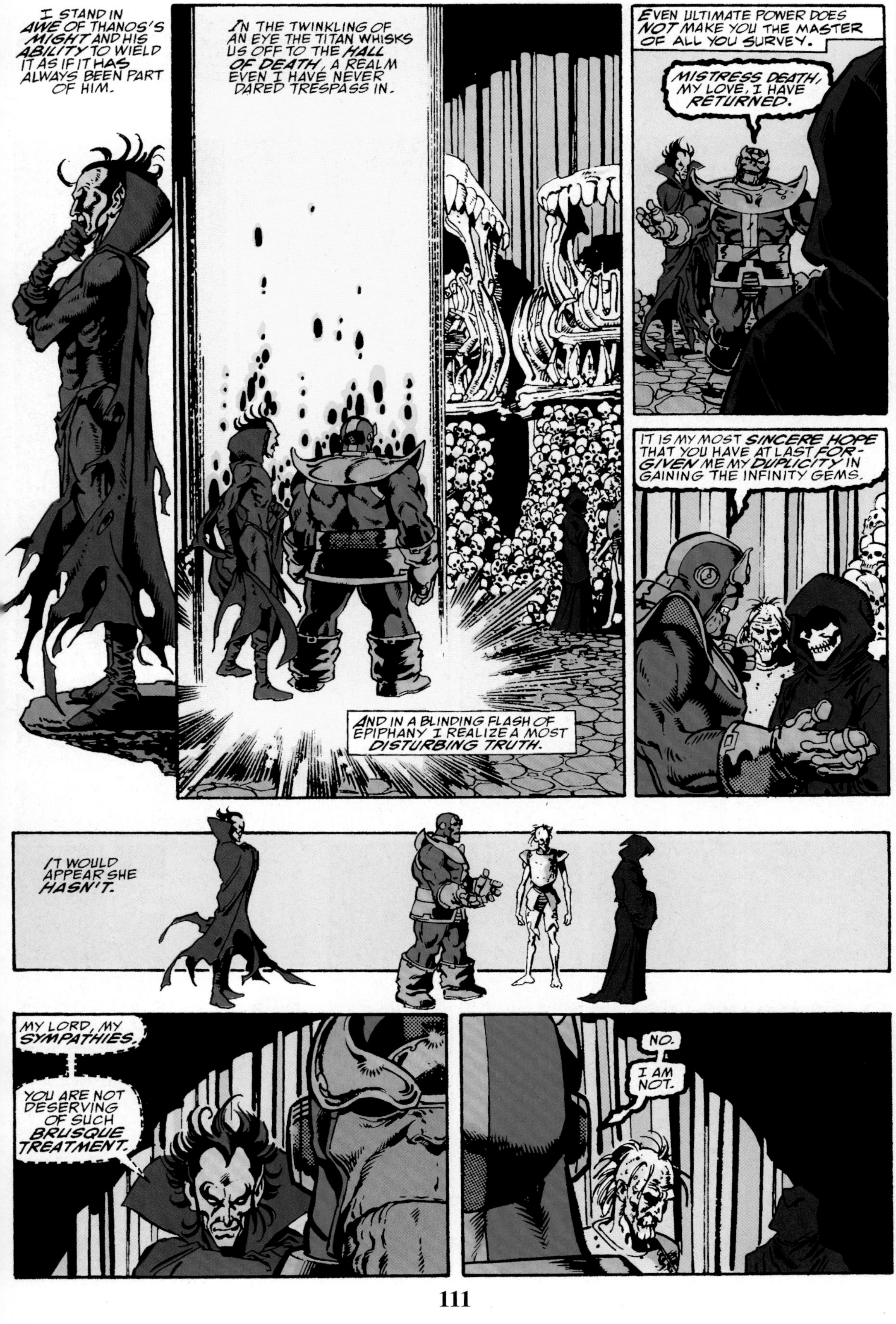
I STAND IN AWE OF THANOS'S MIGHT AND HIS ABILITY TO WIELD IT AS IF IT HAS ALWAYS BEEN PART OF HIM.
IN THE TWINKLING OF AN EYE THE TITAN WHISKS US OFF TO THE HALL OF DEATH, A REALM EVEN I HAVE NEVER DARED TRESPASS IN.
AND IN A BLINDING FLASH OF EPIPHANY I REALIZE A MOST DISTURBING TRUTH.
EVEN ULTIMATE POWER DOES NOT MAKE YOU THE MASTER OF ALL YOU SURVEY.
MISTRESS DEATH, MY LOVE, I HAVE RETURNED.
IT IS MY MOST SINCERE HOPE THAT YOU HAVE AT LAST FORGIVEN ME MY DUPLICITY IN GAINING THE INFINITY GEMS.
IT WOULD APPEAR SHE HASN'T.
MY LORD, MY SYMPATHIES.
YOU ARE NOT DESERVING OF SUCH BRUSQUE TREATMENT.
NO.
I AM NOT.

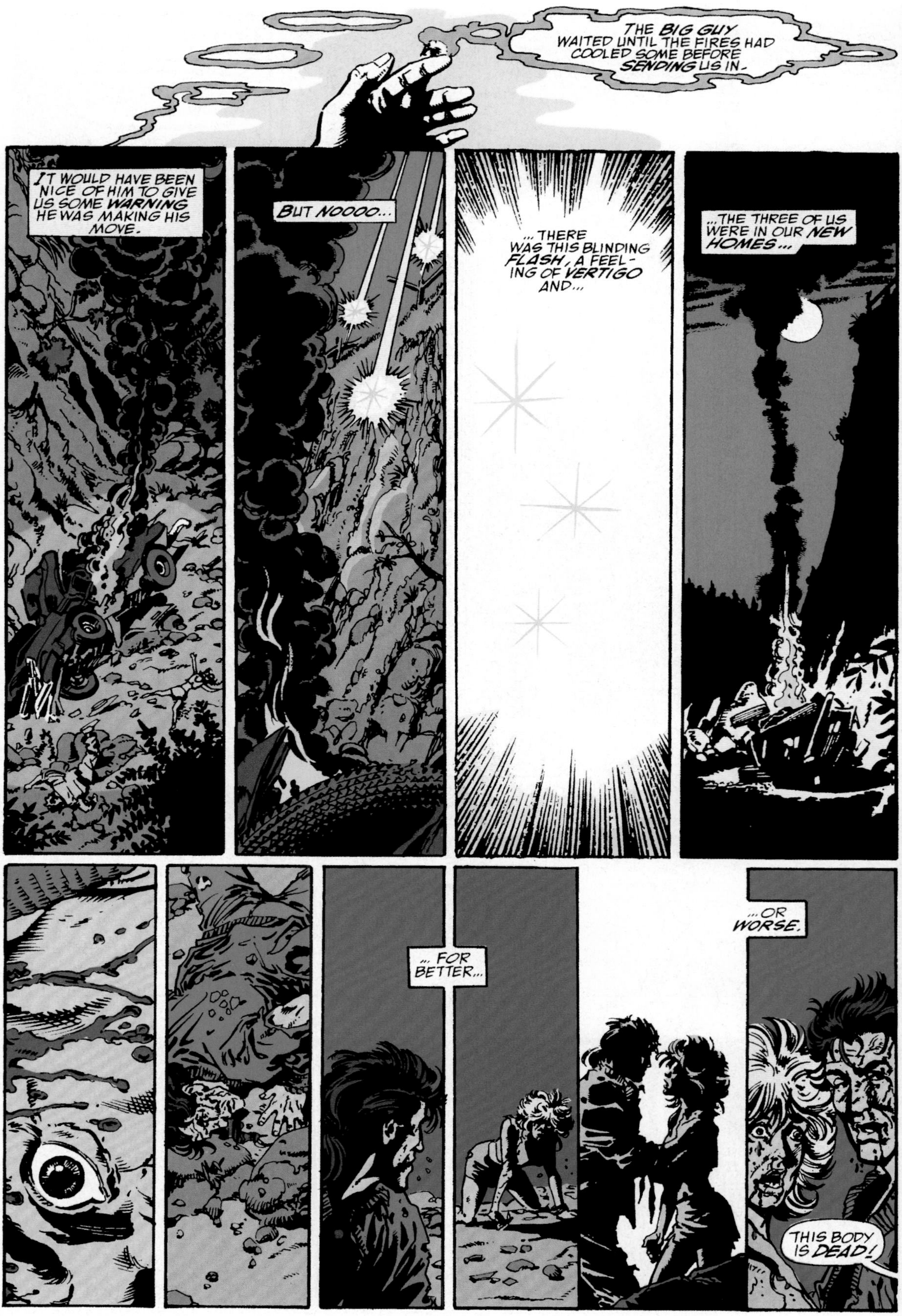

THE BIG GUY WAITED UNTIL THE FIRES HAD COOLED SOME BEFORE SENDING US IN.
IT WOULD HAVE BEEN NICE OF HIM TO GIVE US SOME WARNING HE WAS MAKING HIS MOVE.
BUT NOOOO...
...THERE WAS THIS BLINDING FLASH, A FEELING OF VERTIGO AND...
...THE THREE OF US WERE IN OUR NEW HOMES...
...FOR BETTER...
...OR WORSE.
THIS BODY IS DEAD!

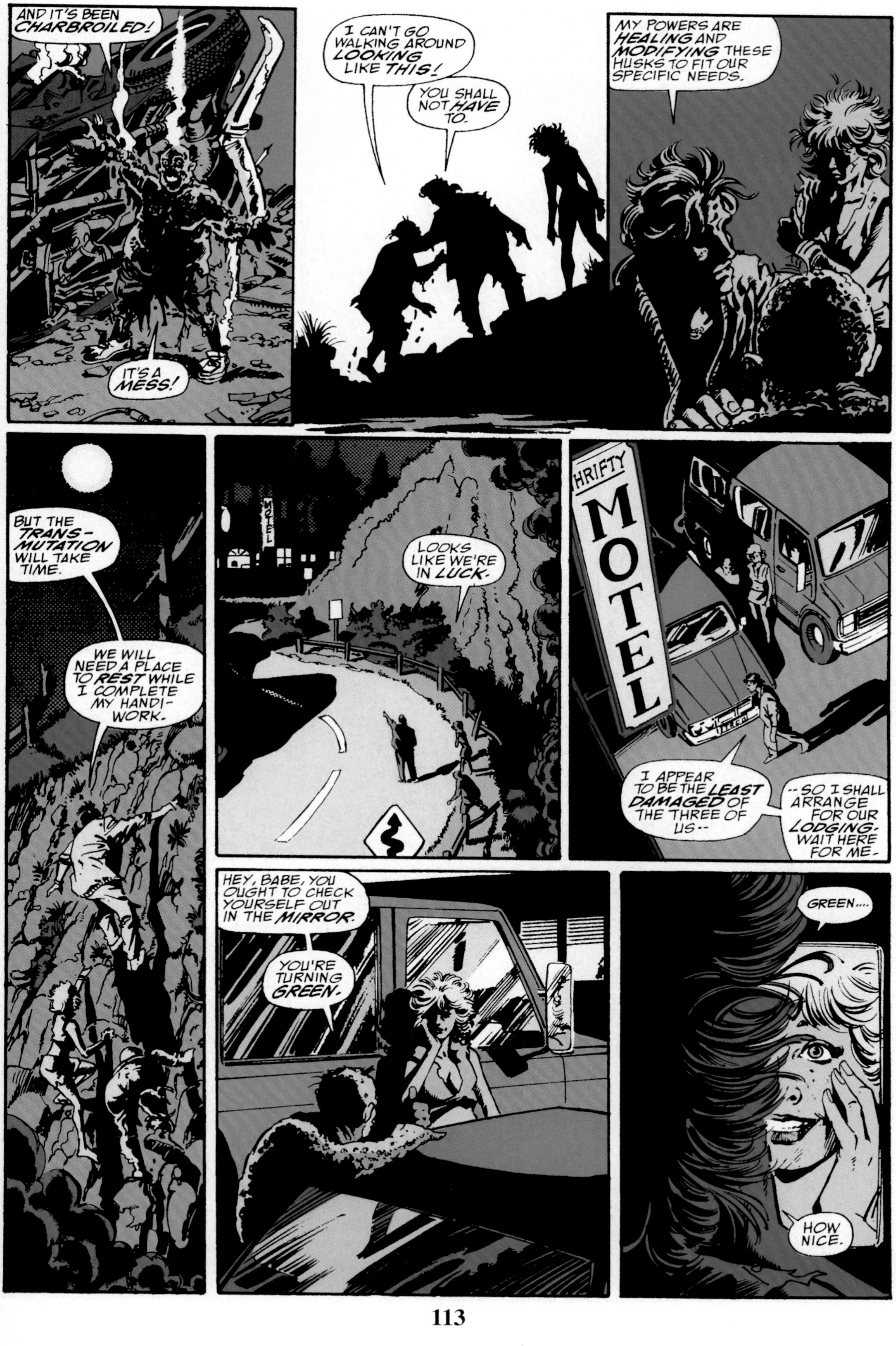
AND IT'S BEEN CHARBROILED!
IT'S A MESS!
I CAN'T GO WALKING AROUND LOOKING LIKE THIS!
YOU SHALL NOT HAVE TO.
MY POWERS ARE HEALING AND MODIFYING THESE HUSKS TO FIT OUR SPECIFIC NEEDS.
BUT THE TRANSMUTATION WILL TAKE TIME.
WE WILL NEED A PLACE TO REST WHILE I COMPLETE MY HANDIWORK.
MOTEL
LOOKS LIKE WE'RE IN LUCK.
HRIFTY
MOTEL
I APPEAR TO BE THE LEAST DAMAGED OF THE THREE OF US--
--SO I SHALL ARRANGE FOR OUR LODGING. WAIT HERE FOR ME.
HEY, BABE, YOU OUGHT TO CHECK YOURSELF OUT IN THE MIRROR.
YOU'RE TURNING GREEN.
GREEN....
HOW NICE.

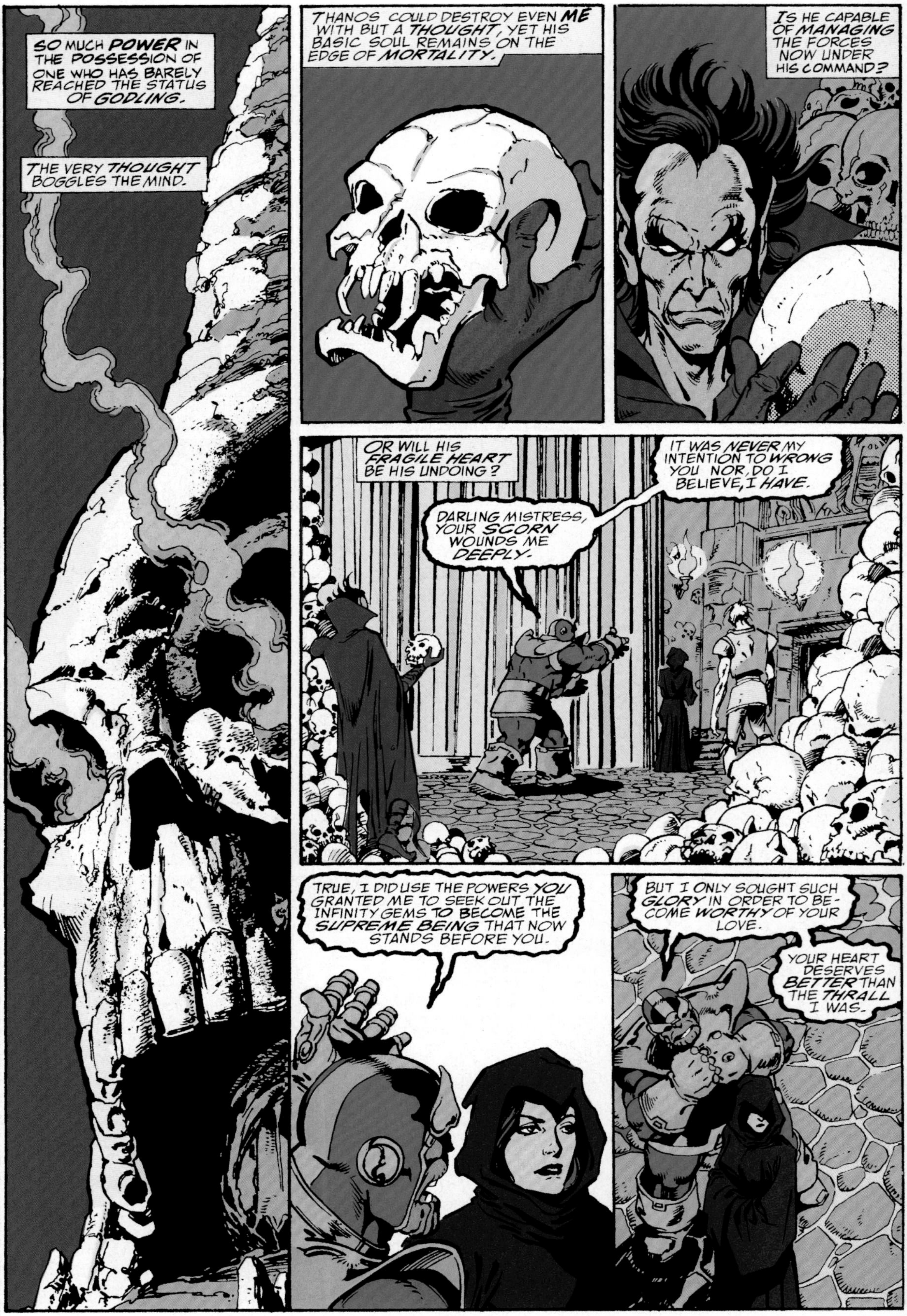
SO MUCH POWER IN THE POSSESSION OF ONE WHO HAS BARELY REACHED THE STATUS OF GODLING.
THE VERY THOUGHT BOGGLES THE MIND.
THANOS COULD DESTROY EVEN ME WITH BUT A THOUGHT, YET HIS BASIC SOUL REMAINS ON THE EDGE OF MORTALITY.
IS HE CAPABLE OF MANAGING THE FORCES NOW UNDER HIS COMMAND?
OR WILL HIS FRAGILE HEART BE HIS UNDOING?
DARLING MISTRESS, YOUR SCORN WOUNDS ME DEEPLY.
IT WAS NEVER MY INTENTION TO WRONG YOU NOR, DO I BELIEVE, I HAVE.
TRUE, I DID USE THE POWERS YOU GRANTED ME TO SEEK OUT THE INFINITY GEMS TO BECOME THE SUPREME BEING THAT NOW STANDS BEFORE YOU.
BUT I ONLY SOUGHT SUCH GLORY IN ORDER TO BE-COME WORTHY OF YOUR LOVE.
YOUR HEART DESERVES BETTER THAN THE THRALL I WAS.

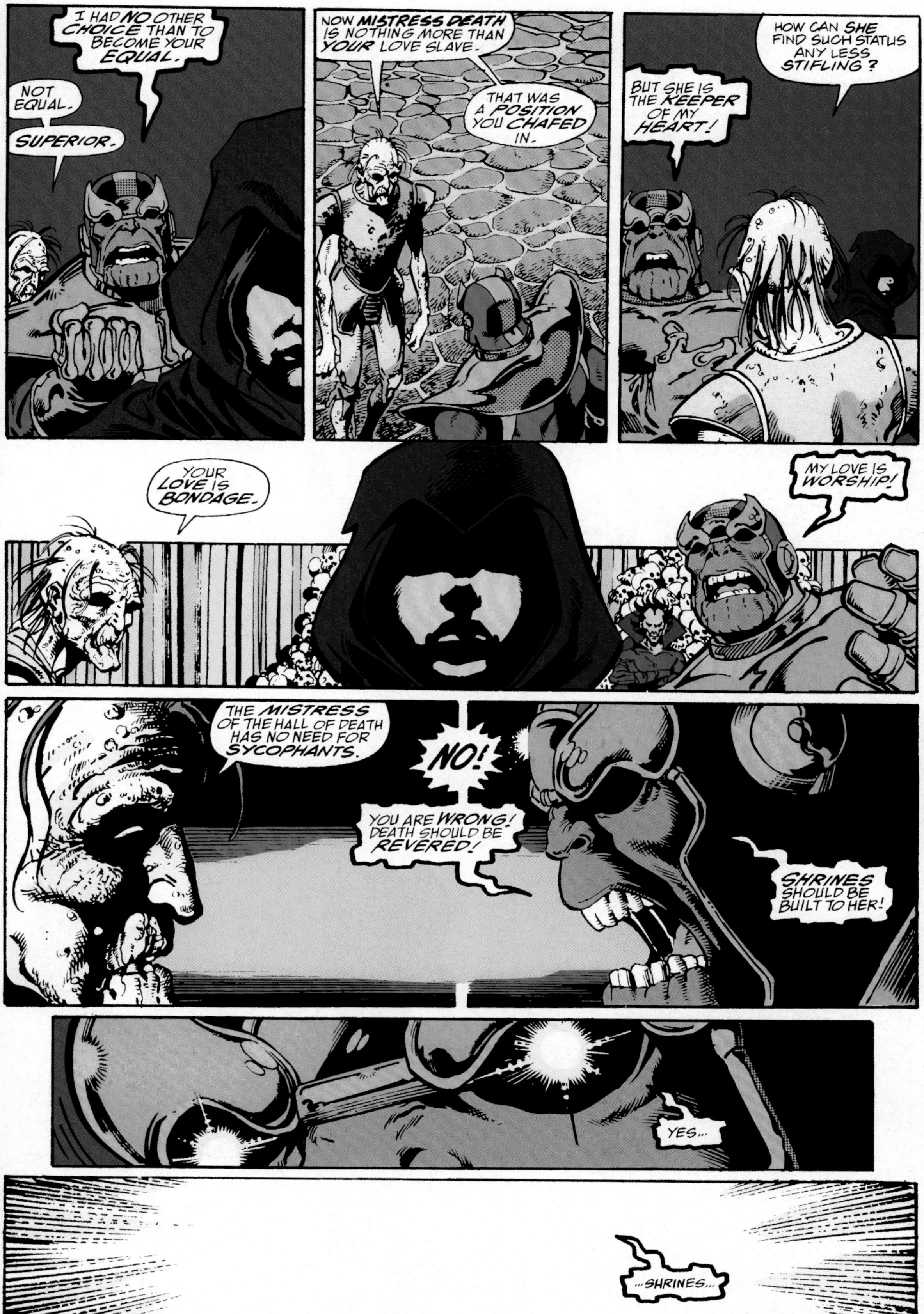

I HAD NO OTHER CHOICE THAN TO BECOME YOUR EQUAL.
NOT EQUAL.
SUPERIOR.
NOW MISTRESS DEATH IS NOTHING MORE THAN YOUR LOVE SLAVE.
THAT WAS A POSITION YOU CHAFED IN.
BUT SHE IS THE KEEPER OF MY HEART!
HOW CAN SHE FIND SUCH STATUS ANY LESS STIFLING?
YOUR LOVE IS BONDAGE.
MY LOVE IS WORSHIP!
THE MISTRESS OF THE HALL OF DEATH HAS NO NEED FOR SYCOPHANTS.
NO!
YOU ARE WRONG! DEATH SHOULD BE REVERED!
SHRINES SHOULD BE BUILT TO HER!
YES...
...SHRINES...

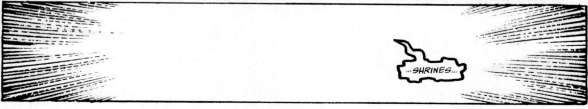

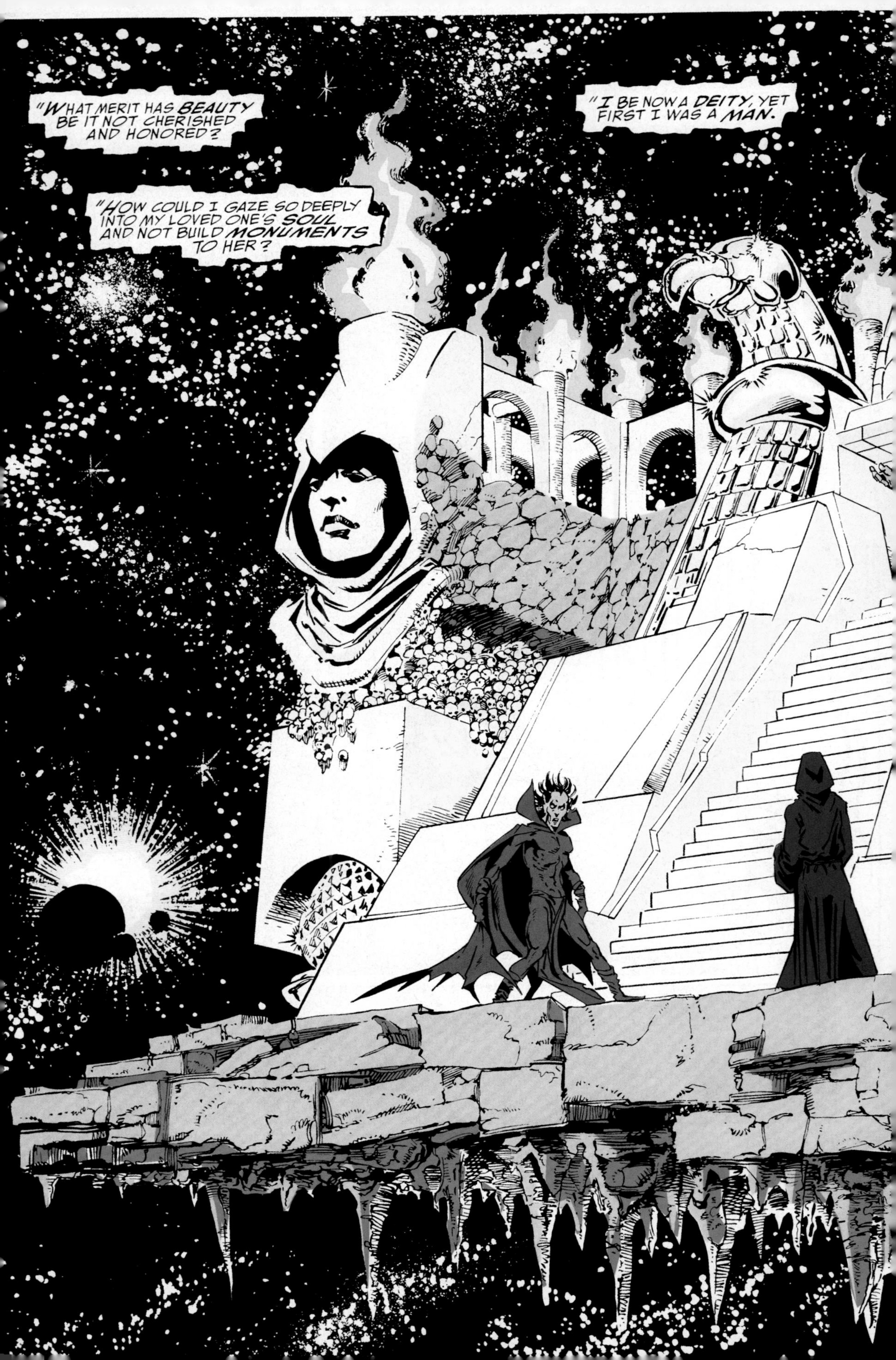
"WHAT MERIT HAS BEAUTY BE IT NOT CHERISHED AND HONORED?
"HOW COULD I GAZE SO DEEPLY INTO MY LOVED ONE'S SOUL AND NOT BUILD MONUMENTS TO HER?
"I BE NOW A DEITY, YET FIRST I WAS A MAN.

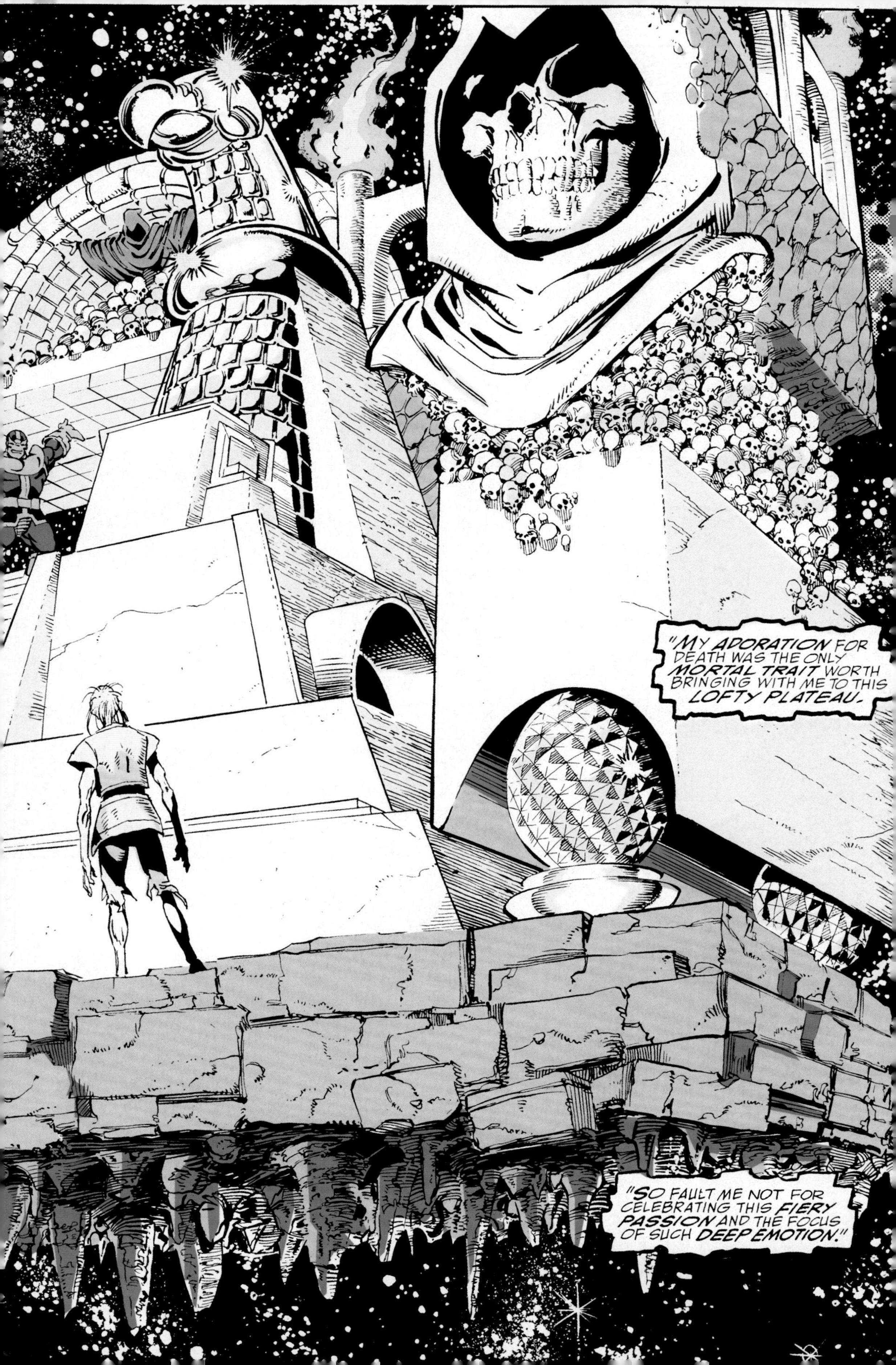
"MY ADORATION FOR DEATH WAS THE ONLY MORTAL TRAIT WORTH BRINGING WITH ME TO THIS LOFTY PLATEAU.
"SO FAULT ME NOT FOR CELEBRATING THIS FIERY PASSION AND THE FOCUS OF SUCH DEEP EMOTION."

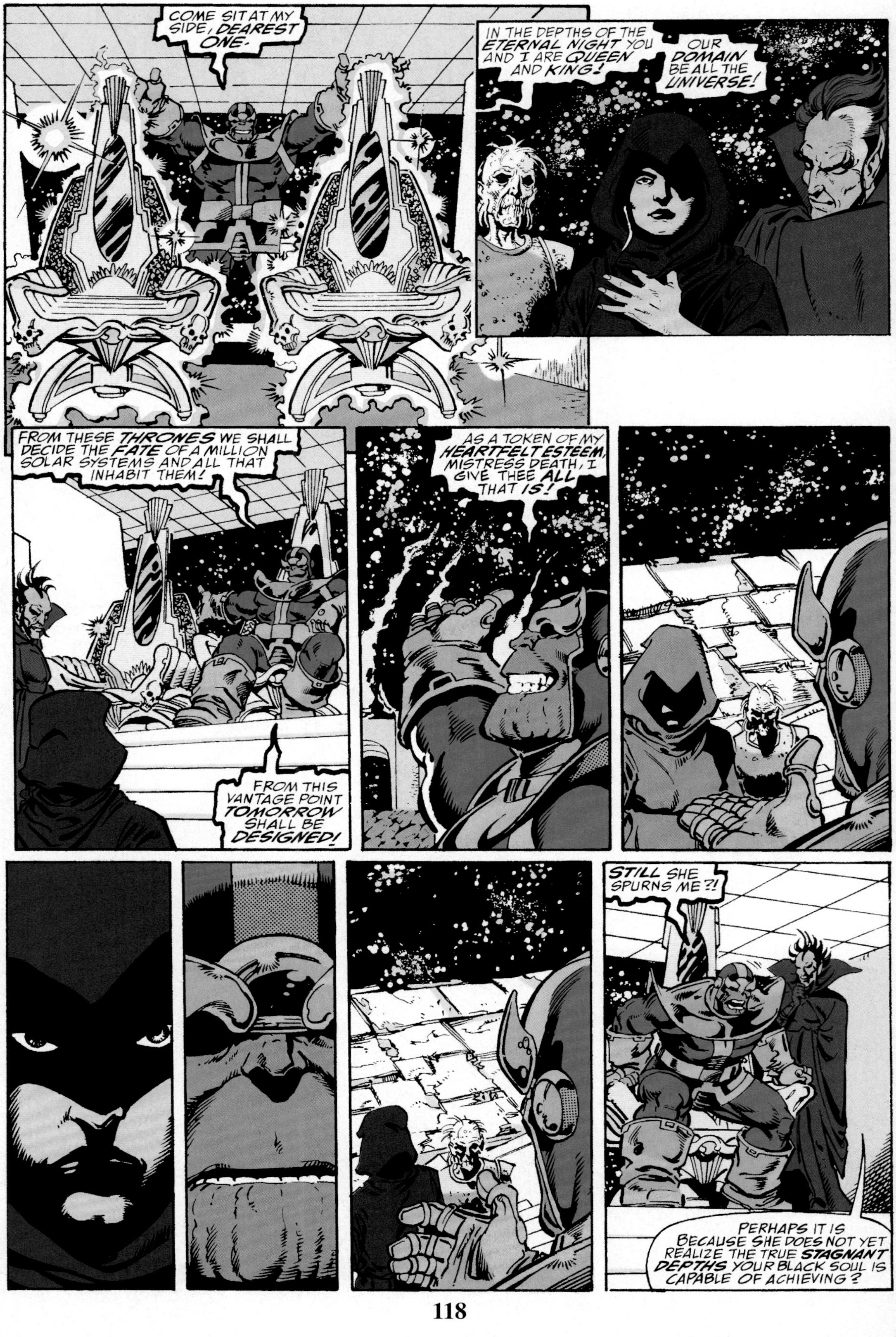

COME SIT AT MY SIDE, DEAREST ONE.
IN THE DEPTHS OF THE ETERNAL NIGHT YOU AND I ARE QUEEN AND KING!
OUR DOMAIN BE ALL THE UNIVERSE!
FROM THESE THRONES WE SHALL DECIDE THE FATE OF A MILLION SOLAR SYSTEMS AND ALL THAT INHABIT THEM!
FROM THIS VANTAGE POINT TOMORROW SHALL BE DESIGNED!
AS A TOKEN OF MY HEARTFELT ESTEEM, MISTRESS DEATH, I GIVE THEE ALL THAT IS!
STILL SHE SPURNS ME?!
PERHAPS IT IS BECAUSE SHE DOES NOT YET REALIZE THE TRUE STAGNANT DEPTHS YOUR BLACK SOUL IS CAPABLE OF ACHIEVING?

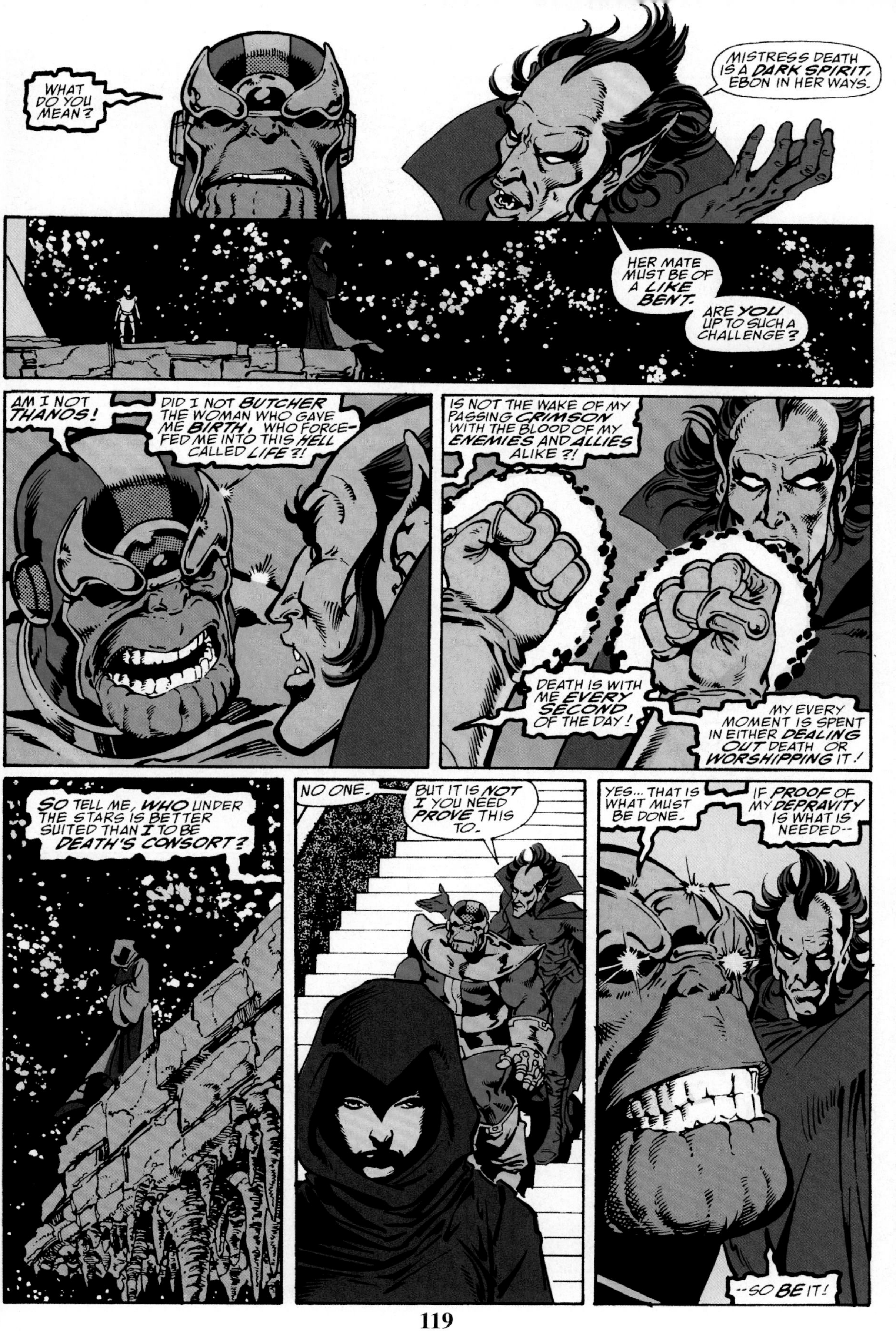
WHAT DO YOU MEAN?
MISTRESS DEATH IS A DARK SPIRIT, EBON IN HER WAYS.
HER MATE MUST BE OF A LIKE BENT.
ARE YOU UP TO SUCH A CHALLENGE?
AM I NOT THANOS!
DID I NOT BUTCHER THE WOMAN WHO GAVE ME BIRTH, WHO FORCE-FED ME INTO THIS HELL CALLED LIFE?!
IS NOT THE WAKE OF MY PASSING CRIMSON WITH THE BLOOD OF MY ENEMIES AND ALLIES ALIKE?!
DEATH IS WITH ME EVERY SECOND OF THE DAY!
MY EVERY MOMENT IS SPENT IN EITHER DEALING OUT DEATH OR WORSHIPPING IT!
SO TELL ME, WHO UNDER THE STARS IS BETTER SUITED THAN I TO BE DEATH'S CONSORT?
NO ONE.
BUT IT IS NOT I YOU NEED PROVE THIS TO.
YES... THAT IS WHAT MUST BE DONE.
IF PROOF OF MY DEPRAVITY IS WHAT IS NEEDED--
--SO BE IT!

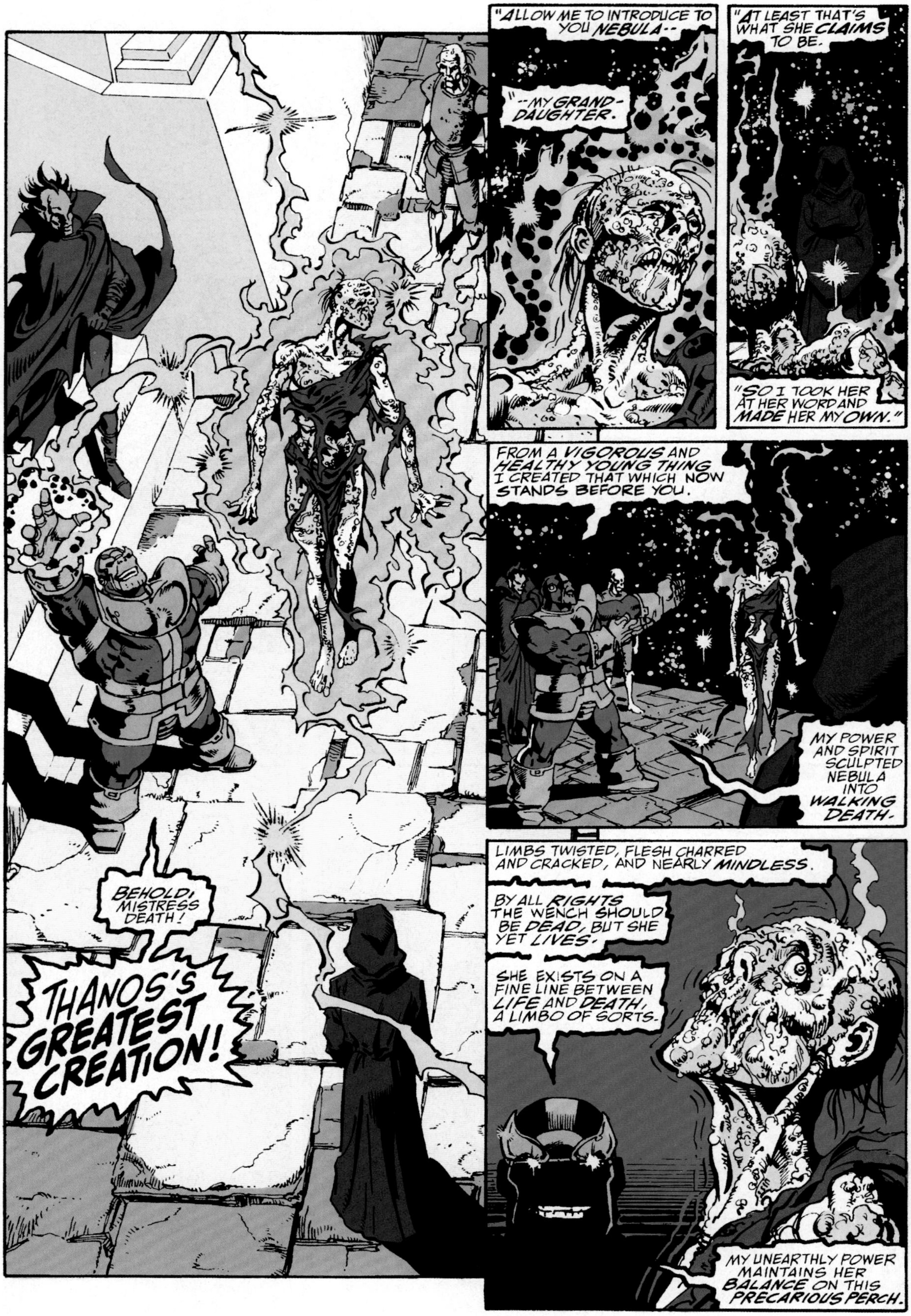
BEHOLD, MISTRESS DEATH!
THANOS'S GREATEST CREATION!
"ALLOW ME TO INTRODUCE TO YOU NEBULA--
"--MY GRAND-DAUGHTER.
"AT LEAST THAT'S WHAT SHE CLAIMS TO BE.
"SO I TOOK HER AT HER WORD AND MADE HER MY OWN."
FROM A VIGOROUS AND HEALTHY YOUNG THING I CREATED THAT WHICH NOW STANDS BEFORE YOU.
MY POWER AND SPIRIT SCULPTED NEBULA INTO WALKING DEATH-
LIMBS TWISTED, FLESH CHARRED AND CRACKED, AND NEARLY MINDLESS.
BY ALL RIGHTS THE WENCH SHOULD BE DEAD, BUT SHE YET LIVES.
SHE EXISTS ON A FINE LINE BETWEEN LIFE AND DEATH, A LIMBO OF SORTS.
MY UNEARTHLY POWER MAINTAINS HER BALANCE ON THIS PRECARIOUS PERCH.

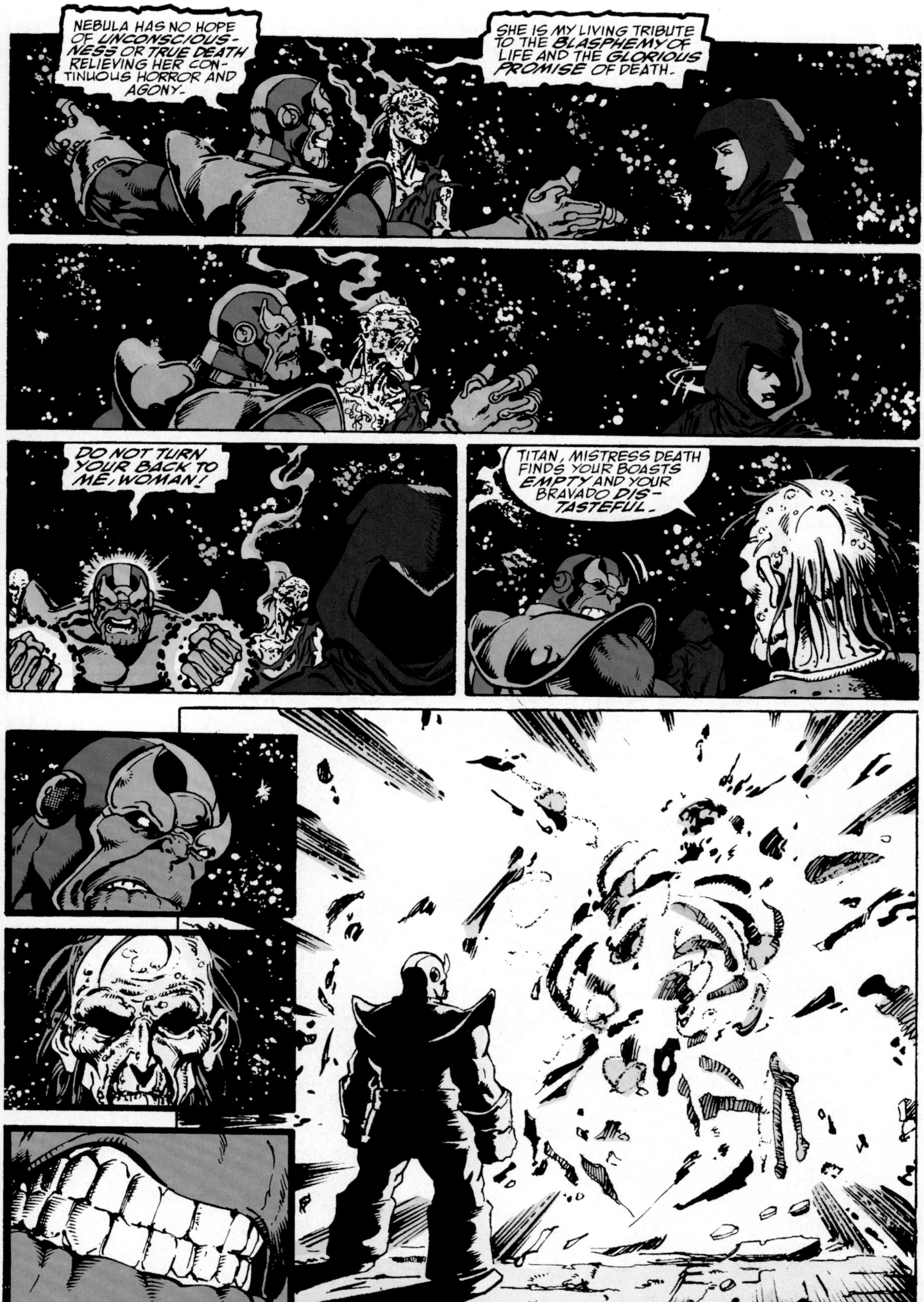
NEBULA HAS NO HOPE OF UNCONSCIOUS-NESS OR TRUE DEATH RELIEVING HER CON-TINUOUS HORROR AND AGONY.
SHE IS MY LIVING TRIBUTE TO THE BLASPHEMY OF LIFE AND THE GLORIOUS PROMISE OF DEATH.
DO NOT TURN YOUR BACK TO ME, WOMAN!
TITAN, MISTRESS DEATH FINDS YOUR BOASTS EMPTY AND YOUR BRAVADO DIS-TASTEFUL.

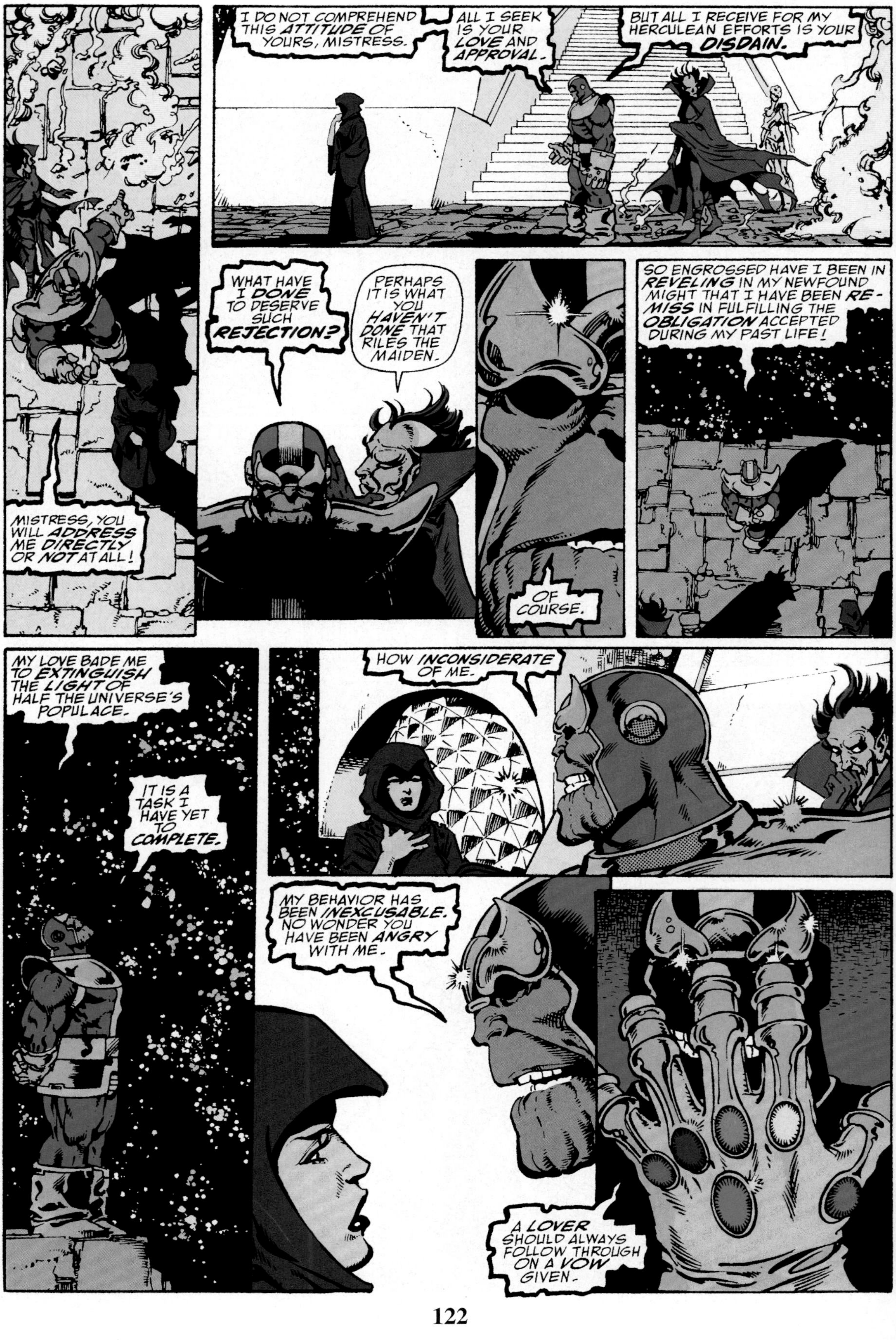
I DO NOT COMPREHEND THIS ATTITUDE OF YOURS, MISTRESS.
ALL I SEEK IS YOUR LOVE AND APPROVAL.
BUT ALL I RECEIVE FOR MY HERCULEAN EFFORTS IS YOUR DISDAIN.
MISTRESS, YOU WILL ADDRESS ME DIRECTLY OR NOT AT ALL!
WHAT HAVE I DONE TO DESERVE SUCH REJECTION?
PERHAPS IT IS WHAT YOU HAVEN'T DONE THAT RILES THE MAIDEN.
OF COURSE.
SO ENGROSSED HAVE I BEEN IN REVELING IN MY NEWFOUND MIGHT THAT I HAVE BEEN RE-MISS IN FULFILLING THE OBLIGATION ACCEPTED DURING MY PAST LIFE!
MY LOVE BADE ME TO EXTINGUISH THE LIGHT OF HALF THE UNIVERSE'S POPULACE.
IT IS A TASK I HAVE YET TO COMPLETE.
HOW INCONSIDERATE OF ME.
MY BEHAVIOR HAS BEEN INEXCUSABLE. NO WONDER YOU HAVE BEEN ANGRY WITH ME.
A LOVER SHOULD ALWAYS FOLLOW THROUGH ON A VOW GIVEN.

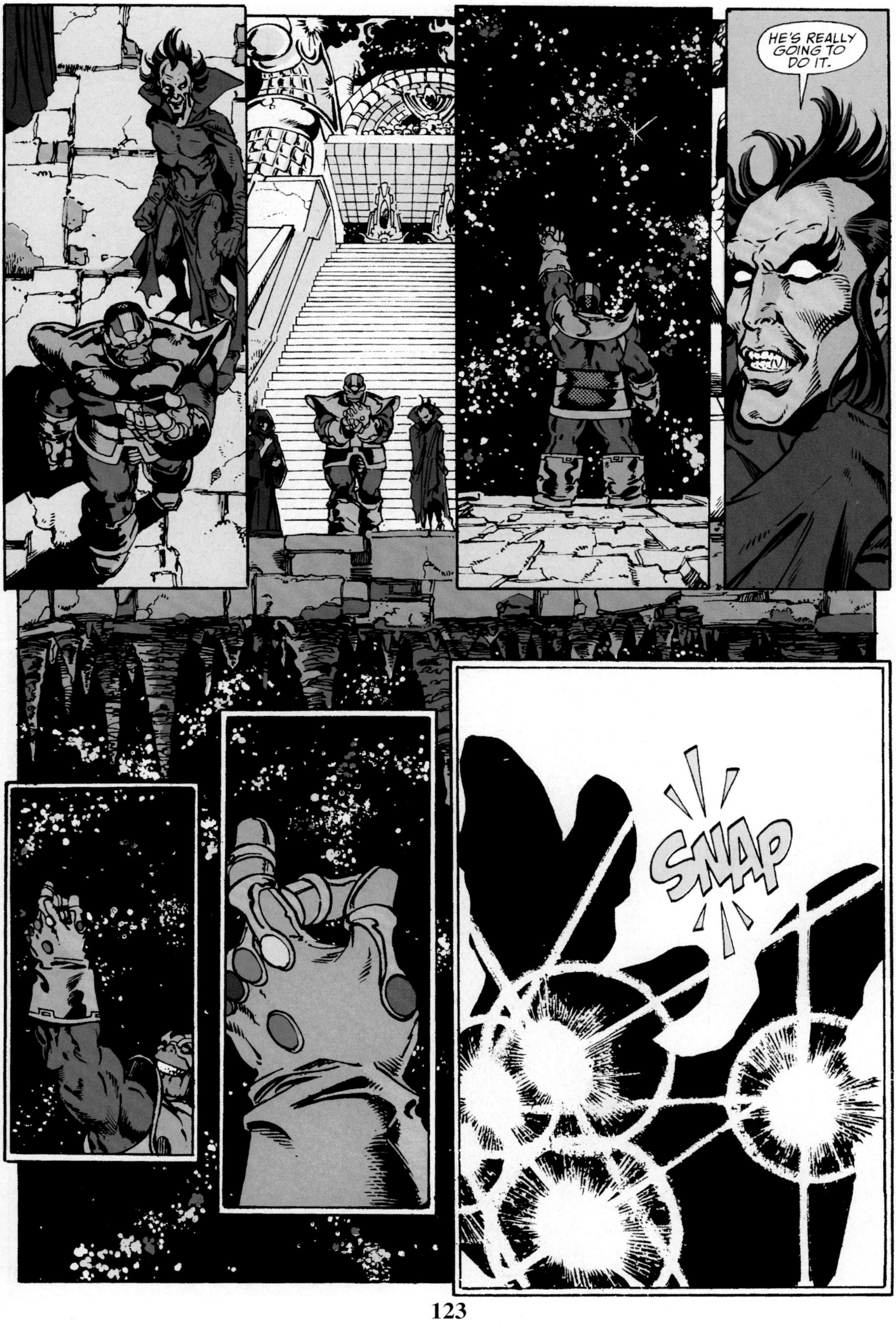
HE'S REALLY GOING TO DO IT.
SNAP

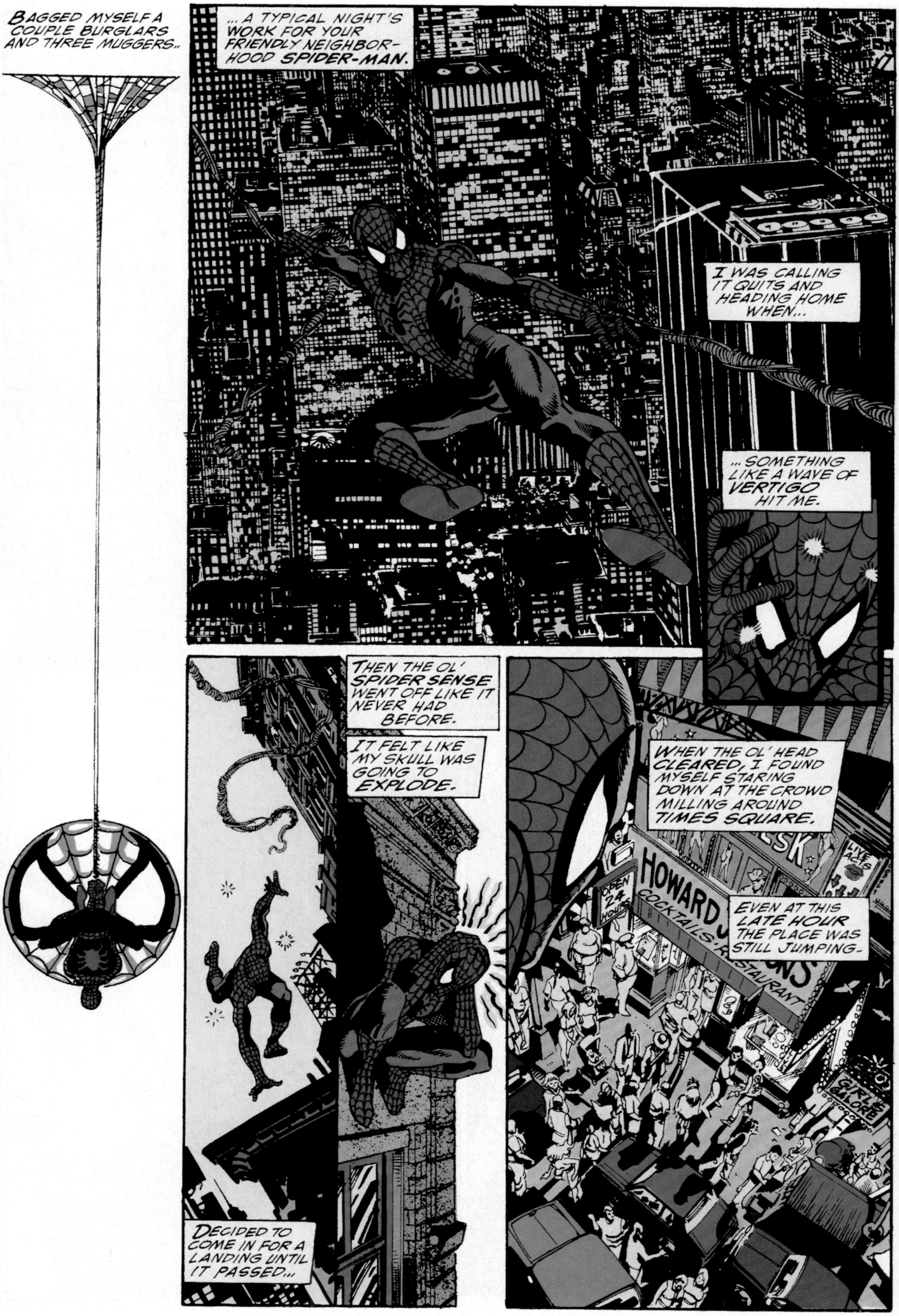
BAGGED MYSELF A COUPLE BURGLARS AND THREE MUGGERS..
...A TYPICAL NIGHT'S WORK FOR YOUR FRIENDLY NEIGHBOR-HOOD SPIDER-MAN.
I WAS CALLING IT QUITS AND HEADING HOME WHEN...
...SOMETHING LIKE A WAVE OF VERTIGO HIT ME.
THEN THE OL' SPIDER SENSE WENT OFF LIKE IT NEVER HAD BEFORE.
IT FELT LIKE MY SKULL WAS GOING TO EXPLODE.
DECIDED TO COME IN FOR A LANDING UNTIL IT PASSED...
WHEN THE OL' HEAD CLEARED, I FOUND MYSELF STARING DOWN AT THE CROWD MILLING AROUND TIMES SQUARE.
OPEN 24 HOURS
LIVE ACTS
EVEN AT THIS LATE HOUR THE PLACE WAS STILL JUMPING-
GIRLS GALORE

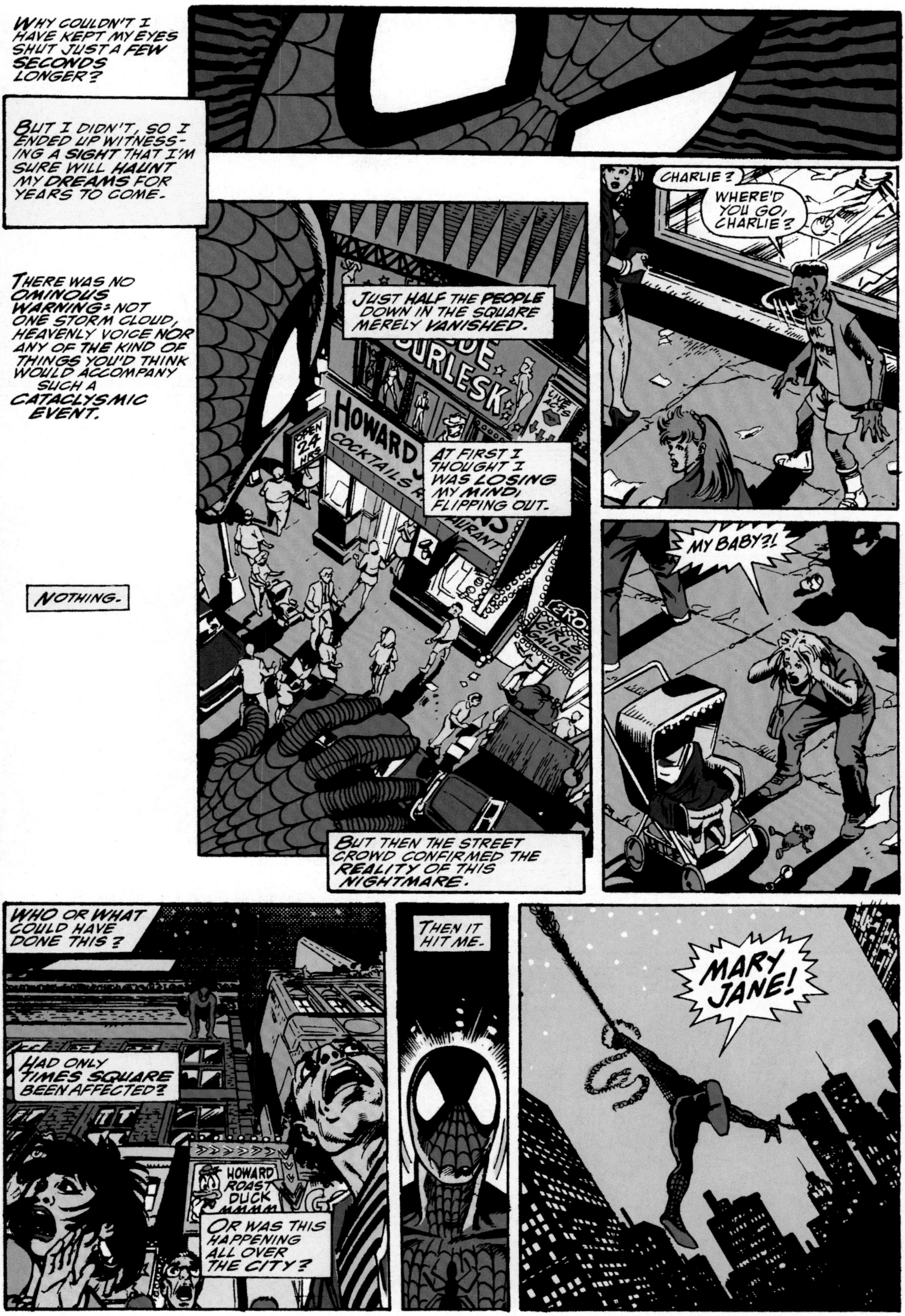
WHY COULDN'T I HAVE KEPT MY EYES SHUT JUST A FEW SECONDS LONGER?
BUT I DIDN'T, SO I ENDED UP WITNESSING A SIGHT THAT I'M SURE WILL HAUNT MY DREAMS FOR YEARS TO COME.
CHARLIE?
WHERE'D YOU GO, CHARLIE?
THERE WAS NO OMINOUS WARNING: NOT ONE STORM CLOUD, HEAVENLY VOICE NOR ANY OF THE KIND OF THINGS YOU'D THINK WOULD ACCOMPANY SUCH A CATACLYSMIC EVENT.
JUST HALF THE PEOPLE DOWN IN THE SQUARE MERELY VANISHED.
BURLESK
HOWARD J
COCKTAILS
OPEN 24 HRS
LIVE ACTS
AT FIRST I THOUGHT I WAS LOSING MY MIND, FLIPPING OUT.
NOTHING.
MY BABY?!
GIRLS GALORE
BUT THEN THE STREET CROWD CONFIRMED THE REALITY OF THIS NIGHTMARE.
WHO OR WHAT COULD HAVE DONE THIS?
HAD ONLY TIMES SQUARE BEEN AFFECTED?
HOWARD ROAST DUCK MMMM
OR WAS THIS HAPPENING ALL OVER THE CITY?
THEN IT HIT ME.
MARY JANE!

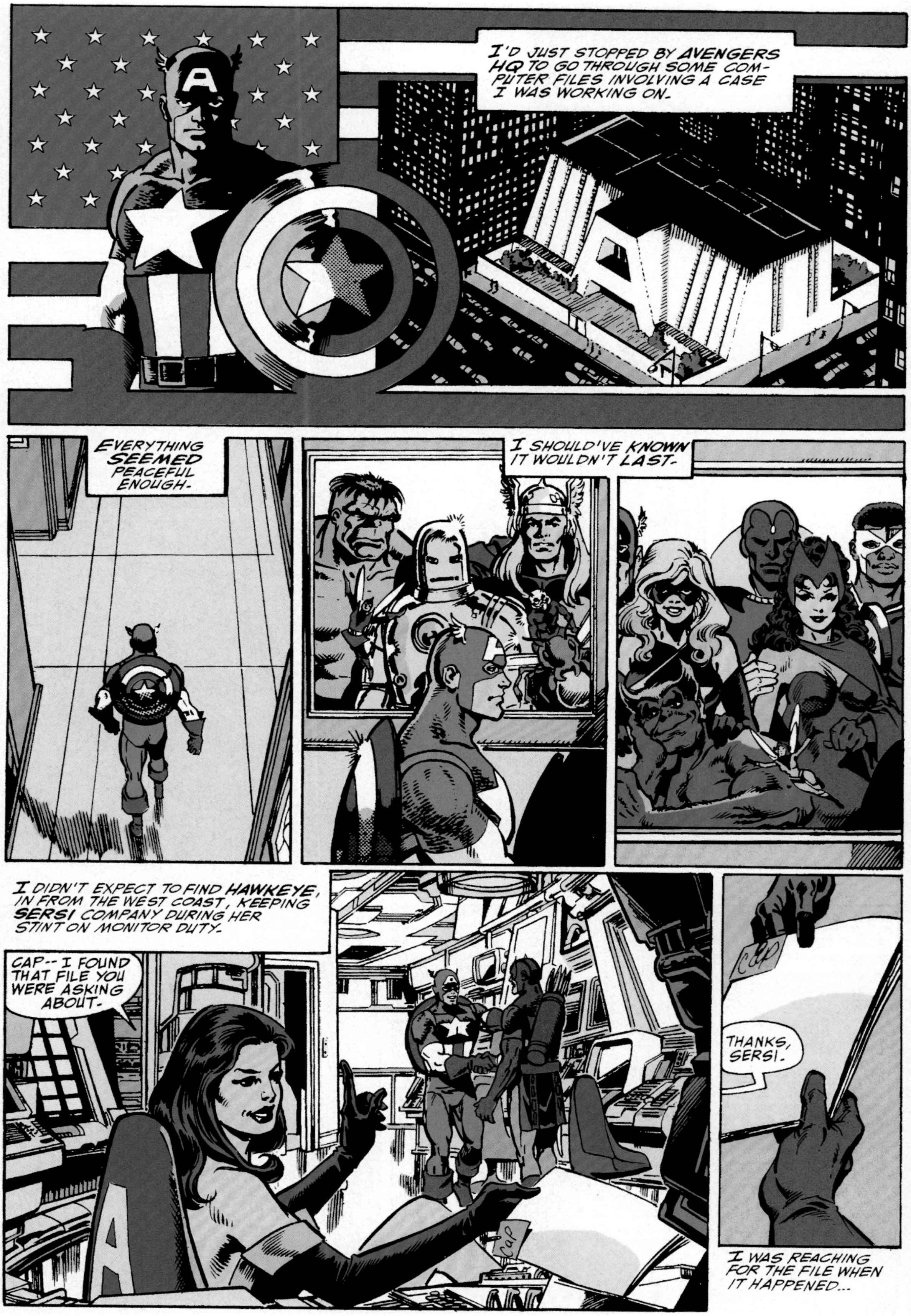
I'D JUST STOPPED BY AVENGERS HQ TO GO THROUGH SOME COMPUTER FILES INVOLVING A CASE I WAS WORKING ON.
EVERYTHING SEEMED PEACEFUL ENOUGH.
I SHOULD'VE KNOWN IT WOULDN'T LAST.
I DIDN'T EXPECT TO FIND HAWKEYE, IN FROM THE WEST COAST, KEEPING SERSI COMPANY DURING HER STINT ON MONITOR DUTY.
CAP-- I FOUND THAT FILE YOU WERE ASKING ABOUT.
CAP
THANKS, SERSI.
CAP
I WAS REACHING FOR THE FILE WHEN IT HAPPENED...

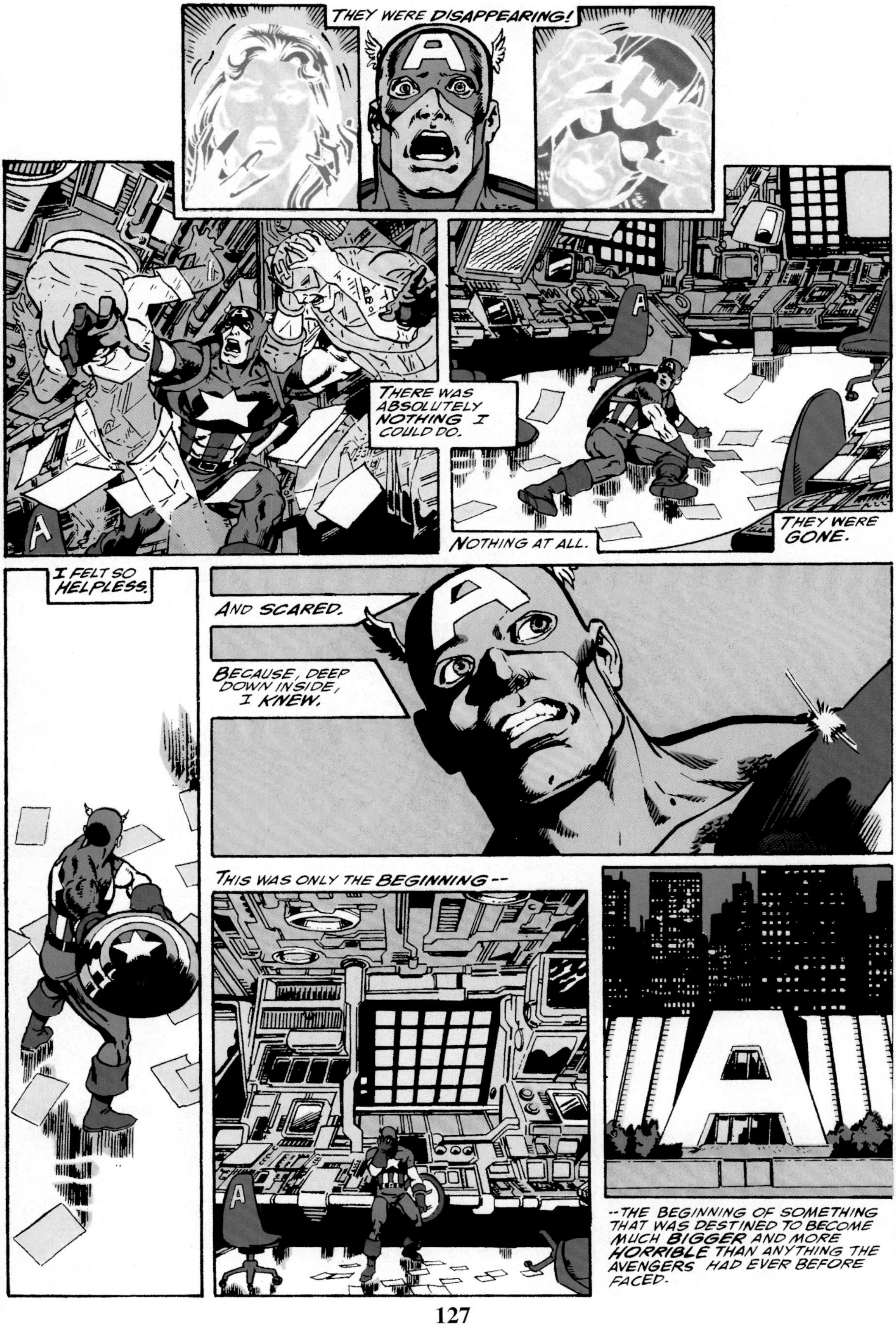
THEY WERE DISAPPEARING!
THERE WAS ABSOLUTELY NOTHING I COULD DO.
NOTHING AT ALL.
THEY WERE GONE.
I FELT SO HELPLESS.
AND SCARED.
BECAUSE, DEEP DOWN INSIDE, I KNEW.
THIS WAS ONLY THE BEGINNING --
--THE BEGINNING OF SOMETHING THAT WAS DESTINED TO BECOME MUCH BIGGER AND MORE HORRIBLE THAN ANYTHING THE AVENGERS HAD EVER BEFORE FACED.

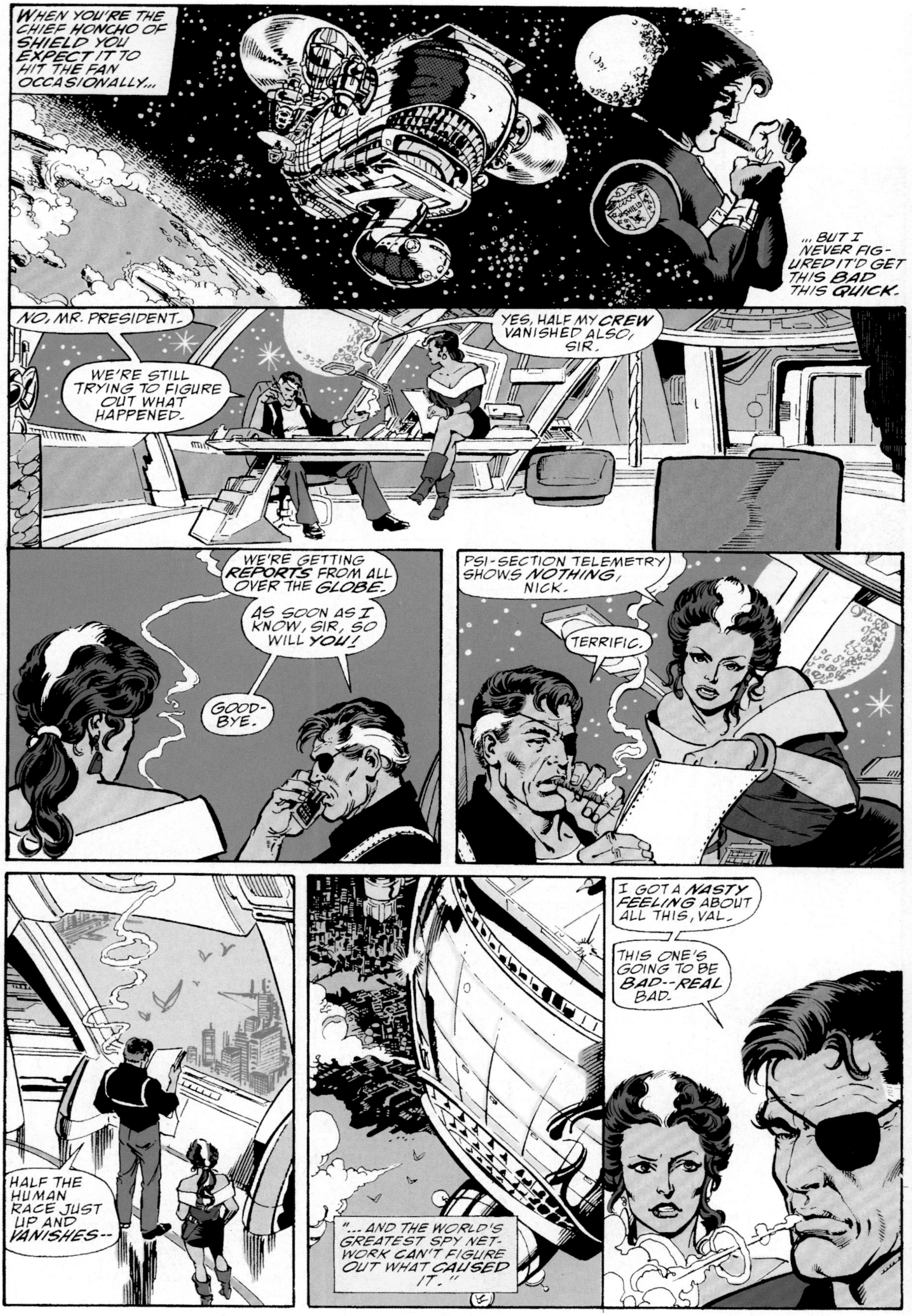
WHEN YOU'RE THE CHIEF HONCHO OF SHIELD YOU EXPECT IT TO HIT THE FAN OCCASIONALLY...
...BUT I NEVER FIGURED IT'D GET THIS BAD THIS QUICK.
NO, MR. PRESIDENT.
WE'RE STILL TRYING TO FIGURE OUT WHAT HAPPENED.
YES, HALF MY CREW VANISHED ALSO, SIR.
WE'RE GETTING REPORTS FROM ALL OVER THE GLOBE.
AS SOON AS I KNOW, SIR, SO WILL YOU!
GOOD-BYE.
PSI-SECTION TELEMETRY SHOWS NOTHING, NICK.
TERRIFIC.
HALF THE HUMAN RACE JUST UP AND VANISHES--
"...AND THE WORLD'S GREATEST SPY NET-WORK CAN'T FIGURE OUT WHAT CAUSED IT."
I GOT A NASTY FEELING ABOUT ALL THIS, VAL.
THIS ONE'S GOING TO BE BAD--REAL BAD.

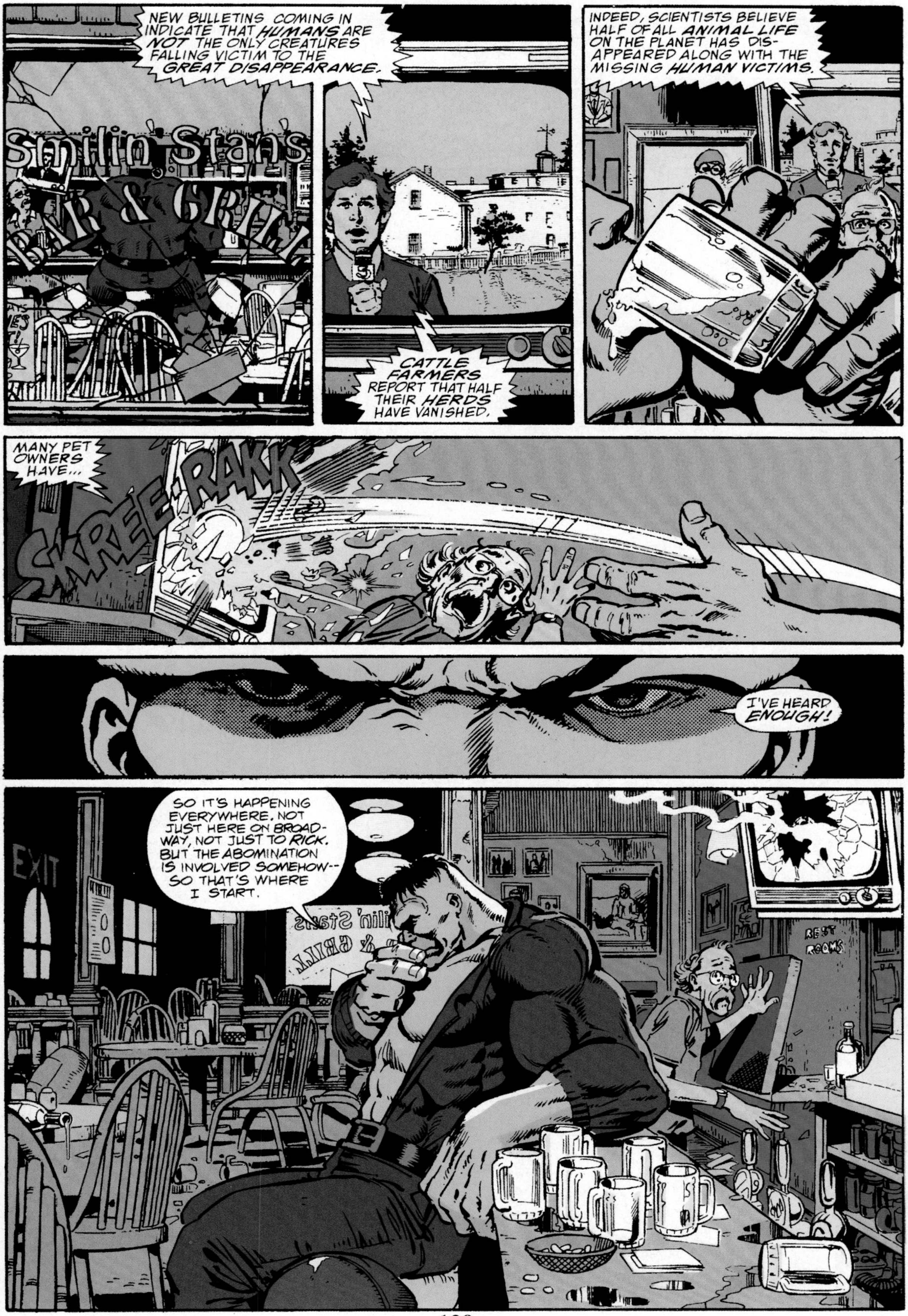
NEW BULLETINS COMING IN INDICATE THAT HUMANS ARE NOT THE ONLY CREATURES FALLING VICTIM TO THE GREAT DISAPPEARANCE.
Smilin' Stans
BAR & GRILL
CATTLE FARMERS REPORT THAT HALF THEIR HERDS HAVE VANISHED.
INDEED, SCIENTISTS BELIEVE HALF OF ALL ANIMAL LIFE ON THE PLANET HAS DISAPPEARED ALONG WITH THE MISSING HUMAN VICTIMS.
MANY PET OWNERS HAVE...
SKREE-RAKK
I'VE HEARD ENOUGH!
SO IT'S HAPPENING EVERYWHERE. NOT JUST HERE ON BROADWAY, NOT JUST TO RICK. BUT THE ABOMINATION IS INVOLVED SOMEHOW-- SO THAT'S WHERE I START.
EXIT
REST ROOMS

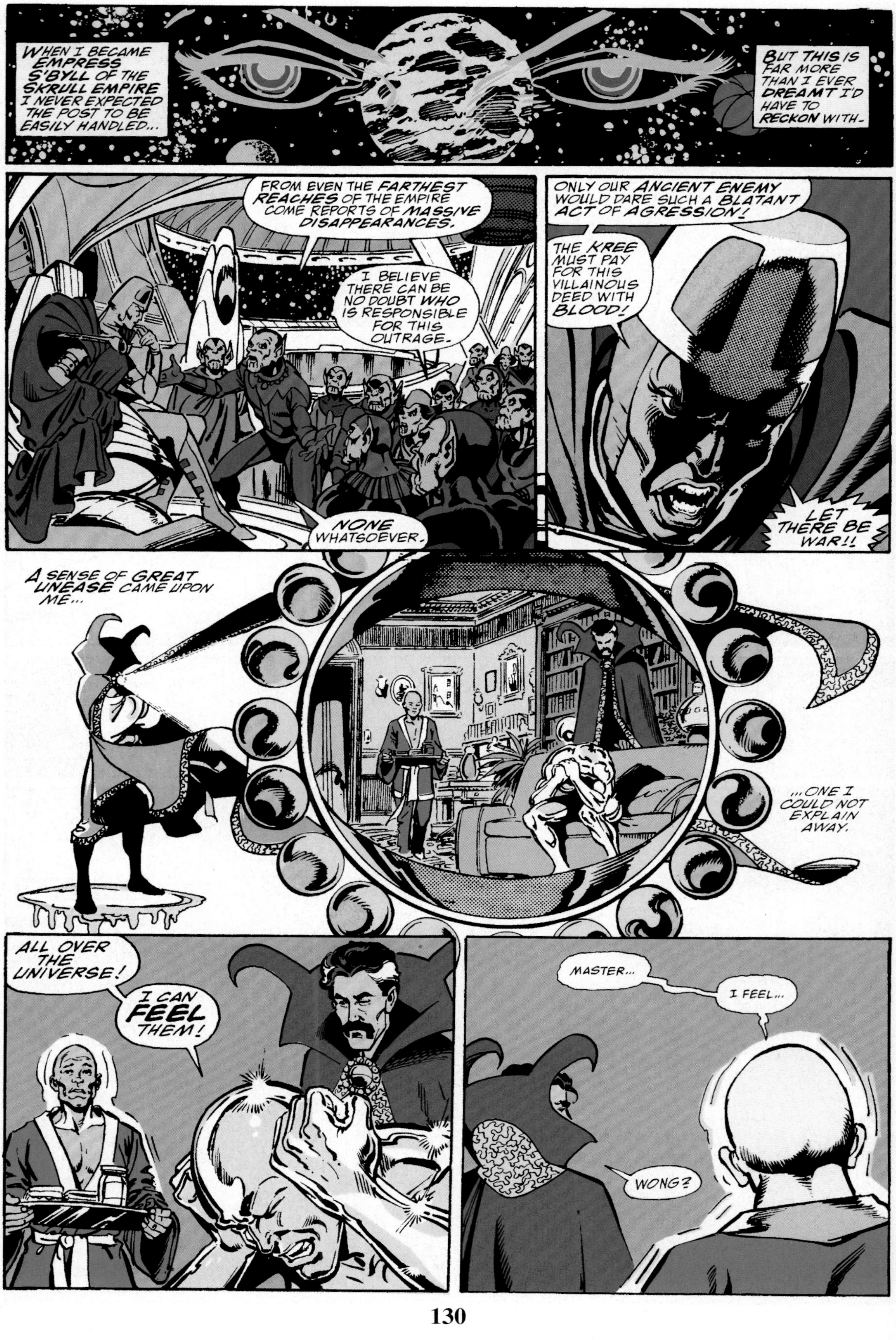
WHEN I BECAME EMPRESS S'BYLL OF THE SKRULL EMPIRE I NEVER EXPECTED THE POST TO BE EASILY HANDLED...
BUT THIS IS FAR MORE THAN I EVER DREAMT I'D HAVE TO RECKON WITH-
FROM EVEN THE FARTHEST REACHES OF THE EMPIRE COME REPORTS OF MASSIVE DISAPPEARANCES.
I BELIEVE THERE CAN BE NO DOUBT WHO IS RESPONSIBLE FOR THIS OUTRAGE.
NONE WHATSOEVER.
ONLY OUR ANCIENT ENEMY WOULD DARE SUCH A BLATANT ACT OF AGRESSION!
THE KREE MUST PAY FOR THIS VILLAINOUS DEED WITH BLOOD!
LET THERE BE WAR!!
A SENSE OF GREAT UNEASE CAME UPON ME...
...ONE I COULD NOT EXPLAIN AWAY.
ALL OVER THE UNIVERSE!
I CAN FEEL THEM!
MASTER...
I FEEL...
WONG?

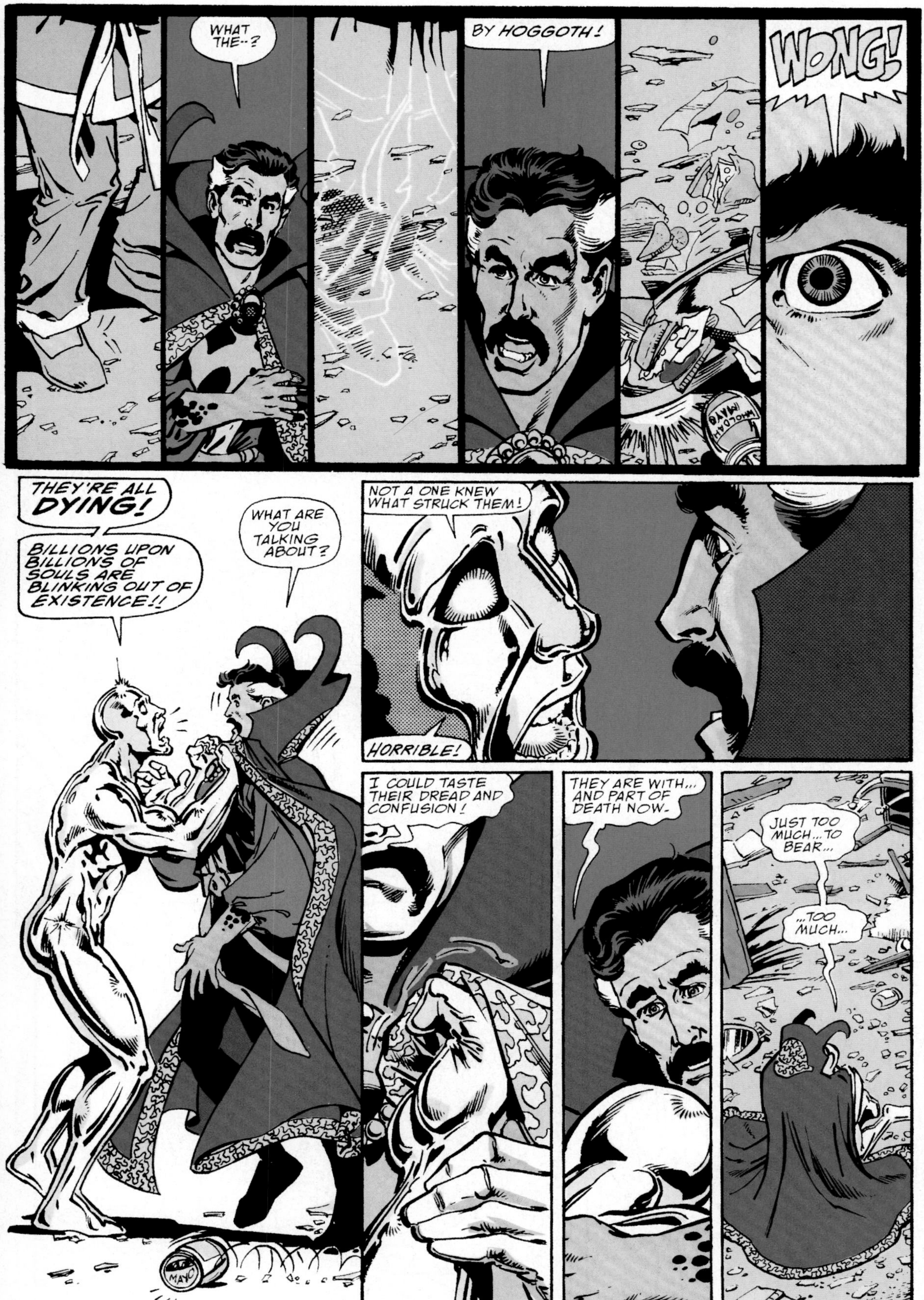
WHAT THE--?
BY HOGGOTH!
WONG!
WHOLOAH MAYO
THEY'RE ALL DYING!
BILLIONS UPON BILLIONS OF SOULS ARE BLINKING OUT OF EXISTENCE!!
WHAT ARE YOU TALKING ABOUT?
NOT A ONE KNEW WHAT STRUCK THEM!
HORRIBLE!
MAYO
I COULD TASTE THEIR DREAD AND CONFUSION!
THEY ARE WITH... AND PART OF DEATH NOW.
JUST TOO MUCH... TO BEAR...
...TOO MUCH...

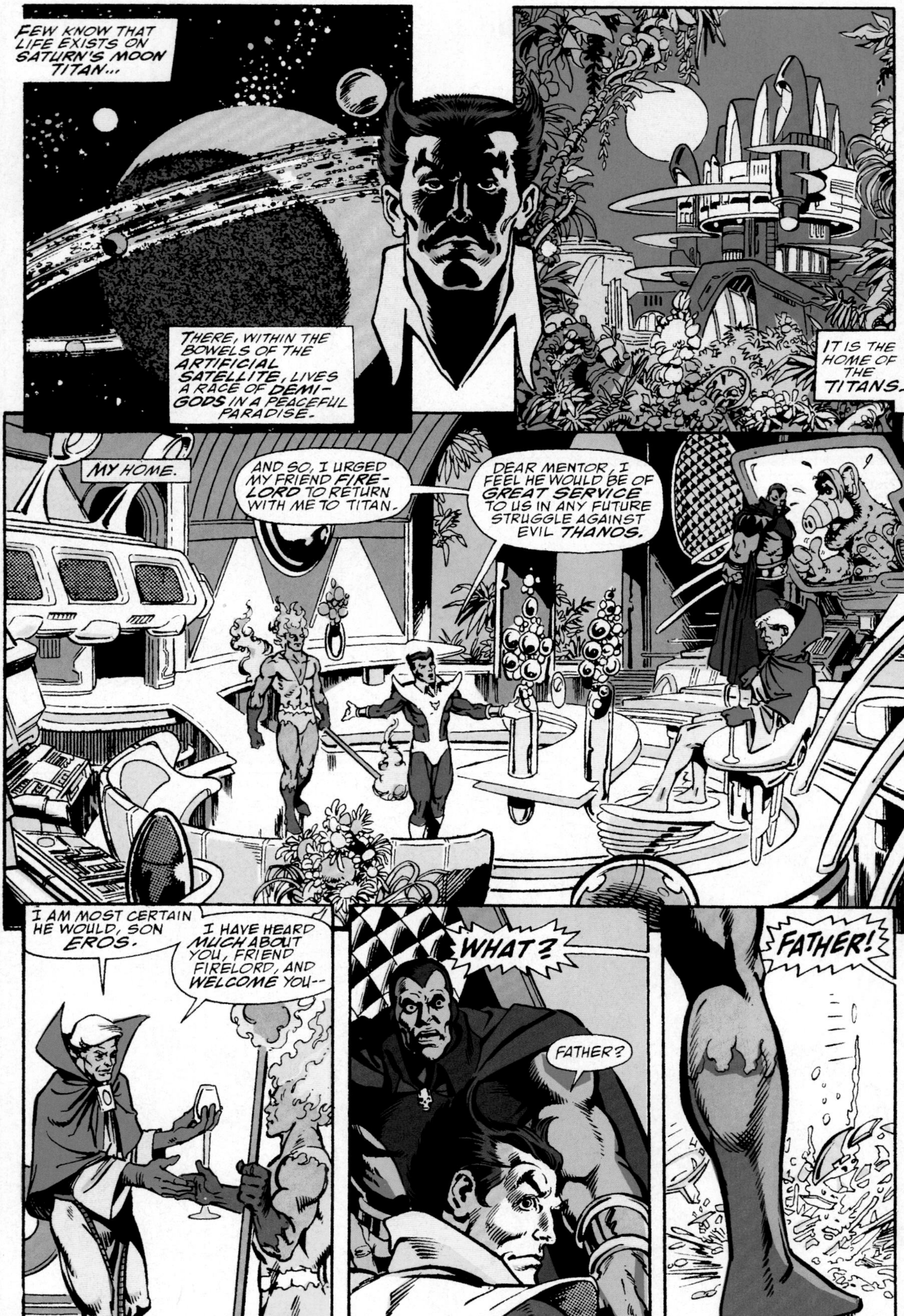

FEW KNOW THAT LIFE EXISTS ON SATURN'S MOON TITAN...
THERE, WITHIN THE BOWELS OF THE ARTIFICIAL SATELLITE, LIVES A RACE OF DEMI-GODS IN A PEACEFUL PARADISE.
IT IS THE HOME OF THE TITANS.
MY HOME.
AND SO, I URGED MY FRIEND FIRE-LORD TO RETURN WITH ME TO TITAN.
DEAR MENTOR, I FEEL HE WOULD BE OF GREAT SERVICE TO US IN ANY FUTURE STRUGGLE AGAINST EVIL THANOS.
I AM MOST CERTAIN HE WOULD, SON EROS.
I HAVE HEARD MUCH ABOUT YOU, FRIEND FIRELORD, AND WELCOME YOU--
WHAT?
FATHER?
FATHER!

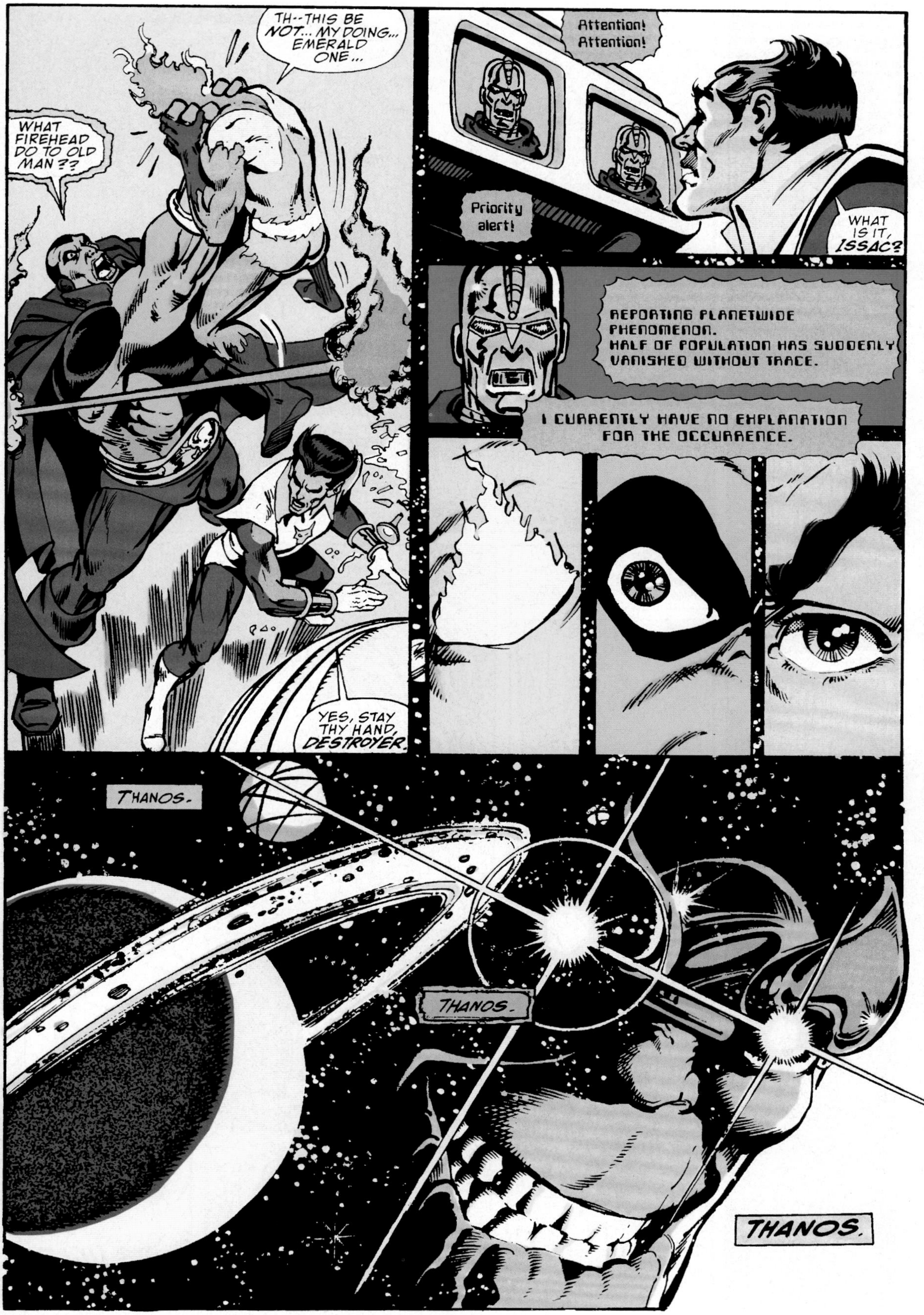
TH--THIS BE NOT... MY DOING... EMERALD ONE...
WHAT FIREHEAD DO TO OLD MAN ??
YES, STAY THY HAND, DESTROYER.
Attention! Attention!
Priority alert!
WHAT IS IT, ISSAC?
REPORTING PLANETWIDE PHENOMENON.
HALF OF POPULATION HAS SUDDENLY VANISHED WITHOUT TRACE.
I CURRENTLY HAVE NO EXPLANATION FOR THE OCCURRENCE.
THANOS.
THANOS.
THANOS.

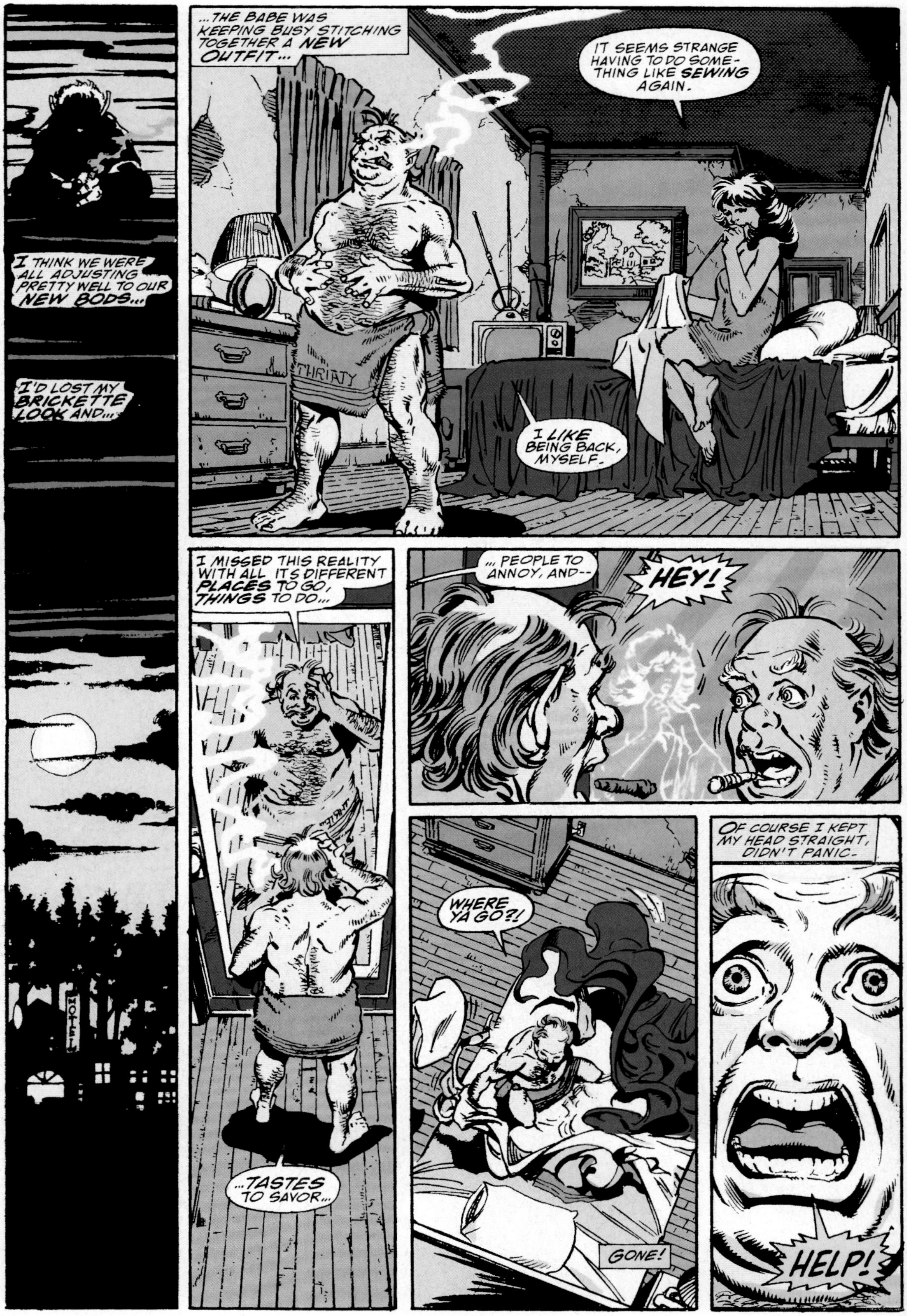
...THE BABE WAS KEEPING BUSY STITCHING TOGETHER A NEW OUTFIT...
IT SEEMS STRANGE HAVING TO DO SOMETHING LIKE SEWING AGAIN.
I THINK WE WERE ALL ADJUSTING PRETTY WELL TO OUR NEW BODS...
I'D LOST MY BRICKETTE LOOK AND...
I LIKE BEING BACK, MYSELF.
THRIATY
I MISSED THIS REALITY WITH ALL ITS DIFFERENT PLACES TO GO, THINGS TO DO...
...TASTES TO SAVOR...
...PEOPLE TO ANNOY, AND--
HEY!
WHERE YA GO?!
GONE!
OF COURSE I KEPT MY HEAD STRAIGHT, DIDN'T PANIC-
HELP!
MOTEL

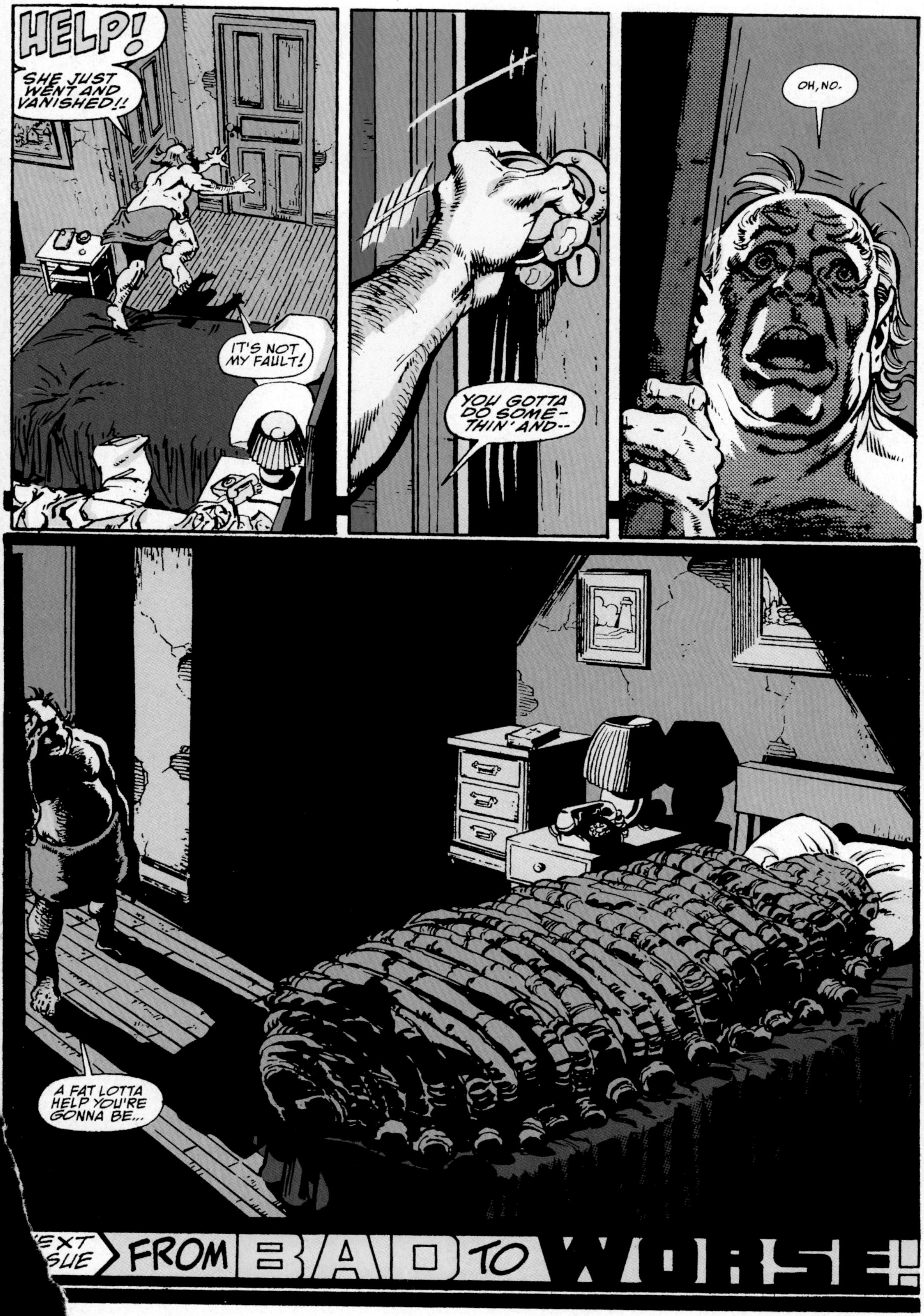
HELP!
SHE JUST WENT AND VANISHED!!
IT'S NOT MY FAULT!
YOU GOTTA DO SOMETHIN' AND--
OH, NO.
A FAT LOTTA HELP YOU'RE GONNA BE...
EXT SUE
FROM BAD TO WORSE!

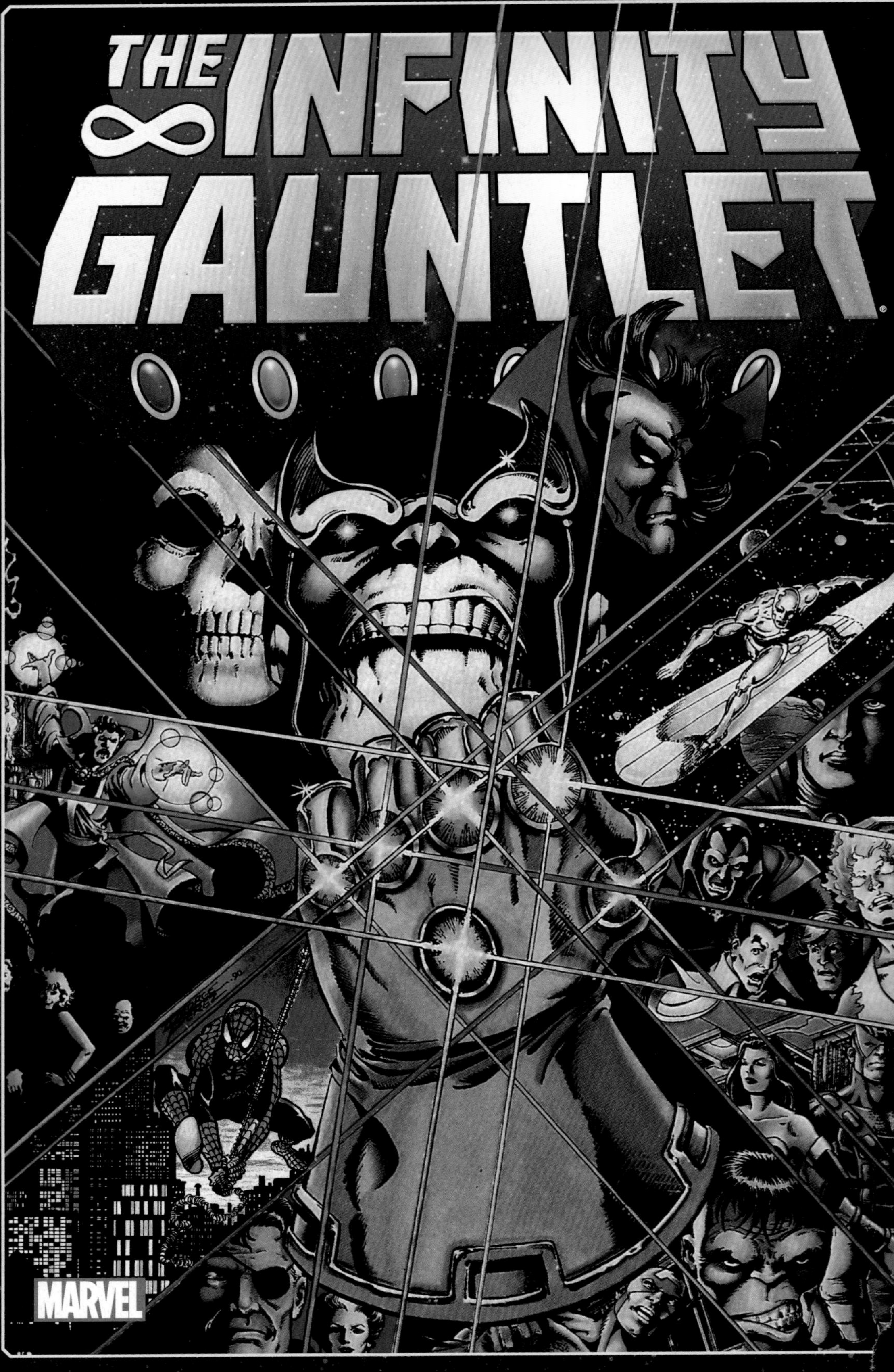
THE INFINITY GAUNTLET
MARVEL